DR. KATHARINE BROOKS is director of Liberal Arts Career Services at the University of Texas at Austin. A nationally recognized career coach, trainer, professor, and counselor for more than twenty years, she is the creator of the National Association of Colleges and Employers Career Coaching Intensives. She has a doctorate in educational psychology.

"In times like these it's crucial to look at entering the workplace from a whole new perspective and *You Majored in What?* accomplishes this! Who cares what your college major is? What is more important are your dreams, values, and strengths and this book helps any young person figure these things out and find a career that fits. Buy it now! It's great!"

—Julie Jansen, author, *I Don't Know What I Want,*
But I Know It's Not This!

"Kate Brooks addresses the key challenges faced by many college students as they attempt to bridge the chasm between sixteen years of education and the largely unknown world of work. *You Majored in What?* is truly a great guide for the soon-to-be-launched student. At a time when all job-hunters are going to need to raise their level of job-getting skills, Kate Brooks has provided the liberal arts grad with exactly what they need to compete and succeed."

—Jaye R. Roseborough, executive director,
Career Services, Middlebury College

"A fresh and encouraging voice in the liberal arts job search wilderness. Extremely helpful exercises and examples. Will be very useful to both students and career counselors. I plan to use it a lot."

—Carolyn Couch, associate director, Career Services,
Wake Forest University

"*You Majored in What?* is a lifeline for parents and students who value a liberal arts education. Katharine Brooks offers smart and accessible insights that turn the apparent chaos of a liberal arts major into a 'wandering map' to illuminate many routes toward a fulfilling career and life."

—James H. Madison, professor of history, and director,
Liberal Arts and Management Program, Indiana University

"Students of all ages will gain valuable insight into their own interests, goals, and career aspirations from this book, even if all they do is skim the first two chapters. *You Majored in What?* helps young people find the connections between their interests and the inexhaustible career options available to them. This book should be sent to every student with their letter of admission or given to every first-year student at the start of orientation. I hope to share it with my graduate students."

—Paul Binkley, director, Career Development Services,
George Washington University

"The wisdom contained in this book could not have become available at a better time for the millions of Gen Y college students and recent graduates who are simultaneously struggling with crushing levels of student debt and the desire to find a career where they can do meaningful work that is of benefit to society."

—Steven Rothberg, president and founder,
CollegeRecruiter.com

"An amazing, refreshing new perspective on an ancient question that does not leave sage advice behind! This book takes tried-and-true concepts and adds meaning and organization. One can't but help but think, engage, and be encouraged by Kate's valuable wisdom! Useful as a course text, a journal, a job search manual, or what it reads like: a personal career companion, mentor, or friend. Born of chaos theory, this book is ready to deliver into the hands of the yearning who are eager to absorb it.

Loaded with images, constructive strategies, and meaningful advice, *You Majored in What?* is intellectual but practical, and readers will deepen their appreciation of their majors. With its many examples, exercises, reflections, and real-life stories, this book has something for every reader to grab a hold of to achieve not only career success, but life and work success."

—Denise Dwight Smith, director, University
Career Services, University of North Carolina at Charlotte

YOU MAJORED IN WHAT

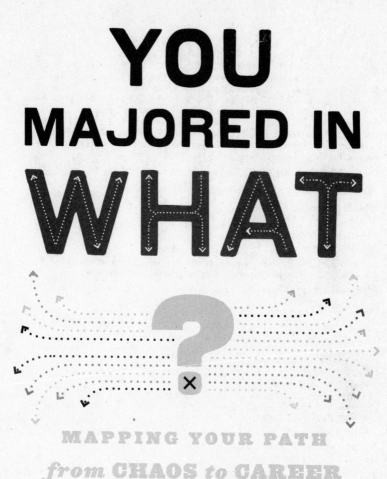

MAPPING YOUR PATH
from CHAOS *to* CAREER

KATHARINE BROOKS, ED.D.

A PLUME BOOK

PLUME
Published by the Penguin Group
Penguin Group (USA) Inc., 375 Hudson Street, New York, New York 10014, U.S.A. • Penguin Group (Canada), 90 Eglinton Avenue East, Suite 700, Toronto, Ontario, Canada M4P 2Y3 (a division of Pearson Penguin Canada Inc.) • Penguin Books Ltd., 80 Strand, London WC2R 0RL, England • Penguin Ireland, 25 St. Stephen's Green, Dublin 2, Ireland (a division of Penguin Books Ltd.) • Penguin Group (Australia), 250 Camberwell Road, Camberwell, Victoria 3124, Australia (a division of Pearson Australia Group Pty. Ltd.) • Penguin Books India Pvt. Ltd., 11 Community Centre, Panchsheel Park, New Delhi – 110 017, India • Penguin Group (NZ), 67 Apollo Drive, Rosedale, North Shore 0632, New Zealand (a division of Pearson New Zealand Ltd.) • Penguin Books (South Africa) (Pty.) Ltd., 24 Sturdee Avenue, Rosebank, Johannesburg 2196, South Africa

Penguin Books Ltd., Registered Offices: 80 Strand, London WC2R 0RL, England

Published by Plume, a member of Penguin Group (USA) Inc.

First Plume Printing, April 2010
20 19 18 17 16

Ⓟ REGISTERED TRADEMARK — MARCA REGISTRADA

The Library of Congress has catalogued the Viking edition as follows:

Brooks, Katharine.
You majored in what? / Katharine Brooks.
    p. cm.
Includes bibliographical references and index.
ISBN 978-0-670-02082-9 (h.c.)
ISBN 978-0-452-29600-8 (pbk.)
1. Job hunting—United States. 2. Employment interviewing—United States. 3. College graduates—Employment—United States. 4. College majors—United States. I. Title.
HF5382.75.U6B755 2010
650.14—dc22   2008046687

Printed in the United States of America
Original hardcover design by Sabrina Bowers

PUBLISHER'S NOTE
While the author has made every effort to provide accurate telephone numbers and Internet addresses at the time of publication, neither the publisher nor the author assumes any responsibility for errors, or for changes that occur after publication. Further, the publisher does not have any control over and does not assume any responsibility for author or third-party Web sites or their content.

To my parents and teachers,
on whose shoulders I stand:

infinite gratitude for shaping and guiding
my work and my life.

And

to singer, songwriter, and daydream believer
John Stewart (1939–2008):

thanks for providing the soundtrack.

CONTENTS

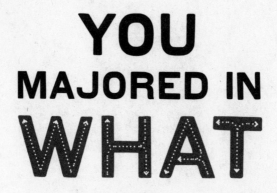

YOU
MAJORED IN
WHAT

CHAPTER 1

A BUTTERFLY FLAPS ITS WINGS AND YOU FIND A JOB

CHAOS AND YOUR CAREER PLANS

You need chaos in your soul to give birth to a dancing star.
—**FRIEDRICH NIETZSCHE,** *THUS SPAKE ZARATHUSTRA*

Has it happened yet? Have you been asked **THE QUESTION?**

You know the one: it's the question that cuts to the core of your existence, the question that haunts you pretty much from the time you decide to be a college student to months, even years, after you graduate. It starts so innocently. Someone asks you what your major is, so you tell them.

There's a slight pause. Then comes **THE QUESTION:**

"WHAT ARE YOU GOING TO DO WITH THAT?"

OK, think fast.

"I'm going to law school," you say, even though you aren't really sure you want to, but it sure sounds good. Or "I'm thinking about med school," even though you have no interest in science classes.

The questioner's face relaxes; maybe he even smiles. He pats you on the shoulder. "Wow, that's great!"

And that's how the lie begins . . .

Do you feel sometimes there's a cosmic joke at work? That you chose this really interesting major but now you're wondering, was it worth it? Or perhaps you're just starting college and **THE QUESTION** is already making you nervous.

THE PRESSURE OF THE LINEAR PATH

The problem behind **THE QUESTION** is that it assumes a linear path between your major and your career. And the lure of the linear path is powerful. It's embedded in our thinking. From the time you played with fire trucks and people asked you if you wanted to be a firefighter, linear paths to careers have been assumed to be the natural state of things. So it seems only logical that you would pursue a major that would become your ultimate career. Business majors go into business. Engineering majors become engineers, philosophy majors become . . . ? Hmm . . .

Your parents would probably be thrilled if you had a glitch-free linear path from school to work all worked out. You know, "I'm studying accounting so I can be an accountant," or "I'm going to be an English major so I can teach English." *You* might be secretly relieved as well.

But that's early twentieth-century thinking—1909 to be exact, when the trait-and-factor approach was designed to determine the best career choices for people. As America shifted from an agricultural to an industrial society, vocational researchers sought ways to determine the best fit between individuals and their jobs. Career tests were designed to match people's interests and skills with potential vocations. Society placed additional restraints on employment, with women and minorities relegated to narrow fields. Most people pursued education to learn a specific trade, and a college education was reserved for the elite few who would likely go on to teaching, medicine, law, or the ministry.

In the twenty-first century, a college education is wide open to many more individuals regardless of gender, race, or career goal. Many students now choose a college education because of the interesting subjects they can study, not necessarily because of a specific career plan.

Whatever your reason for pursing your major, you, like many others, are probably struggling with **THE QUESTION**: What do I *do* with this degree? Where is *my* linear path?

To help you envision such a path, here's a list of the actual careers of some recent graduates, drawn from alumni surveys from three institutions. Note the relatively direct relationship between their majors and their careers.

MAJOR	JOB
Art	Cartoonist
Asian American Studies	Teaching English as a second language in Korea
Chemistry	Veterinarian
Classics/Archaeology	Latin teacher
Dramatic Arts	MTV program developer
Economics	Bond trader on Wall Street
English	Editor, major publishing house
French and Spanish	Foreign service officer
Geography	High school geography teacher
Government	Special prosecutor, district attorney's office
Government	Republican National Committee PR staff
Psychology	Psychotherapist
Religion	Minister, single adults program

Can you see the linear relationship that exists between a major and a career? The symmetry between the job duties and the use of the graduates' skills? The English major is using her writing skills. The psychology major is helping people. The economics major is working on Wall Street. It's reassuring, isn't it? Not only can you get a job, your job can be directly related to your major.

There's only one problem with the list: *it's all wrong.* These are the *actual* careers of graduates with those majors:

MAJOR	JOB
Art	Special prosecutor, district attorney's office
Asian American Studies	Bond trader on Wall Street
Chemistry	Teaching English as a second language in Korea
Classics/Archaeology	Foreign service officer
Dramatic Arts	Republican National Committee PR staff
Economics	Veterinarian
English	Psychotherapist
French and Spanish	Latin teacher
Geography	Editor, major publishing house
Government	Minister, single adults program
Government	High school geography teacher
Psychology	Cartoonist
Religion	MTV program developer

Oops.

Is something wrong here? No, something's actually right. Clearly, reality doesn't always match up to that traditional linear career path. These graduates, whether by design or by accident, have channeled the real, deep value of their academic and life experiences, and taken them beyond traditional thinking.

The linear career path hasn't disappeared. Some psychology majors do become psychologists and some English majors become English professors. But linear thinking can keep you from thinking broadly about your options and being open-minded to new opportunities.

LINEAR THINKING ABOUT CAREERS

Right about now you're probably thinking that pursuing an education that directly relates to a career, and vice versa, seems so stable and easy. Wouldn't it make more sense to follow a more direct path? After all, if you try to use that second chart as a guide, you really have no idea where you might end up. And doesn't most of the advice out there on career planning focus on that direct path?

As we saw earlier, the roots of modern-day career counseling lie in the early twentieth century, 1909 to be exact, when Frank Parsons, an engineering professor, developed his trait-and-factor approach to making career decisions. Parsons defined a *trait* as a characteristic of a person that could be discovered by testing, and a *factor* as a characteristic of a job. He described his approach as "matching men to jobs" and believed there was one right career for each worker.

This approach to career analysis was designed to reduce any elements of chance or uncertainty in the process, just like those books and Web sites that neatly outline the "five steps to your career" and ask you to quickly set a goal and move toward it. Career assessments are integral to this method to further eliminate the element of chance, on the assumption that a test will help you determine the exact fit between your traits and the workplace factors.

Now, any theory that has hung around for a hundred years can't be all bad, and it *is* important to know how your strengths and skills fit into the workplace (and you'll explore these in the next few chapters), but many career systems and assessment instruments follow the trait-and-factor approach too literally, leading you down the linear path using traditional linear thinking and reasoning. They are too simplistic for twenty-first-century career planning.

For instance, if you use traditional deductive reasoning, where you start with one personal trait and expand it to a career factor, you might follow this logical train of thought:

- Pilots must have strong attention to detail.
- I have strong attention to detail.
- I should be a pilot.

Or

⇒ The Peace Corps helps people.

⇒ I want to help people.

⇒ I should work for the Peace Corps.

One particular challenge with deductive reasoning is that it assumes the first statement is true. If the first statement is inaccurate, then the reasoning quickly falls apart. On the other hand, if you rely on traditional inductive reasoning, where you start with a large factor like a field of employment and reduce it to a simple trait, you might follow this train of thought:

⇒ Every lawyer I've met has been untrustworthy.

⇒ Therefore all lawyers are untrustworthy.

⇒ I can't be a lawyer.

Or

⇒ My insurance salesperson is boring.

⇒ Therefore the insurance industry is boring.

⇒ I won't look at careers at an insurance company.

While these traditional reasoning methods are simple and (on the surface) logical, they could actually impede your career planning. You might choose a career field or employer based on one arbitrary skill or characteristic (trait) you possess, which might ultimately not work for you, or conversely, you might completely avoid a career field because you have developed a global perception of it (factor) based on your limited personal experience.

For instance, if you speak with Peace Corps recruiters, they will tell you that the Peace Corps volunteer position is extremely tough, demanding, and often frustrating. They don't want people who just want to "help." They need practical people with their heads on their shoulders who see the big picture of providing service but aren't there to save the world.

And did you know that the insurance industry offers fascinating positions for people with all sorts of interests? In the field of underwriting, for example, special knowledge or expertise is often called for to make important judgments about the value of property. An art history major, for example, works with a major insurance firm valuing the oriental carpets and art holdings of major corporations. A geology major evaluates beach properties for an insurance company, determining the odds of hurricanes or other natural phenomena destroying them. She spends much of her time traveling to beachfront communities, sometimes to review new developments and other times to assess damage after a hurricane or other tragic event. Is that a "boring" job?

Wandering off:

MY DEGREE EQUALS MY EARNING POWER

Want to know the number one most requested piece of information from college career centers? The employment figures from alumni surveys. Everyone, from students to parents to government agencies, wants to know what percentage of students found jobs by graduation. And how much were they earning. And their major. There seems to be a theory that if sociology majors found jobs in X field, making X dollars, then I, a sociology major, can find a job in X field making X dollars. While there's some truth to that theory, there's less truth than you might imagine.

Study after study show poor correlations between students' undergraduate majors and their income. Get that? *Weak* correlation. You're working off a common myth that your degree equals your earning power.

Your earning power is much more affected by where you live, your field of work, and your job title. An accounting major working for a small nonprofit organization in the Midwest will likely earn less than an English major working as an investment banker in New York City. Get the point?

Is it true that engineers generally make higher salaries than liberal arts majors? Yes. But—hello—they're *engineers*. Do you want to be an engineer? Then go to engineering school and be one. Problem solved.

So take a minute to think about what you've said and heard about career planning. You can catch yourself (or your parents) thinking linearly about careers if you're harboring any of these thoughts:

- "My major equals my career."
- "If I can just combine the right skills and the right values, I'll know what I want to do."
- "I can't do much with a liberal arts degree."
- "I guess I should go to grad school."
- "I guess I should go to law school."
- "Career tests will tell me what to do"
- "Career counselors can tell me what to do"
- "I should wait until I know what I want to do before starting my job search."
- "I should wait until I graduate to start my job search."

So if this linear approach doesn't really work all that well in the twenty-first century, what model do you turn to if you're multitalented, multifaceted, or just not sure?

HOW COLLEGE STUDENTS *REALLY* FIND JOBS

It's ridiculous to ask liberal arts students what they plan to do in five years. They don't even know what they plan to have for dinner.

—ANONYMOUS COLLEGE CAREER COUNSELOR

As we've noted, if you listen to most people and read most career books or Web sites, you might assume that the job search is a linear logical process: you set a specific career goal, follow clearly outlined steps, and arrive at the perfect job. But try asking graduates how they actually arrived at their current jobs. You'll get replies like this one:

I don't know exactly. I majored in psychology and thought I'd pursue a Ph.D. and maybe become a professor. But I also liked my anthropology classes, and a professor told me about a summer internship in a museum. I helped create an exhibit on Native American art and I really enjoyed the work. Then an alumna spoke at a career program on her work at the Smithsonian Institution. It sounded interesting so I went up and introduced myself to her. We kept in touch and she called me during my senior year to see if I would be interested in a fund-raising position for the Smithsonian's new Native American exhibit. So here I am using my psychology skills to ask important business and community leaders to fund our research and exhibits. And I love it. And now that I know how museums work and how to raise money, my goal is to open an art gallery/museum on a Native American reservation.

Notice how this story starts out in a linear way: the student was studying psychology so she could become a psychology professor. But then a totally unpredictable event occurred: her internship at a museum caused her to start thinking about other choices. And then a chance meeting with an alumna resulted in a job opportunity. If you had asked her at age eighteen, "What are you going to do with that psychology major?" do you think she would have said, "I'm going to open an art gallery/museum in New Mexico"?

Clearly the linear approach isn't at work here. Unplanned events and emerging conditions changed this individual's circumstances. We need a theory that fits this more typical situation, a theory that recognizes that just like the life of the psychology major above, yours isn't unfolding in a straight line either, and the job search seems chaotic and messy at best. Enter chaos theory—a nonlinear and much more relevant career theory for you. Now, that sounds daunting and complicated, not to mention, well, chaotic. But it's really rather simple. And believe it or not, once you learn the key elements of chaos theory, which form the basis of the Wise Wanderings system you will learn in this book, you'll find you can relax and go with the flow of your job search instead of wanting to force and control everything.

In fact, you have just witnessed a key element of chaos theory: the butterfly effect. The butterfly effect states that a small incident at the beginning of a process (such as a butterfly flapping its wings or a graduate speaking at a career event) can produce a large variation in the long-term outcome (ultimately causing a tornado or a new career). A chaos-based career system allows for change and the unexpected. It takes into account your diverse interests and broad scope of knowledge, and takes advantage of how the job search really works today. You might be surprised to learn that in one study of university graduates almost 70 percent reported that their careers were significantly influenced by unplanned events—in other words, the butterfly effect (Krumboltz and Levin, 2004).

What if you could actually harness the power of the butterfly? You can. Let's start by learning more about chaos theory.

English Literature at Work:

CHARLES DICKENS EXPLAINS THE BUTTERFLY EFFECT

In Charles Dickens's book *Great Expectations*, the lead character Pip makes the following observation:

> *"That was a memorable day to me, for it made great changes in me. But, it is the same with any life. Imagine one selected day struck out of it, and think how different its course would have been. Pause you who read this, and think for a moment of the long chain of iron or gold, of thorns or flowers, that would never have bound you, but for the formation of the first link on one memorable day."*

Sounds a lot like the butterfly effect doesn't it? With a twist though: instead of thinking about an event that happened, Dickens is asking you to think about something that didn't happen. How would your life be different if a particular event had not occurred?

CHAOS THEORY

People usually smile when you tell them that careers follow chaos theory rather than linear theory. Chaos theory conjures up thoughts of craziness and being out of control: the notion that there is no rhyme or reason to one's career path. The irony is that despite its name, chaos theory is anything but chaotic. It's just complex—as you and you career can be. The order is there, but it's just not immediately visible on the surface.

Chaos theory is based on mathematical formulas originally designed to develop a better weather prediction model. Think about it: how successful are we at predicting the weather? Sometimes we're pretty good. When the conditions are foreseen, when nothing changes, and when we know certain physical laws are being followed, we can predict the weather. If we see a front moving across the map, we know a storm is coming. But what happens when something interrupts the pattern? What if the front coming from the west suddenly encounters another storm coming up the East Coast? When and where will they meet? How well can we predict a tornado's path? Not too well generally. We know it's coming (sometimes) but we can't tell where it's going. Chaos theory helps us understand that too many variables in a complex system make it hard to predict the outcome.

We also know from chaos theory that the greater the distance between now and the future, the weaker our prediction will be. For instance, we're pretty good at predicting the weather today. Maybe even tomorrow or within the next week. But after that our predictions get shaky. We may notice trends, or make logical inferences such as if it's August, it will be hot (at least in most of the United States), but chaos theory helps us understand we can't predict the future in greater detail.

CHAOS THEORY AND YOUR CAREER

Just as complex factors influence the weather, the path to a career can be complex with all sorts of intervening variables, including family origin, level of education, individual skills and talents, the job market, and so on. And just like weather forecasting, career planning is a form of prediction, right? Aren't you trying to guess the career path you'll pursue in the future based on the degree you're pursuing, the experiences you've had, or what you like or dislike? And isn't it easier to predict what you'll do this evening (or even this semester) than what you'll be doing in two years?

Traditional chaos theory is a mathematical model that serves as an excellent basis and metaphor for the Wise Wanderings system. To see how this works, let's consider five basic tenets of chaos theory and how they apply to career planning:

1. Chaos theory helps us predict the outcome of complex situations by asking us to *assess what we currently know, what we cannot know, and what we can learn.* Then we can make reasonable choices based on that information. So instead of trying to predict a future you can't see, you can start your career planning by focusing on what you know right now, what you don't know, and what you can learn. What you probably know right now is that you have a variety of interests and talents and you aren't ready to make a decision. You aren't ready to—and cannot—predict the future, but you can also see that it's not total anarchy: you do have some ideas and interests you could pursue if you wanted to. So instead of having to make a career choice right now, consider yourself in an information-gathering phase. Is the pressure lessening already?

2. Chaos theory relies on abductive reasoning (as opposed to simple deductive and inductive reasoning of linear theory), which says *we can't base decisions on single factors or traits.* We make better decisions when we look at the big picture, stay open-minded, and consider a variety of perspectives. And chaos theory even has a nice term for changing your mind: it's called phase shifting. So you don't need to base your career plans on one piece of information, such as your major, or find the simple answer to **THE QUESTION**. You can find the patterns and connections between your interests, knowledge, and experiences and know that a variety of career choices are available to you—and during your lifetime you may try them all! You will not only tolerate but also welcome the ambiguity, recognizing that what others might call cluelessness you can call open-mindedness, because you know lots of unexpected opportunities await and you're not ready to limit yourself.

3. Chaos theory assumes that change occurs constantly and that the unexpected and unpredicted will occur. As you develop your career plans, you'll encounter changes (or what chaos theory calls emergent variables) that will lead to new paths. Just think back to the psychology major who planned to teach psychology. She went through a series of events (what chaos theory calls recursive changes): an interesting class, internship, and job offer that resulted in her plans to open an art gallery. And who knows where she'll be in ten years? This is one of the most fun aspects of applying chaos theory to careers. All you have to do is pay attention and take advantage of those emerging variables. Isn't it great that something's coming up that will propel you forward in ways you haven't even considered yet?

4. Now, just in case you're getting a little nervous about all these changes that seem out of your control, chaos theory comes to the rescue because it holds that *systems will ultimately reveal an order*. This is a key piece of knowledge: what looks like chaos isn't always chaotic. You may just be too close to it to see the organizing patterns. Chaos looks orderly from afar and so will your career. By using the Wise Wanderings system, you'll begin to see the order to your seeming career chaos. And while you may not see a coherent pattern in what you're doing right now, you'll learn to think about the connections you're building between your classes, your experiences, and so on. You get to create your future, and suddenly the major that seemed to be a problem and a source of concern might actually be a part of the solution. You will start to see this more clearly when you create the Wandering Map in Chapter 2 and perform other exercises in this book.

5. Finally, chaos theory describes several attractors that grab our attention and control our behavior. *Point attractors* move us toward or away from something; for instance, a party is usually a point attractor for college students and a raise or promotion is a point attractor for someone at work. Point attractors cut through the chaos because they keep you focused on one specific item and not the whole chaotic scene. Later in this book you'll learn to analyze your point attractors and develop new ones that will help you move forward without the stress. *Pendulum attractors* are two or more points that we move between. Attending graduate school or working after graduation might be two pendulum attractors that you move between. Or perhaps you are stuck between two seemingly opposing goals, such as "I want to help people but I want to make money" or "I should start a career but I'd really like to take a year off."The Wise Wanderings system will help you look for creative ways to resolve the tension that keeps you from making a choice or, for that matter, feeling as if you to have to choose. (You don't, by the way.) *Strange attractors* are unpredictable or random events that don't repeat. Later, you'll identify your strange attractors and use them to your advantage or keep them from distracting you. Finally, *torus attractors* represent cycles of behavior we repeat. By analyzing your torus attractors you'll be able to break cycles of behavior (like procrastination) that might impede your job search or career plans.

On the surface, chaos theory seems more complicated than linear theory. And perhaps it is. Life is more complicated now than in 1909. But you're smart and, as you've already discovered, applying linear theory to your future is a joke—and a bad one at that. The chaos theory tenets behind the Wise Wanderings system give you the confidence to welcome the seeming chaos of your future as you learn that what appears chaotic is actually well organized and ordered. Linear approaches get thrown off by change; chaos theory harnesses the power of change. Linear approaches can make you nervous: Are you limited by your choice of major? Do you have to have a career goal? And what do you do if you don't have one? Chaos theory says, "Relax." A world of possibilities is within your grasp and you don't need a specific goal. And you don't need to answer **THE QUESTION**. Chaos theory says, "Let's get going—a butterfly awaits."

The Classics at Work:

CAREERS, CHAOS, AND THE ANCIENT GREEKS

Did you know the ancient Greeks had a word—*metos*—for your career path?

In her book, *Learning to Think Strategically*, Julia Sloan defines *metos* as "the ability to oscillate or steer a course between the world of order (cosmos), of forms and laws, and to deal with the world of chaos, which includes the multiple, the unstable, and the unlimited nature of affairs."

The Greeks didn't strive for certain knowledge. They knew that there would always be tension between order and chaos. Their goal was to take into account the conflicting information and be willing to bend the course of action to take advantage of opportunities and avoid problems. Odysseus was highly respected for his ability to use forethought and planning to chart courses in chaotic environments. To see a modern adaptation of *The Odyssey*, watch *O Brother, Where Art Thou* and study how the character of Ulysses (played by George Clooney) manages the many chaotic events in his journey back to his wife.

WISE WANDERINGS INTO YOUR FUTURE

So what do you think about this new approach? Is it helping you relax a little? Are you less worried about where your degree might lead? Are you psyched about the "butterfly" that might be just around the corner? Maybe you've even started to think the career that seemed unrealistic just a day or so ago might actually be a possibility.

Or do you have some concerns? The most common question or concern expressed, aside from the complexity of the theory, is "Isn't this method simply random trial and error? After all, if you can't predict the future, and you're waiting for a butterfly effect, isn't that a rather passive approach?"

Not at all. Trial and error implies a thoughtless and random experimental process. Throughout this book you will weigh evidence, take note of what works and what doesn't, and draw mindful conclusions. Everything is potentially revealing—you just have to focus your thinking to start drawing helpful information from your experiences. And there's nothing passive about what you will be asked to do in your job search. You will be constructing powerful stories, résumés, and letters. You are going to actively wander, try out new ideas, and take advantage of unknown opportunities, but you will be doing so in a directed, mindful manner. That's why the system is called Wise Wanderings and not simply Wanderings. Thanks to this new approach, you will:

- use your knowledge of chaos theory to create a resilient career strategy that will serve you throughout your life;

- adapt to change and not be defeated by it;

- be open to possibilities, without simply going any way the wind blows;

- know you are in charge and can create each and every day of your life;

- have a direction, even though you're not arrogant or mindless enough to think that life will be served up in one neat linear package.

- embrace the chaos of your life and take it as a source of pride.

In the next chapter you will put your new knowledge of chaos theory to work and create a Wandering Map that will help you organize all the experiences, skills, and knowledge you have developed. You just need to be willing to try them out. There is a wonderful Spanish saying, "La vida es corta pero es ancha," which means "Life is short, but it is wide." You have a breadth and depth of worlds to discover thanks to your education, so let's start wandering into it. Wisely.

WISDOM BUILDERS

BUTTERFLY MOMENTS IN YOUR LIFE SO FAR

As you look back on your life, can you identify what Dickens called "memorable days" or occurrences in your life that started you on a new and unexpected direction?

- Maybe it was the day you decided which college to attend.
- Maybe it was the day someone gave you a valuable piece of advice.
- Maybe it was a day you learned a new skill.
- Maybe it was a decision your parents made.

How does this new knowledge about your life affect your job search or career plans? Take a few minutes to write down those experiences and what changed in your life as a result.

Unexpected event:_____

_____

_____

Result:_____

_____

_____

Unexpected event:_____

_____

_____

Result:_____

_____

_____

You will have days like this in the future. The trick is to be aware of them when they happen and take advantage of the opportunity offered to you at that time.

ARE YOU ON A LINEAR PATH?

Have you already decided the career you plan to pursue? Describe the connections between the courses you're taking and your experiences so far that connect you to this career.

_____

_____

_____

_____

_____

_____

_____

_____

_____

Jot down some ideas for future classes and experiences:

_____

_____

_____

_____

_____

_____

_____

_____

_____

CHAPTER 2

CONNECTING THE DOTS

UNCOVERING THE POWER OF YOUR WANDERINGS

Not all those who wander are lost.
—**J.R.R. TOLKIEN,** *THE LORD OF THE RINGS*

hen you think about the future, do you sometimes feel

Overwhelmed?

Clueless?

Stuck?

Join the crowd. If you're like most college students or recent grads, you've done a lot of different things in your life and sometimes it's hard to know where and how to direct your focus. After all, you certainly don't want to miss anything. But the chaos created by so many choices can leave you feeling like a pinwheel: spinning in the wind and going nowhere fast.

➔ What if you had a way to organize your past so that you could more clearly see your future?

•> What if you could discover new empowering information about yourself?

•> What if there was a simple way to help you identify what makes you special and interesting to employers?

You're one blank piece of paper away.

You already learned from the explanation of chaos theory in Chapter 1 that there is always order despite the chaos. You just have to step away from it to see it. The exercise you're about to complete will help you uncover the most important factors in your life so far, and then give you the priceless opportunity to step away from them, look at them from above, and see the connections.

In this chapter, you're going to make a Wandering Map: a simple, yet surprisingly powerful tool for organizing the chaos of your life. It won't serve as a literal map, of course, but it will help you focus on your strengths, identify significant themes and moments in your life, and maybe even start you on a future path. The Wandering Map will help you develop your reflective thinking skills as you look to your past to find your future.

MAKING SENSE OF THE CHAOS

Have you ever noticed that the knowledge you acquire in one area of your life can be applied to a completely different setting? You may have already seen that in your classes—how what you study in one class seems to dovetail with what you're learning in another. For instance, you might be studying the behavior and culture of a tribe in anthropology class only to find that the way you're analyzing the tribe could apply to what you're learning in your business class about behavior in a corporation. Your business professor might not ever mention the words "culture" or "anthropology" but you see the connections. When we take what we learn in one sphere of our life and apply it to another, our knowledge and understanding increase substantially and we open the door for creative thinking and brilliant new insights and ideas.

Nobel Laureate Dr. Herbert Simon, who developed the field of artificial intelligence, discovered the same thing. His degrees in economics, computer science, and psychology gave him the unique vision to see what others had missed. He used the phrase "network of possible wanderings" to describe the value of multidisciplinary perspectives. He said that the more you know about different disciplines and are able see the connections between those disciplines, the more you are able to create innovative solutions to problems. Your mind is able to wander into many territories. Your knowledge of chemistry, for example, might improve your thinking in the field of biology. Or your understanding of poetry might make you a better therapist.

Charles Munger, vice chairman of Berkshire Hathaway and business partner of Warren Buffet, the richest man in the world, calls this approach to thinking "mental latticework" and applies it to investing. He believes that to fully understand the stock market and investments, you need to apply knowledge from disparate fields, including philosophy, physics, psychology, history, economics, biology, and literature. He states that only by understanding the key elements of each of these fields and then pulling them together into a cohesive latticework can one develop what he calls "worldly wisdom," an invaluable means of making intelligent decisions.

The Wandering Map you're about to create combines the thinking behind Herbert Simon's network of possible wanderings, the basic principles of chaos theory, Munger's latticework, and the visual mapping work of Joseph Novak and Tony Buzan. You'd probably rather get started on the map than read a lot of research, but if you'd like to learn more about these ideas, see the References and Resources section at the end of the book. To put it succinctly, the power and value of the Wandering Map lies in its ability to help you

- ◆ brainstorm new ways of viewing and understanding your past;
- ◆ identify previously hidden themes and threads in your life;
- ◆ break away from linear thinking to look for creative connections;
- ◆ make meaningful order of the chaos;
- ◆ create a powerful vision for planning your future; and
- ◆ get excited about your talents, interests, and possible future.

So I have one question for you: *Is it worth thirty minutes of your time and a blank piece of paper to rise above the chaos and find direction?*

Self-discovery requires time and focus. You can't think clearly in the midst of cell phones ringing, e-mail arriving, friends dropping in, worrying about exams, and so on. So to get the most out of this exercise set aside some time when you won't be interrupted—thirty minutes is great. If possible, leave your room and go to the library or a park or your local coffeehouse—anywhere you won't be disturbed. Let's get started.

SHOW ME THE CHAOS: CREATING YOUR WANDERING MAP

Let's start by getting your brain ready to create this map. This exercise may seem unusual to you, particularly if you're more comfortable making lists or writing outlines. It may even seem kind of silly. Trust me: the students who complain the most at first usually tell me it turns out to be the most valuable activity they have ever tried. So suspend your judgment for a few minutes and give it a try. Keep the following thoughts in mind as you create your Wandering Map:

- It will always be a work in progress. You may add items to it anytime you want and we will revisit it in future chapters.

- There are no rules, so don't sabotage yourself by creating arbitrary rules, such as

  - "I must figure out the answer to all my questions."

  - "I must know by two o'clock this afternoon what I plan to do when I graduate."

  - "I must make the perfect map that includes absolutely everything that's important."

  - "I have to be some kind of artist to create this map."

  - "I should include _____ because my parents think it's important."

So unburdened by rules and perfectionist thinking, here we go . . .

First, get a big sheet of blank paper and something to write with. Poster board or newsprint paper (available in the art section of your college bookstore) or 11 × 17 inch paper is ideal, but you can also work with a regular piece of plain 8½ × 11 inch paper if you wish. Try to avoid using paper with lines because that will increase your tendency to list and organize. We're working with chaos here, remember. You can use pencils or pens, but I find that people get really creative when they use crayons or colored markers. Something about the bright colors and the fun of using crayons opens up your mind to all kinds of new ideas. It's more fun if you like the materials you're using.

Second, start thinking about all the interesting and significant things you've done or have happened to you. Go back as far in your life as you wish. If a significant event occurred at age five, include it. Have you had unique jobs or taken unusual classes? Did you have a memorable summer experience? What are you most proud of in your life? Do you have hobbies you've pursued for a while? What awards or honors have you received during your life? Can you think of a particularly valuable lesson you've learned? What knowledge do you rely on that you have developed from your experiences or education? What successful experiences can you recall?

To help you visualize a Wandering Map, there's a sample created by Bill on page 24, a senior majoring in finance. You can copy the style of map he created or develop your own. Add any shapes or colors or graphics you would like.

Notice that there's no rhyme or reason to what Bill selected or the order in which he put it on the paper. He just selected some key events from his life and placed them randomly on the paper.

Third, start writing down your thoughts. At this point you are probably buzzing with ideas. If something has meaning to you, write it down anywhere on the paper. It's important to write what comes to mind, not just what you think is career related. You don't need to write any long explanations; just jot down a few keywords. For instance,

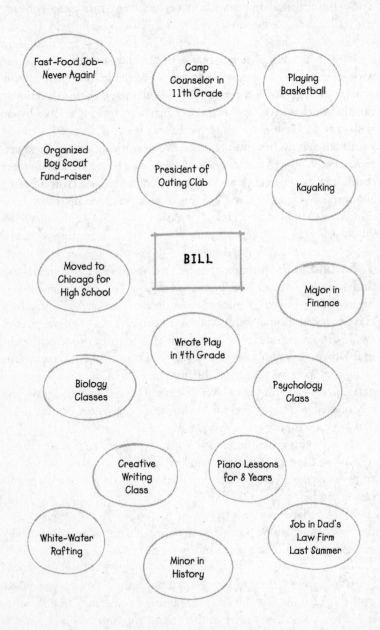

if you learned something from working at a camp one summer, just write "summer camp counselor" or whatever the position was. If you have read several biographies of Martin Luther King Jr.and find you quote him or follow his beliefs, write down his name. There will be time later to expand your thoughts. You can even draw little pictures if you prefer. The important thing is to just dump everything that's in your head onto the map.

Fourth, as you continue to write down significant aspects of your life, *don't try to organize them in any way.* Just write them down, draw a circle or other shape around them, and keep going. You can put down ten items or forty items or four hundred items; it's up to you.

Fifth, staring at a blank piece of paper can be daunting. Just in case you're stuck or still not quite sure what to put on your map, here are some final prompts that may help you remember key moments in your life:

→ **Objects** you use and/or enjoy
- Computers
- Musical instruments
- Books
- Binoculars
- Skateboards
- Telescopes or microscopes
- Sailboats
- Paintbrushes
- Journals

→ **Events** in your life, whether a moment in time or lasting for years
- Jobs you've held—awful to wonderful
- Taking a fantastic class
- Tutoring a child
- Baking cookies for the holidays

- Designing a Web site or your Facebook page
- Acting in a school play
- Running for office in a school election
- Playing sports
- Creative projects
- Adventures/risks you've taken
- Assignments, papers, or projects you're proud of
- Family heritage/culture
- Hobbies
- Ideas you have developed
- Internships
- Places you've lived or traveled
- Summer activities or vacations
- Volunteer activities

So if you haven't started already, get out your blank piece of paper and start mapping.

Remember:

- *Quickly* write whatever comes to mind and keep going. Get as much as you can on the paper.

- Don't waste time erasing or making it look perfect.

- Don't worry about spelling. As long as you can read it, that's all that matters.

- Use short words, phrases, or even drawings if you prefer.

- Don't censor yourself or try to make the map look a certain way. For instance, if you've been thinking about becoming a lawyer, but you notice you are putting down items more related to music, *don't* start thinking "I'd better put something down that relates to being a lawyer."

- Don't worry about organizing your thoughts—just get them down on the paper.

Congratulations!

You did it. Does it look a little chaotic and crazy? So many different things—and all seemingly unrelated? Don't be stressed—we'll fix that soon.

⇨ **Take another look to see if you want to add anything.**
Remember, you can always add things at any time and we'll keep building your map throughout the book.

⇨ **If you're out of time, you can quit now as long as you promise to return for the analysis.**

ANALYZING YOUR NETWORK: FINDING YOUR THEMES AND THREADS

Creativity is connecting the unconnected.

—**JOHN MAXWELL,** *THINKING FOR A CHANGE*

Now the fun begins. We're going to step back and look for some connections. If creativity is connecting the unconnected, as author John Maxwell says, we're going to be very creative. And trust me, there's a gold mine in here.

STEP 1: IDENTIFY THE BASIC CATEGORIES

Let's start by making some obvious connections. Look over your map. Would some of the items you wrote down fit into a particular category? For instance, did you list several jobs, vacation spots, friends, or classes you liked? Draw lines on your map to connect the different categories.

On page 30 you'll see how Bill drew his lines to connect the categories.

From this map, Bill can now create a list of categories:

1. Jobs

2. Creativity

3. Money-related items

4. Classes

5. Sports

Write down your list of categories from your Wandering Map. See if you can identify at least five below, or if you prefer, write them on the back of your map or on a separate piece of paper.

1. _____

2. _____

3. _____

4. _____

5. _____

> Are you surprised by your list of categories?

> Are there categories you weren't expecting to see?

> Is there a pattern to your categories?

> Does any one category have a lot of items?

Note anything that you find interesting or possibly significant.

STEP 2: DIG DEEPER: IDENTIFY THEMES AND THREADS IN YOUR LIFE

This time you're going to look at your map again, but instead of focusing on the obvious categories you noted above, ignore them and dig deeper to see if you can find some new connections beyond the simple categories you identified earlier.

For instance:

- ⇥ Do you see a thread that follows you from elementary school through college?

- ⇥ Is there a pattern to the types of jobs you've held?

- ⇥ What might some of your seemingly disparate experiences have in common?

- ⇥ What did you learn or what strengths did you acquire by pursuing a particular activity?

Before you try this yourself, let's revisit Bill's Wandering Map on page 32 to see how he redrew his lines and connected themes and threads rather than categories:

Bill's list of themes and threads follows:

1. Leadership is shown by his time in the Boy Scouts, his outing club work, and his role as a camp counselor. Bill has discovered that he likes to be a leader and the person in charge. He had to solve a lot of problems when he was in his leadership roles and he did them well.

2. Teamwork is exemplified by his baseball experience and his work with the outing club. Bill enjoys activities where he can interact with others. He can work alone as well, but he prefers the energy he gets from working closely with others.

3. Bill had to demonstrate practice and discipline consistently in practicing the piano and at baseball practice. He had to learn to put up with a sometimes dull routine. He learned that some things don't come quickly and that learning one small part (like four measures on a line of music) can be a big accomplishment.

4. Notice that Bill has drawn arrows that go from biology to history to creative writing to psychology and then end with his major in finance. He connected them because he realizes that *he learned key concepts in these courses that have been valuable to his understanding of finance.* He also discovered that he tended to focus on financial elements of

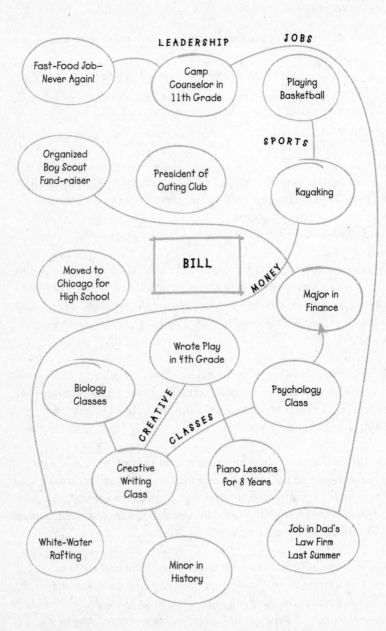

each subject he was studying, such as when he studied the Great Depression in history class or gambling behavior in psychology.

5. He enjoys writing, as illustrated by his taking an elective creative writing course. This is a long-term thread in his life; he even wrote a play back in elementary school. He likes being creative, and writing is relaxing and something he would do even if he weren't paid to do it.

6. Risk taking is shown in his kayaking and white-water rafting hobbies. He believes that his ability to take risks, while at the same time knowing how to remain safe, is a unique skill.

7. Bill is starting to identify the kind of work he doesn't want: working in a hotel or a law firm. He will want to analyze further the specific aspects of those jobs he didn't like.

Now it's your turn. What new connections can you make? See if you can *identify any themes or threads* that run through your life. For instance:

- ⇥ You, too, might see examples of an interest in writing: you created a neighborhood newsletter when you were a kid, and then you got an A in creative writing in high school and are now working on your college newspaper staff.

- ⇥ Maybe you've worked with children in one capacity or another for a long time.

- ⇥ Maybe you do a lot of physical or hands-on activities, such as playing sports or building things.

- ⇥ Maybe you've always been the peacemaker in your family or with your friends.

- ⇥ Maybe you've done lots of activities that involve international themes.

Can you identify at least four or five themes or threads in your Wandering Map? If so, draw lines connecting the different entries on your map and then make a list of your basic themes below, on the back of your map, or on a separate piece of paper.

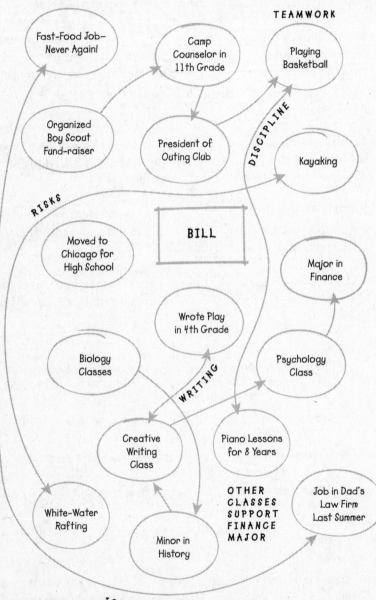

1. _____
2. _____
3. _____
4. _____
5. _____

This part of the process is challenging and it's not always easy to spot the themes and threads that run through your life. If you're stuck, here are some more ideas for possible themes and threads:

Achievement/ Awards

Alone or with others

Animals

Art

Computers

Creative ideas

"Doing" or "Thinking"

Drama

Equipment or tools I use

Family

Fun

Hobbies

Indoors or outdoors

Internally or externally rewarded

Knowledge I've acquired

Learning

Locations

Music

Physically active or deskbound

Reading

Research

Risky or safe

Roles I've played in family or elsewhere

Solving problems

Subjects—topics of interests

Things I want to change

Types of people

What comes naturally to me

Maybe your themes fall under specific skill areas such as these:

Analytic

Artistic

Communication

Computer

Counseling

Creative thinking

Detail/Follow-through

Interpersonal/People skills

Research/Investigative

Leadership/Management

Manual

Negotiating

Mathematical/Financial

Organizational

Outdoor/Athletic

Presentation/Performing

Problem-solving skills

Serving/Helping

Teaching/Instruction

Thinking strategically

Sometimes your themes can reveal what's important to you. Do any of these themes show up consistently?

Adventure: taking risks, frequent change, trying new things

Challenge: testing skills, seeking stimulating physical/mental experiences

Contribution: making a difference, helping victims, solving problems

Creativity: self-expression, ideas; art, music, and/or drama; beauty

Diversity: being around people from many cultures, appreciating differences

Expertise: possessing knowledge or skills, having authority

Family: nurturing, children, appreciating relatives

Friendship: close friends, collegial environment, friends at work

Harmony: peace, orderliness, calm surroundings, meditation

Health: time for exercise, eating well, safe work environment

Independence: freedom, autonomy, acting on own terms

Joy: pleasure, humor, happiness

Justice: helping society, equality, fairness, important causes

Leadership: organizing, delegating, managing, inspiring, influencing

Learning/Knowledge: acquiring education or training, teaching, expertise

Leisure: finding time to relax, pursuing hobbies

Physical Work: using your hands, building, physical fitness

Power: exerting personal power, controlling, influencing, assigning

Prestige and Recognition: being successful, attaining a high status

Productivity: accomplishing, hardworking; excellence; efficiency

Security: safety, stability, secure job

Spirituality: practicing religion, meditating, spiritual exploration

Variety: different tasks, exploring new territories

Wealth: acquiring money, economic security, high-paying positions

How are you doing? Have you been able to find some new connections? Have you discovered a skill that has served you in more than one location? If the preceding lists have helped you identify new themes or threads in your life, be sure to add them to your list.

Or are you finding this challenging—perhaps you can see a few connections, but you're not really seeing a bigger picture? Then move on to Step 3.

Wandering Off:

CAN'T I JUST TAKE A CAREER TEST THAT WILL TELL ME WHAT TO DO?

Does it seem as if you've had to work pretty hard in this chapter? You're probably wondering why you couldn't just take a test. Career tests have been around for many years and they continue to develop and improve. But no career test can tell you what to do. At best, they take the responses you provide (usually in a forced-choice format, so you can't argue or explain the nuances of your thinking behind the answer), compare those responses with others who work in particular career fields, and then tell you how you compare to those people. For instance, you might find that you answered the questions in a similar manner to veterinarians. Does that mean you should be a veterinarian? Not necessarily. And the tests won't tell you whether you have the skills, education, or talent to be one either. So there are limits to testing.

That said, there are some excellent tests on the market that can provide more information that might be helpful. As long as you're not asking a test to predict your future, you might find some of these tests give you more information about yourself that you can use to your benefit in interviews or graduate school essays. Contact your career center or counseling center to see if they administer them—the fees charged (if any) will be much less than the fees you would pay in a private counseling setting.

Recommended tests you can take in a career counseling setting:

Myers-Briggs Type Indicator

Strong Interest Inventory

Campbell Interest and Skill Survey

Excellent tests you can take on your own:

Values in Action (http://www.authentichappiness.sas.upenn.edu/)

The Strengths Inventory from the book *Now, Discover Your Strengths* by Marcus Buckingham and Donald Clifton.

STEP 3: SHARE YOUR MAP

Try sharing your map with someone who can help you identify more themes or might see some connections you're missing. Wandering Maps can be even more valuable when someone else helps you see the connections. Try showing and talking about your map to friends, roommates, classmates, parents, a counselor, supervisor, professor, or anyone who might help you see connections you're missing. Review some of the items you placed on the map and tell them why you included them. Ask them if they see any other connections. Tell them you're on a hunt to find hidden treasures in your life.

STEP 4: EXPAND AND COMPLETE YOUR THEME CHART

Complete the chart opposite (or use a separate piece of paper) by filling in the themes or threads you've identified from your map. Add descriptions or comments that will help you identify what these themes might ultimately mean to you. Your chart allows you to compile up to ten themes. If you have more, feel free to add them; if you have fewer, that's fine. There is no magic number here; it's just a starting point to isolate the themes. By the way, don't judge them either. It's OK if you write down a theme you don't particularly like or don't wish to continue. *You might even find that a theme that initially seems negative (perhaps you had a difficult childhood or experienced a significant trauma in your life) might actually become a positive theme because of how you overcame it.*

Don't pressure yourself to make any career decisions yet based on your themes, and don't worry if your themes don't seem to be career related. Remember, we're still gathering information.

Themes or Threads

1. _____

2. _____

3. _____

4. _____

5. _____

6. _____

7. _____

8. _____

9. _____

10. _____

If you want, check or highlight the themes above that you'd like to continue developing. *Remember that you will be adding to or changing your Wandering Map and themes as you go through the Wise Wanderings system.*

You saw Bill's map earlier; here are a few more examples of themes uncovered by college students completing their Wandering Maps:

→ Jim's Wandering Map (pp. 38–39) illustrates what chaos theory calls pendulum attractors: his two main interests seem to oppose each other. He enjoys helping others in time of crisis, and he enjoys work related to money and finance. Jim felt pulled by these seemingly opposite themes. He enjoyed working in banks, studying economics, and had a strong desire to work on Wall Street. He liked the excitement and hustle of the trading floor. At the same time, he had a long history of helping people in need from staffing emergency centers during the Katrina hurricane to volunteering at local shelters, to working with the police department's victims unit supporting and consoling the families of crime victims. He could also see himself working in a nonprofit setting because it was important to give back. How could he resolve these seemingly disparate interests? When he analyzed the

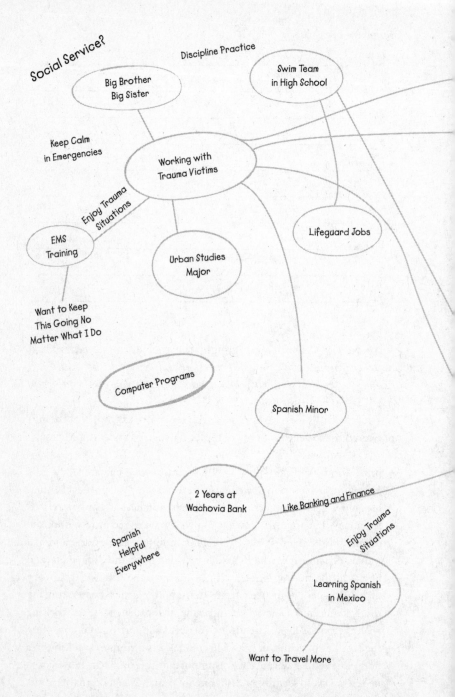

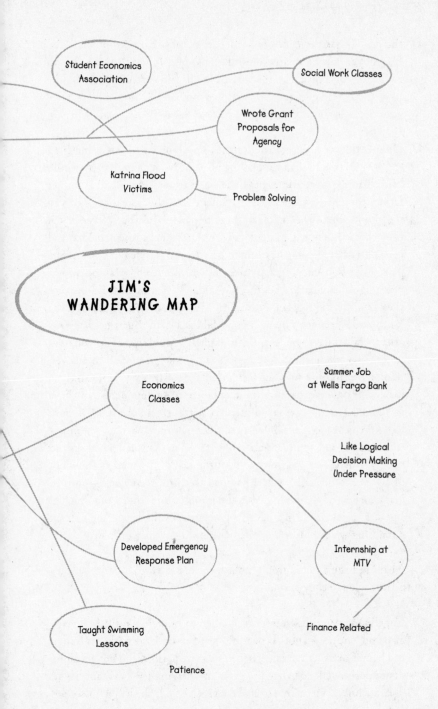

themes in his experiences, he realized that they shared commonalities: he enjoyed taking charge of situations, he is good at dealing with challenges and obstacles, he thrives in chaotic surroundings, and he likes to help people in crisis. Jim plans to use this information as he goes through the job search process.

➜ One of the more interesting entries on Danielle's Wandering Map (pp. 42–43) is her talent for playing pool, or what chaos theory would call a strange attractor. Danielle learned to play eight ball from her father (they had a table in the basement) and she honed her skills to the point where she regularly beat her older brothers, even when they cheated! She has entered and won many pool tournaments, and even admitted to some hustling in bars to earn money in college. She placed her pool-playing activities on her Wandering Map because it was a significant part of her life, but said it was "kind of silly" because she certainly didn't plan a career as a pool hustler, even though she joked about it always being a good fallback plan. But when she was asked, "What have you learned from playing pool? What do you have to know or understand to be good at it?" she was quick to answer. "You have to think on your feet, you have to strategize constantly—both your own moves and the likely moves of an opponent—you have to stand up to men who think they're better than you, and you have to hold your own independently in a competition when no one else is rooting for you." Hmm. Sounds like pool playing is not a bad skill to have. Danielle then began to look at the rest of her map and quickly discovered other areas where she had to think strategically both in her favorite classes and in her summer jobs. She realized that she had a powerful talent she had never appreciated. Danielle is going to start pondering ways to use her strategic thinking in the workplace.

Although their maps aren't included, here are two more examples of the knowledge they can uncover.

➜ Angelina's map illustrates the challenge of being pulled by two disparate entities—another pendulum attractor. Her mother is Italian and her father is Armenian. Their respective families did not get along particularly well, so Angelina grew up viewing the two families in separate boxes, virtually unrelated to each other. She loved both sides of her family but because of the constant conflict between them, she tended to judge each one based on the standards of the other. After completing her Wandering Map and noting the many family-related activities she had placed on it, she discovered that family influences were strong. She started to think about what she had learned from each side of the family. Both sides had actually encouraged strong, loving ties. From the Armenian side of the family she learned the importance of hard work, of responsibility and keeping your word. From the Italian side of her family she learned the importance of enjoying life, taking time for eating and sharing conversations, and appreciating beauty. She realized that she was a blend of these two cultures and could use the strengths of each in the workplace. Angelina began to feel much stronger and less torn by the differences in her family. She learned to make use of the gifts she had acquired from each and to understand how different cultures could conflict and yet, if given the proper mindset, could learn to value differences and get along. She's going to think about this newly discovered aspect of herself and see how she might parlay it into a career.

➔ Rachel discovered that her themes were writing, travel, imagination, ethnography, and enjoying change. Even though writing was a strong theme, she decided she couldn't be a journalist because she found the structure of journalistic writing too limiting. She prefers the ethnographical style she learned in her anthropology major, which allows creativity and can delve into the unknown and unseen—two themes she finds fascinating. She doesn't know yet how all this will tie into a career, but she suspects something interesting is just around the corner.

Congratulations! You've now completed the whole Wandering Map process. Did reading about other people's stories help you? Remember, this map is designed to help you identify key themes, skills, interests, values, and other important aspects of your life, but it is not meant to point you directly to a career. If you find career-related themes at this point, by all means feel free to pursue them. But if you don't see a career path from your map, don't worry. You have been mining for gold, and you have already uncovered nuggets even if you aren't sure how you'll use them or what their value might be.

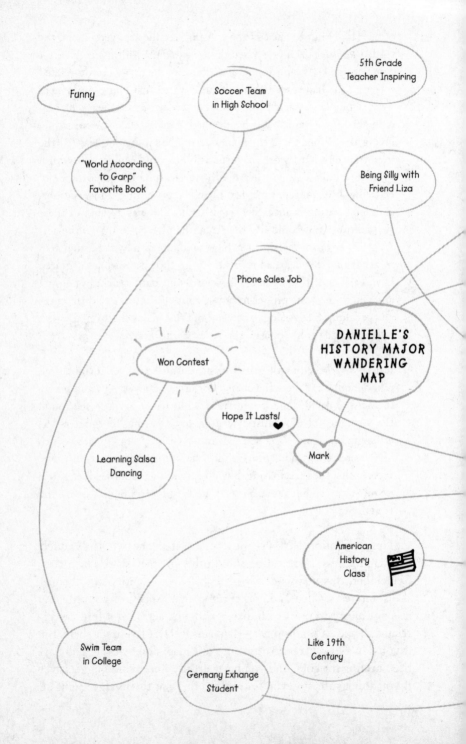

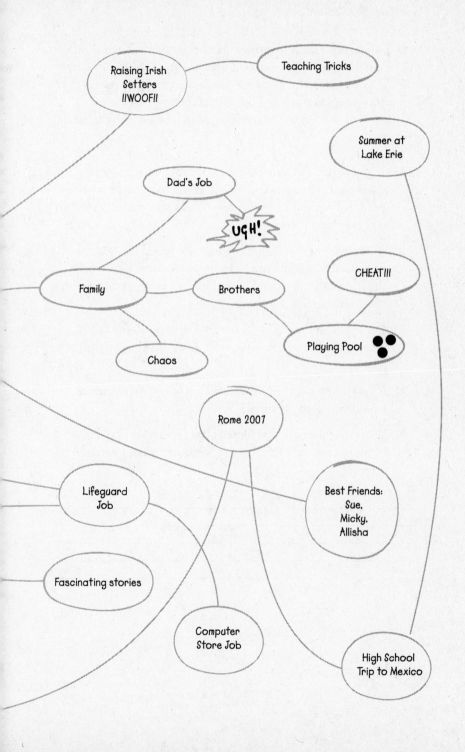

Your Wandering Map is just the start of your process and soon you will be combining the information you've uncovered in this chapter with the knowledge you'll acquire in the next few chapters to begin designing your plans for a captivating and compelling future.

Before you leave your Wandering Map, consider the following questions:

1. If you're having trouble seeing your themes, try asking yourself these questions: "What would happen if a miracle occurred tonight and suddenly I could see the themes? What do I think they would be?"

2. What two or three items are you most proud of? What skills or behaviors did you use to accomplish them? Can you begin thinking of ways to use those skills or behaviors now or in a work setting?

3. On a scale of 1 to 10, with 1 being least important and 10 being most important, which theme would you rank as the most important? Why?

4. If you knew you couldn't fail, which one of these themes would you keep pursuing?

5. What theme would you like to take a step toward pursuing in the next twenty-four hours? What step would you take?

_____

_____

_____

_____

_____

WISDOM BUILDERS

· ⟩

I. GETTING THE MOST FROM YOUR STUDY-ABROAD EXPERIENCE: WHAT GRADUATES HAVE DISCOVERED

Many students and recent graduates include their study-abroad experience in their Wandering Maps. When surveyed about their college experiences, graduates almost always rank their study-abroad experience as one of the best and most fulfilling times in their lives. They cite the unexpected benefits they received from the experience and the many skills and talents they acquired, almost without realizing it. Here's a list of the common strengths graduates say they acquired through the study-abroad experience:

- Established rapport with individuals from other cultures
- Functioned well in ambiguous situations and handled difficult situations
- Achieved goals (despite lots of challenges)
- Showed initiative and took risks
- Managed time well enough to both study and travel
- Responsible for all personal actions (no one else to rely on)
- Learned the language quickly
- Learned to be comfortable while relocating often in a job
- Learned through listening and observing
- Developed good decision-making skills . . . after making some errors

How might this list of skills interest an employer?

Can you think of some skills you derived, or might get, from studying abroad? Make some notes here: _____

_____

_____

2. HOW DO MY RELATIVES FIT INTO MY CAREER PLANS?

Another common component of a Wandering Map is the influence of family. Your parents and other relatives can be influential sources of information and attitudes about careers. Whether it's a family business or career such as medicine, performing arts, and the law, it's not uncommon for family traditions to develop around careers. What you need to decide is whether your family's career field works for you. Here are some questions to consider as you think about the influence of your family:

- What do my parents say about their work?
- Did they choose their careers or did circumstances influence them?
- Would they do the same work again?
- Is there a career field that runs through my family?
    - Am I interested in continuing this family tradition?
    - What will happen if I do or don't follow the tradition?
- What suggestions or advice have my parents given me about my career?
- What are my siblings doing?
    - Do they enjoy the careers they're in? Why or why not?
    - What advice or guidance have they given me?
- What assumptions about work might I have made based on what I heard or observed in my family?

Summarize any significant messages you've received about work from your family: _____
_____
_____

3. HOW DO I DEFINE SUCCESS?

When you look at the experiences on your Wandering Map that you consider successful, how did you define success? Did it involve winning? Helping others? Achieving?

How might you define success in the future? Complete any of these sentences that appeal to you (no need to do them all):

As my life progresses, I will consider myself successful when I

HAVE THIS JOB TITLE: _____

OWN _____

RETIRE AT AGE _____ IN _____ (LOCATION)

USE MY TALENT IN _____ TO _____

AM IN LOVE WITH _____

SPEND MY TIME _____

VOLUNTEER TO _____

RECEIVE AN AWARD FOR _____

AM ASKED FOR MY AUTOGRAPH BECAUSE I _____

HAVE PURSUED _____

DO _____

HAVE _____ DOLLARS IN THE BANK OR IN INVESTMENTS

FILL IN THE BLANKS WITH YOUR OWN IDEAS:

_____

_____

Now, reward yourself for the hard work you've already done, and relish the order you're finding in the chaos. You've already mined your past for gold; in the next chapter you're going to get the most from an extremely valuable possession: your brain.

CHAPTER 3

MENTAL WANDERINGS

YOUR MIND CAN TAKE YOU ANYWHERE OR NOWHERE

The universe is full of magical things, patiently waiting for our wits to grow sharper.

—EDEN PHILLPOTTS, *A SHADOW PASSES*

THE VALUE OF THINKING

Two college deans stepped off the curb to cross a street when a pickup truck with a gun rack whizzed by, slowing down just long enough for the passenger to lean out the window, look at the two men, and yell, "Hey, smart guys!" before driving on. The two deans looked at each other, unsure how to react. Was that an insult or a compliment?

Our society sends mixed messages about being smart. From popular movies such as *Dumb and Dumber,* the TV show *Jackass,* and even book series such as ——— *for Dummies,* we seem to be much more comfortable putting down our thinking power than promoting it. This tendency to downplay intelligence and thinking even rubs off on clearly intelligent career fields like Web development. A popular Web design book title, *Don't Make Me Think,* succinctly sums up the prevailing philosophy about Web sites: the worst thing you can do is design a Web site that will require people to think. Part of the problem seems to be that people simply don't have time to think anymore. We need short and quick Web sites and books that spell out everything so we don't have to waste our time thinking.

College is supposed to be a time for thinking, but again, if you watch movies about the college scene (*Animal House* anyone?), you sure wouldn't know it. The students who are serious and thoughtful never seem to be the cool or popular ones. So it's not surprising that when I ask my students in class what mindsets or types of thinking they've developed through their classes, I get blank stares. They'll tell me they haven't had time to think about it. Ironic, isn't it?

Does the "don't make me think" philosophy mirror your time in college? Have you been acquiring a lot of knowledge and information without thinking of its value? Are you finding it hard to articulate to employers what you have learned or are not even sure why they'd want to know about your classes? After all, those job openings for philosophers or sociologists have been few and far between.

There's no mixed message in this chapter—your knowledge and thinking skills *are* your power. Employers are begging for intelligent workers who possess and use the right mindsets: specific ways of thinking. The way you choose to think about your classes, your experiences, and your job search is the key to your success in the hiring process and beyond. But good luck finding a career book that gives thinking or mindsets more than a cursory glance.

In the last chapter you developed your Wandering Map, which highlighted past achievements, talents, and themes running through your life. In this chapter we're going to *dig deeper and look specifically at the brain power behind those talents and themes*: the mindsets you've developed that will help you ace your interview, get a job, and move up in whatever career path you follow. And if you haven't developed all of these mindsets yet, you will learn enough to start adding them to your repertoire of skills and talents.

What if you possessed a secret power that would change your job search completely? What if that power was in your mind?

It's time to get wise.

RIGHT MIND: THE KEY ELEMENT OF GOOD THINKING

We don't think of thoughts as tangible, because we can't see them with our eyes any more than we can see the electricity that powers our computers or the vibrations that travel from our cell phones. Yet your e-mail arrives and your friend answers the cell phone. Thanks to increasingly powerful medical technology, we are beginning to "see" and measure thoughts—or at least see the parts of the brain that light up when certain thoughts or images are active. And as a result, our knowledge of the brain and how it thinks is growing exponentially. Your thinking skills are as real and identifiable as your more visible skills, such as athletic, musical, or artistic talents.

If you consider your thoughts to be just as tangible as the book you're holding, then you can examine them and make deliberate choices in how you think. The field of cognitive behavioral psychology has demonstrated that how we think directly influences how we feel. When our attitude changes, our behaviors change, and this in turn influences our performance. So how you choose to think about your classes, experiences, the job search, and your job directly affects your success before and after graduation.

> When you change the way you look at things, the things you look at change. **—WAYNE DYER,** *THE POWER OF INVENTION*

Good thinking will help you change how you interpret a situation. Zen philosophers have a nice phrase for good thinking: right mind. Right-mind thinking creates a positive chain of success in whatever endeavors you pursue even when you're in less than desirable situations. Right-mind thinking doesn't mean you ignore challenges or pretend that something bad is really good. Instead, you take what is challenging and find a way to mentally approach the challenge so that ultimately you succeed in the situation.

Let's look at this in terms of a common student situation: you're required to take a class you really don't want to take. There are two tracks your thinking can follow:

	NEGATIVE THINKING	RIGHT-MIND THINKING
THOUGHT	"I have to take this required class I'm going to hate."	"I have to take this required class. I don't think I'm going to like it, but because I want to do well I'm going to see what I can do to make it a good experience."
BELIEF	"I shouldn't have to take this class. I'll never need this information. This is ridiculous. It's a complete waste of time and a stupid requirement."	"I can't control the class, but I can control my experience of it."
EXPECTATION	"This class will be boring and useless."	"I'm going to see what I can learn from this class."
ATTITUDE	"There's no point in putting much effort into it. I'm just going to do the minimal amount of work to survive and suffer through the semester until it's over."	"I'm going to make this a personal challenge. Because it's a required class, someone must think it's valuable. And the professor must think there's something valuable in what we're studying. I'm going to find out why. If nothing else, I'll have a great story for an interviewer about how I survived a difficult class."
BEHAVIOR	Cut class. Sit in the back row. Use the time to instant-message (IM) friends or play a game on your laptop. Do minimal work on assignments.	Attend class. Take good notes. Study for the tests. Keep looking for something interesting about the course—even if it's just the professor's bad wardrobe!
PERFORMANCE	Get a C or worse.	Get an A or the best possible grade in the situation.
WHAT YOU'VE LEARNED	"I'm helpless and at the mercy of ridiculous rules."	"I'm in control. I can make the best of a bad situation. I can challenge myself."

Notice that at no time did the right-mind thought process become Pollyannaish or lapse into happy talk. The thinker didn't lie to herself and say. "Oh, this class will be wonderful. I can't wait to take it.

I love the professor." Quite the opposite. The thinker took a realistic perspective: "The class is what it is. I can choose to suffer through it or I can make the best of it."

Aside from causing pain and leading you down a path to a poor outcome and uninspiring future, negative thinking has a particularly fatal flaw: it presumes you are a fortune-teller. How do you know you'll never need the information from that class? Maybe a required science class sounds awful now, but what if two years later you decide to become a psychologist and need that science knowledge to get better grades in your psych classes, ace the Graduate Record Examination (GRE), or get into a master's degree program? How do you know that you won't suddenly enjoy that class and end up majoring in the subject? The right-mind thinker understands the power of the butterfly effect and remains open to the possibility that something good might come from an experience. The Chinese philosopher Lao-tzu was on to something when he said, "Know that you don't know. That's superior."

Remember: you're thinking all the time, and the thoughts you choose can propel you forward or hold you back. Take a moment and refer to your Wandering Map. Look at some of your achievements and successes. What thoughts were behind the positive actions you took? What thinking skills did you need to be successful at what you did? If you can name them, write them down on the back of your map or on a separate piece of paper. If you're not so sure, you'll have a chance to process this more thoroughly later in the chapter.

ACTION: THE CORNERSTONE OF WISDOM

There is no try. There is only do. —**YODA** IN *STAR WARS*

A comedian once described discovering a magazine totally devoted to running. He said he could understand the first couple of issues—maybe some articles about the best running shoes, suggestions for warm-ups and cooldowns, and maybe even the most scenic places to run. But after the first couple of issues, he asked, "Shouldn't the magazine just say 'Run!'"

He has a point. We can go on and on about knowledge, wisdom, and mindsets, but without taking action with each mindset, we're wasting time. We have a saying in Texas: "I'm fixin' to do that." It's a joke, of course, based on the premise that we all have lots of things we plan to do but haven't done yet. Thinking is the first step, but to get results you have to take action. In the next section of this chapter, as you focus on the ten key mindsets employers are seeking, start considering which mindsets you have already put into action and which ones you want to start using.

Music at Work:

THE MUSIC MAN

In the musical *The Music Man*, con man bandleader "Professor" Harold Hill promotes the "Think System" to his pupils. Not wanting to let on that he doesn't know how to play an instrument, he tells his students they don't need to practice; they only need to "think the Minuet in G and you will play the Minuet in G." Recent psychological research says he may have been on to something: visualization is an important factor in the learning process. Visualizing yourself successfully making foul shots in basketball leads to a greater percentage of successful shots. And visualizing yourself acing the interview helps as well. The successful job search starts in your head.

The easiest way to start taking action is to start **paying attention.** Teach yourself to develop a cycle of action and reflection throughout the day. Try observing your behavior:

- ⇢ What would you like to do?
- ⇢ How much do you talk about doing rather than doing?
- ⇢ Is there a disconnect between what you think (or say) and what you really do?

⇥ What is the first step you could take toward doing?

⇥ Who or what could help you take action?

⇥ How will you feel when you start taking action?

⇥ Imagine that you have taken the action you wanted—how do you now look or feel?

GOOD THINKING WORTH CULTIVATING: TEN MINDSETS EMPLOYERS ARE SEEKING

So you get the message that thinking is vital to your success in life. But what mindsets would be most helpful? Let's examine ten of them that will ensure your success in the job market and beyond. The mindsets may look intimidating, but in truth you will find that you already know about and practice many of them. You just haven't paid attention to them or thought about mentioning them specifically to employers.

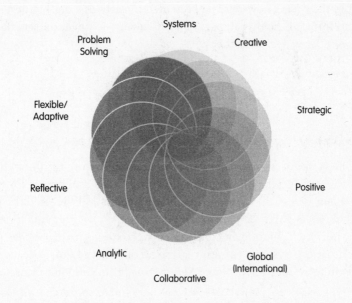

Psychologists and researchers have identified innumerable kinds of "thinking" above and beyond the ten described here. If you have developed other thinking skills or mindsets, by all means note them and be ready to explain to employers how they would make you the best candidate for the job.

The mindsets described here are simply a starting point: a top ten list, if you will, based on years of conversations with employers who are seeking the best talent for their organizations, whether in a profit, nonprofit, education, government, or entrepreneurial setting. Numerous books have been written about these mindsets and others, so in the interest of time, only the elements related to the job search will be covered here. If you want to read more about each mindset, see References and Resources located at the end of the book.

For each of the mindsets presented you will find questions that will help you develop and strengthen your thinking. As you read through these different mindsets, consider how each one becomes more valuable when combined with action. If you find they overlap with one another as in the diagram above, good for you. They do overlap and the best thinkers use them all and more. And don't forget to get out your Wandering Map to look for the mindsets you used in the past. They must be presented linearly in a book, but it's best to think of them as all part of a whole with no one mindset taking precedence over the other.

ARE YOU READY TO GET WISE?

MINDSET I: THE SYSTEMS MINDSET

The systems mindset can also be called Big Picture thinking. It says we have to take different points of view into account to solve a problem or develop an idea, and that the whole is greater than the sum of its parts. The systems approach allows an organization to see how each component contributes to the strength (or weakness) of a situation. Systems thinking says to connect the dots, because everything is connected. Some key systems thinking questions to ask are:

> What do these things have in common?

> How can they work together?

> How does each piece influence the whole?

> What is the perspective of each piece?

> How does the overall structure influence the behavior of its components?

> What is the consequence of a decision in one part of the system on the rest of the system?

A baseball team, for example, can be considered a "system." How does the performance of one player affect the performance of the team? How important is it that they work together? How does each player view the game? How important are the fans to the team? Does the name of the team help its popularity or perhaps cause controversy? And what about the location or quality of the stadium—not to mention unions, salary negotiations, community issues, and so on. Systems thinking will help create the best possible baseball team by considering all the elements in relation to one another.

Why Would an Employer Care About Systems Thinking?

> Workers who use a systems approach are more likely to see connections between divisions and develop stronger relationships.

> A systems mindset is vital to an organization's survival. As customers become more concerned about environmental issues, for instance, the company's "good citizenship" in the world can influence the company's bottom line.

> If organizations focus only on one factor or perspective, their decision making is compromised and limited. Systems thinking results in creative problem solving.

> Internal effects: organizations are comprised of networks of internal relationships between divisions and departments. The systems approach pulls divisions together so that the human resources department is aware of the sales department, which becomes more aware of the manufacturing process, and so on.

➔ External effects: organizations have to consider outside forces as well. For instance, a company like Benetton can't just focus on buying and selling clothes. It must consider environmental impact and related issues; labor conditions for employees, including their standard of living; the source of its products, including whether and how animals are used; geographic locations and climate; political conditions; shareholders; customers, and so forth.

How You Can Develop or Use the Systems Mindset

➔ **You have already begun using a systems mindset:** you used it when you created your Wandering Map in Chapter 2. Chaos theory is an example of a systems perspective.

➔ **Begin noticing connections.** How do seemingly disparate parts of your life connect to and influence one another? How do your classes connect? Why is what you learned in psychology helpful in your history class? How did observing your coach settle a rivalry within the team teach you a way to settle a conflict in your residence hall? Why is it important for you to understand someone else's perspective or viewpoint?

➔ **Look at the systems surrounding you.** What organizations do you belong to or where have you worked? What kind of systems interact at your college or university? How many different departments or groups exist within the system? What are the outside influences? How could you apply a systems approach to better explain and understand conflicts or problems as well as apply new solutions?

➔ **Take courses that allow you to study complex systems** such as anthropology, economics, sociology, or political science, or interdisciplinary courses such as American studies, Asian studies, women's studies, and so on, where you will examine societal problems like poverty or immigration. You know that topics like these can't be studied from only one perspective and why it's silly when a politician proposes a "simple" solution to a complex problem.

On a scale of 1 to 10, how would you rank your use of the systems mindset?

Never Use	1	2	3	4	5	6	7	8	9	10	Constantly Use

If you were going to tell an employer about your strength in systems thinking, what example(s) would you use?

_____

_____

_____

_____

_____

MINDSET 2: THE CREATIVE MINDSET

Quick—answer this question: Are you creative?

How did you answer?

Why?

When I ask this question in classes, about 50 percent to 75 percent of the students raise their hands. When I ask the others why they don't think they're creative, they usually mention their lack of talent in music, writing, or the arts. But this is a myth and an extremely limited view of creativity. The truth is everyone is, and can be, creative. Creativity like any other mindset can be cultivated. You may recall the quote about creativity in Chapter 2 that said, "Creativity connects the unconnected." Creativity is not only talent in the arts, it's also the ability to view circumstances in a new way, to see what others don't see, find a new solution to a problem, or develop a new product or idea. People who are creative question the status quo and wonder how it could be changed or improved. They ask questions such as What if . . .? or What else . . .? or How can we . . .?, any of which can lead to new ideas.

Another myth about creativity is the belief that we have to have unlimited time and/or money to be creative. We conjure up notions of the wonderful creative projects we could do if only we had all the time and money we needed. But research has shown that creativity actually thrives with moderate limitations (like deadlines or budgets) and decreases when unlimited resources of time and money are provided.

Why Would an Employer Care About Creative Thinking?

➔ Organizations need to grow and move forward to keep up with change, and creative people are invaluable to growth.

◆) Creative thinkers will help organizations stay ahead of the competition.

◆) Creative thinkers are the greatest source of innovation and new products.

◆) Creative thinkers will see solutions where others see only problems.

How You Can Develop or Use the Creative Mindset

◆) *Make the most of your talents.* If you meet the more traditional definition of creativity and have a talent in music or the arts, how can that skill assist you in the workplace? For instance, if you studied ballet, what are the behind-the-scenes skills of being a ballerina that might help in the workplace? Did you have to have lots of discipline? Good time management skills? Get over your stage fright? Learn to accept limitations?

◆) *Lighten up.* Taking yourself too seriously and worrying about being perfect are the greatest stumbling blocks to creativity. Too many talented writers, musicians, inventors, and others quit because they view their work as less than perfect. Remember that if something is worth doing, it's worth doing badly, simply because it's worth doing. With practice you will improve but not become perfect, because nothing is perfect. So silence your inner critic and keep taking chances.

◆) *Set limits.* Creative types often feel overwhelmed. From the research presented earlier, you know that creativity thrives in a moderately controlled environment. One creative aspect of the job search is deciding what career to pursue. Have you seen those ridiculously long lists titled "What You Can Do with a Major in———" and followed by two hundred possible careers? Is that helpful? Or is it just overwhelming? Try setting a limit, such as focusing first on careers in a particular category, for example, sports or writing. You've probably heard the saying "Follow your bliss." That's a great idea, but it, too, can be overwhelming. You'll likely be more creative if you set a limit on your bliss. Maybe you'll follow your bliss in New York City. That's the beginning of setting limits that will help you more easily find it.

◆) *Stretch yourself.* Are you in a rut? Do you follow the same schedule, go to class the same way, hang out with the same friends? Maybe it's time to shake things up a little. Sit in a different location in class. Decide to meet one new person this week. Speak up when you would normally be silent. Be silent when you would normally speak up. Attend a club meeting in a new area. Maybe you're into all the political clubs, so try attending a drama club meeting. The two fields have a lot in common, you know. When you stretch yourself, you'll be surprised at what you can do and how seemingly disparate activities have much in common.

> *Consider a weekly "artist's date."* One of the best writers on creativity, Julia Cameron, recommends that everyone set aside a one-hour chunk of time during the week to explore something alone that will get your creative juices going: a museum, a bookstore, an auto parts shop, wandering the aisles of a favorite store, sitting on a park bench, listening to an outdoor concert, and so on.

On a scale of 1 to 10, how would you rank your use of the creative mindset?

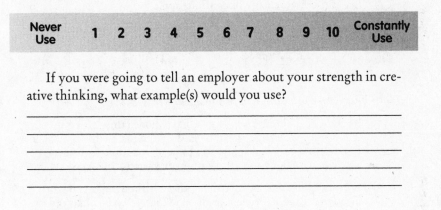

| Never Use | 1 | 2 | 3 | 4 | 5 | 6 | 7 | 8 | 9 | 10 | Constantly Use |

If you were going to tell an employer about your strength in creative thinking, what example(s) would you use?

_____

_____

_____

_____

_____

MINDSET 3: THE ANALYTIC MINDSET

We use the word *analyze* all the time:

> A psychiatrist analyzes his patient.

> An engineer analyzes the traffic patterns on the highway.

> A stockbroker analyzes the stock market.

In the simplest terms, analysis is a breaking down of the whole into distinct parts. By examining each piece using logic and reason, the analytic thinker is able to reassemble the pieces into a greater whole that is better understood and valued. Analytic thinking skills help you convert a large problem into a series of smaller parts, thus making it more understandable and workable. Analytic thinking is the key to better understanding and organization. And with analysis often comes synthesis, where you pull your individual thoughts back into a whole that is greater than the sum of its parts.

Why Would an Employer Care About Analytic Thinking?

- ⟫ Cost-benefit analysis is just one example of a common use of analytic thinking in the workplace. Employers must know how a proposed product, idea, or plan is going to affect the bottom line.

- ⟫ Analysis of key problems or successes in the workplace can help to ensure their remedy or continuation.

- ⟫ Analytic thinking is rational and logical and not governed by emotion. Employers need decision makers who examine the details in a situation before making a decision.

How You Can Develop or Use the Analytic Mindset

- ⟫ Analytic thinking is a skill you've likely honed through your schoolwork. You have probably used analytic skills if you've taken an English course and analyzed a piece of literature. Consider how you developed analytic thinking in various courses.

- ⟫ Writing a research paper requires analytic thought as you work through the main problem or thesis. What have you analyzed in your papers?

- ⟫ Try analyzing a favorite movie. Watch it again and notice the components: the actors selected for the roles, the story, the costumes, the sound effects, the music, the lighting, the scenery, and so forth. Describe the different components and consider why they were chosen. How do they help (or hinder) your enjoyment of the film?

- ⟫ Create metaphors to give meaning to a situation. For instance, what might be your metaphor for your job search? Is it a nightmare? Or are you on easy street? Is your future an abyss? Or is it, as the saying goes, "so bright you have to wear shades"? Analyze how your metaphor affects your behavior.

On a scale of 1 to 10, how would you rank your use of the analytic mindset?

Never Use	1	2	3	4	5	6	7	8	9	10	Constantly Use

If you were going to tell an employer about your strength in analytic thinking, what example(s) would you use?

_____

_____

_____

_____

_____

MINDSET 4: THE STRATEGIC MINDSET

A strategic mindset is first and foremost rational, logical, and practical. The strategic mindset incorporates analytic thinking and draws from a systems perspective of looking at the Big Picture to solve a problem. A strategic mindset provides a specific way of solving problems, often using a method called strategic planning, a common system used by organizations to understand their current position in the marketplace, develop a vision, and plan for the future. Common techniques used in strategic planning are SWOT (an acronym for strengths, weaknesses, opportunities, and threats) analyses, goal setting, vision statements, and gap analysis.

Why Would an Employer Care if You Are a Strategic Thinker?

Strategic thinking can help an organization:

- ➔ set priorities and stick with them;
- ➔ develop focus and keep everyone on the same plan;
- ➔ measure and monitor success and progress;
- ➔ determine what is and isn't working, why it isn't working, and how it can be changed;
- ➔ ensure employee commitment to its plans;
- ➔ focus on action rather than contemplation.

How You Can Develop or Use the Strategic Mindset

⇗ You will learn specific strategic planning techniques later in this book as you develop your career plans and prepare for interviews.

⇗ Read a book on strategic planning and try applying the approach to an organization you're in.

⇗ Look for courses that teach strategic thinking or planning. You can find them in most business, human resources, or organizational behavior programs.

⇗ When you encounter a problem, ask yourself questions such as the following, which will stimulate strategic thinking:

- What strategy will work best to solve this problem?
- What challenges do I need to be aware of?
- What are my strengths?
- Where do I need to improve?

On a scale of 1 to 10, how would you rank your use of the strategic mindset?

Never Use	1	2	3	4	5	6	7	8	9	10	Constantly Use

If you were going to tell an employer about your strength in strategic thinking, what example(s) would you use?

_____

_____

_____

_____

_____

MINDSET 5: THE POSITIVE MINDSET

You began learning about the positive mindset when you read about the right-mind approach at the beginning of this chapter. Most people misunderstand the positive mindset because it seems at odds with analytic or critical thinking. Isn't the point of analysis to find the problems? Why would one focus on the positive aspects of a situation? Positive thinking is not happy talk or blind optimism in the face of reality. Instead, it is a consistent focus on strengths in any situation: what went right, rather than what is wrong. Positive thinkers are using analytic thinking, but they are analyzing the strengths, the learning, and the desired outcomes instead of the problems.

In the last ten years, a new field of positive psychology has evolved to examine what works in peoples' lives, and the research conducted so far overwhelmingly demonstrates the significance and value of a positive (optimistic) mindset. Dr. Martin Seligman is one of the foremost researchers in the field, and he identifies four personal traits that contribute to a positive mindset: well-being, optimism, happiness, and self-determination.

Positive thinking creates a positive future. His studies have found that in virtually all professions (with one notable exception), positive thinking or optimism is a major component of success. For example, optimistic sales representatives experience more sales; optimistic teachers are happier and experience more success in the classroom. What's the one exception? Lawyers. Unfortunately, the field of law doesn't reward optimism: it is the nature of lawyers to seek out problems and constantly consider worst-case scenarios. Dr. Seligman has found that this characteristic wreaks havoc on the personal lives of lawyers, and in true optimistic style, he offers remedies for the situation.

Why Would an Employer Care About Your Positive Mindset?

- As mentioned earlier, research increasingly supports the importance of the positive mindset for success in the workplace. A positive mindset cuts stress, boosts morale, and improves productivity.

- The most successful leaders have positive mindsets, and a positive mindset helps you motivate yourself and others. Motivating workers is an ongoing challenge in many workplaces, and positive psychology research offers valuable advice and solutions.

- Optimistic workers are more resilient, less likely to quit or give up, and more likely to achieve goals and focus on their strengths.

➔ Individuals with positive mindsets are more likely to take responsibility for themselves and work independently.

How You Can Develop or Use the Positive Mindset:

➔ Consider a time when you experienced a setback. How did you handle it? What would a person with a positive mindset have done? When you're faced with a setback, ask yourself: "How would the 'perfect' me at my all-time best handle this situation?"

➔ What strengths did you discover in your Wandering Map? How can you use or build on them today?

➔ Think about times when you've been "in the flow"—when time just flew by because you were so caught up in your experience. What were you doing? Can you increase the time you spend in the flow now?

➔ In his book *Authentic Happiness,* Dr. Seligman writes that "the key is not finding the right job; it is finding a job you can make right." He recommends "recrafting" your job by changing the duties to fit your strengths. Think about the various jobs or activities you've enjoyed. How did you make them right through recrafting?

➔ Name three things that went right today. Better yet, name three things that have gone right with your job search recently. Perhaps reading this book is one of them. What did you do to make them happen?

➔ Develop an "attitude of gratitude" by focusing on what has worked well in your life. Or try thinking of three things you're grateful for today. You might even want to create a gratitude journal, writing down the large and small things you're grateful for, like that great coffee shop that's located on your way to class or work. By the way, this also works when you can't sleep. Instead of thinking about all the things you need to be doing, or haven't done, focus on the three things that went right during the day.

On a scale of 1 to 10, how would you rank your use of the positive mindset?

Never Use	1	2	3	4	5	6	7	8	9	10	Constantly Use

If you were going to tell an employer about your strength in using a positive mindset, what example(s) would you use?

_____

_____

_____

_____

_____

MINDSET 6: THE GLOBAL (INTERNATIONAL) MINDSET

You'd have to have been living in a cave to have missed all the buzz about globalization. The world seems to shrink every day—we are not on an isolated island, nor should we strive to be. A global mindset goes beyond tolerance of another culture to appreciation and understanding. People with global mindsets go out of their way to study other cultures and languages, and immerse themselves in new places and experiences. The global thinker understands that our worlds are enhanced by appreciating, valuing, and incorporating ideas from other countries and cultures. We even understand ourselves better when we understand others.

Why Would an Employer Care About Your Global Mindset?

- ➔ Even small organizations are increasingly international in nature if only because the Internet has created customers or clients from around the world. They have a need for workers with global knowledge and understanding.

- ➔ Leaders, in particular, need to have global mindsets to be able to develop far-reaching visions for their organization.

- ➔ Workers who can speak other languages and understand and appreciate other cultures are highly prized in the workplace. They already have a strategic advantage over employees who don't possess the same skills and knowledge.

- ➔ The organization that is global in its thinking has a strategic and competitive advantage in the marketplace.

How You Can Develop or Use the Global Mindset

➜ Expand your world: seek opportunities to immerse yourself in people, places, and experiences that are new and out of your comfort zone. Deliberately seek experiences that you might find uncomfortable and go in with an attitude for learning.

➜ Study abroad—or better yet, volunteer or work abroad so you are more fully immersed in the culture.

➜ Seek out students at your school who are not native to your country and listen to their perspective. Ask them what they like about college. What do they dislike? What has been hard about adapting to American culture? What mistaken assumptions do Americans possess about their culture?

➜ Seek out courses that will teach you about cultures, languages, and international issues. Go with an open-minded attitude and a desire to learn. Consider studying a language that's completely unknown to you, such as an Asian or Middle Eastern language if you're most familiar with European languages. Download a foreign language podcast and take the first lesson. Understanding someone else's language will help you better understand their culture.

➜ Immerse yourself in an unfamiliar culture or country by reading books or watching films native to that culture or country.

On a scale of 1 to 10, how would you rank your use of the global mindset?

Never	1	2	3	4	5	6	7	8	9	10	Constantly

If you were going to tell an employer about your strength in this area, what example(s) would you use?

_____

_____

_____

_____

_____

MINDSET 7: THE COLLABORATIVE MINDSET

The collaborative mindset can be challenging, particularly for students who have had negative experiences with teamwork in their classes. If you've ever been graded on a team project, you probably know what I'm referring to. Isn't there always someone on the team who doesn't even show up for the meetings? And doesn't someone always get stuck doing the bulk of the work? Bad experiences with working on teams have created a mental block against teamwork for many people. In fact, teamwork often goes against the classic American mindset of rugged individualism and the romantic image of the lone hero. Consider the film *Die Hard,* which in 2007 *Entertainment Weekly* magazine voted the number one action film ever made. Bruce Willis is the lone hero and the only "teams" in the movie are the evil terrorists and the clueless police force. That is, until toward the end of the film when Bruce teams up with one lone-wolf street cop and the two together outsmart the larger groups.

On the other hand, many of you have probably experienced good moments of collaboration: the orchestra you played in, the choir you sang in, the athletic team you were on, or the student committee you formed to change a bad policy at your school.

Most people would agree that collaboration is a good thing. While most conflict can be boiled down to the simple question, "Why aren't you more like me?" the collaborative mindset responds, "Sure we're different; so how can we work together?" Good collaborators know that our thinking expands into new areas when we work with and listen to others.

Why Would an Employer Care About Your Collaborative Mindset?

- ➜ Employers consistently list teamwork as a vital skill in their organization, regardless of the type of organization.

- ➜ Being able to work on a team is a survival skill in the workplace. Workers have to be able to communicate and work together to be efficient.

- ➜ Teams are often responsible for the development of new products, innovations, and ideas. Teamwork results in synergy, where the whole is greater than the sum of its parts.

→ Well-constructed teams can break down "silo thinking," the failure to take into account the opinions and needs of other groups within the organization.

→ Teams foster the sharing of information and cooperation and can draw out the best in each worker.

→ By strengthening communication, teams help to foster a culture of trust within an organization.

How You Can Develop or Use the Collaborative Mindset

→ Consider when you have you been part of a team. Was it a successful experience? What made it a success or failure? What did you learn from working in a team?

→ Seek opportunities to be part of a team. Join an organization, attend the meetings, and be an active participant.

→ Make a point of listening to and valuing the ideas and opinions of others. Ask yourself, "What could I learn from this person or this group?"

On a scale of 1 to 10, how would you rank your use of the collaborative mindset?

Never Use	1	2	3	4	5	6	7	8	9	10	Constantly Use

If you were going to tell an employer about your strength in this area, what example(s) would you use?

_____

_____

_____

_____

_____

MINDSET 8: THE REFLECTIVE MINDSET

During periods of relaxation after concentrated intellectual activity, the intuitive mind seems to take over and can produce the sudden clarifying insights which give so much joy and delight.

—**FRITJOF CAPRA,** *THE TAO OF PHYSICS*

With cell phones, iPods, BlackBerry devices, video games, twenty-four-hour cable, and so on, developing a reflective mindset is probably the most challenging. In fact, when surveyed, students often indicate that it is their least-used mindset, and it is usually in the top five mindsets the students wish to develop. Most of us know the value of taking a moment of reflection particularly when emotions are high—have you ever regretted sending an e-mail or IM in a moment of anger? Taking time to reflect helps us make smarter decisions.

A reflective mindset is extremely powerful and the small amount of time spent in this mode will yield results exponentially. There are two main challenges to reflective thinking: time and noise. You need to have a chunk of time and get into a quiet setting.

Why Would an Employer Care About the Reflective Mindset?

◆ A reflective mindset will help you make sound decisions. By taking the time to reflect, you can avoid errors in judgment or snap decisions made through emotional reasoning.

◆ The reflective mindset helps you stay calm and relieves stress, making you a more productive and healthier worker.

◆ The reflective mindset enhances creativity and makes you more likely to produce ideas and innovations.

◆ The reflective mindset gives you perspective—you won't jump to conclusions as quickly when you take the time to reflect.

How You Can Develop or Use the Reflective Mindset

◆ Try using an online meditation site. You can even download a five-minute podcast of meditative music. One of the myths about reflective thinking is that you need lots of time—sometimes five or ten minutes is all you need.

➔ Try to get into the habit of writing in a journal or creating a portfolio to reflect on your experiences.

➔ Take a creative writing or rhetoric course where you can write opinion or argument papers that will require you to take some time to reflect on your opinions and thoughts.

➔ Invite a coworker or fellow student to lunch and talk about what you're doing at work or what you're learning in your classes. Use this time to reflect on what has been most valuable or what you've enjoyed learning or doing.

➔ Take up a hobby that allows you solitary time to reflect, such as kayaking on a slow river. Even working a jigsaw puzzle can help relax your mind and reduce stress.

➔ Here's an interesting activity: sit in a comfortable place, preferably outdoors on campus or where you can people watch. Sit and observe. Don't interact. What do you notice? What do you see, hear, smell, or feel? What details are you picking up on? How much activity is going on? Are people interacting? Are they on cell phones? Just observe. Is your mind wandering? Bring it back and keep observing. That's all you need to do. Just relax and observe. Give your mind a break from all the analyzing and strategizing.

➔ Take time to reflect on your classes. Ask yourself

- What did I learn?

- How did I add value to something or someone?

- How are things better?

- What did I encounter today that I'd like to think more about?

- What went wrong? What went right?

- What could I do differently next time?

- What do I like about what I'm learning?

- What would be cool to share with someone?

- What is my favorite class so far?

➔ If I weren't attending college right now, what would I do instead?

On a scale of 1 to 10, how would you rank your use of the reflective mindset?

Never Use	1	2	3	4	5	6	7	8	9	10	Constantly Use

If you were going to tell an employer about your strength in reflective thinking, what example(s) would you use?

_____

_____

_____

_____

_____

MINDSET 9: THE FLEXIBLE/ADAPTIVE MINDSET

A famous Zen story tells of a farmer whose horse runs away. His neighbors come over and say, "How terrible!" He simply replies, "Maybe, maybe not." The next day the horse returns accompanied by two wild horses. "How wonderful!" the neighbors say. "Maybe, maybe not," he replies. His son tries to ride one of the wild horses but falls and breaks his leg. "How terrible!" say the neighbors. "Maybe, maybe not," says the farmer. The next day a military officer shows up to round up the men in the village to fight in a war. But the son can't join the military because his leg is broken. "How fortunate!" say the neighbors. The farmer replies, "Maybe, maybe not."

One of the key methods for developing a flexible mindset is to limit judgments and preconceived notions. By detaching yourself from opinions, you are able to listen to information with an open mind and choose your response accordingly. Rigid thinkers often try to place everything in a right or wrong context too quickly and might miss important information.

Flexible thinkers are natural experimenters: curious, alert, and open to change. They don't allow failure or a setback to end their pursuits. Being flexible and adaptable allows you to experiment and roll with the punches. You're more likely to take risks if you know you can cope with whatever the outcome might be.

People often misunderstand Darwin's survival of the fittest theory, assuming that *fittest* means the biggest or the strongest. It actually means the most adaptable. Just consider how the (relatively) small cockroach has survived for millions of years through adaptation, not brute force or size. Or how American car manufacturers have suffered from their inability to be flexible and change with the times.

There is nothing wrong with being organized and having a plan. But the advantage of cultivating a flexible mindset is that you can more easily adapt to changes in your environment and be open to new ideas or opportunities. There's a Yiddish proverb, "Mann trakht und Gott lakht," which translates to "Man plans and God laughs." Like chaos theory, it reminds us that we are not always in control of everything no matter how hard we try, so it's important to be able to adjust to whatever situation we're thrown into.

Why Would an Employer Care That You Are Flexible and Adaptable?

➔ Speed and agility are invaluable in today's working environment. Organizations need to be able to change and react quickly to such factors as global competitiveness, advanced technology, increasing customer expectations, and the changing needs of employees.

➔ Change is a constant, and flexible workers can go with the flow in fast-changing environments. They are also great at customer service, which demands flexible thinking.

➔ Flexible thinkers adapt to both adversity and success because they change their techniques or skills accordingly. They manage change rather than let change manage them.

➔ Workers who are adaptable and flexible ultimately save the organization both money and time. Just think of a bureaucratic organization (the antithesis of flexibility): how much time and money is wasted by employees and supervisors who continue to do their work the same way it's been done for twenty years?

How You Can Develop or Use the Flexible/Adaptive Mindset

➔ Examine your "rules" about things and shake up your routine. Do you always order the same thing at your local coffee shop?

Try something different. Or skip the coffee and put your money in a charity donation jar or give it to a homeless person. What changes occur throughout the day when you make that small change?

→ Go to a bookstore but wander into sections you never normally visit. Do you traditionally head toward the true crime books? Try the computer book section. Are you a psychology or self-help addict? Visit the mysteries section. A science junkie? Try the art and architecture section. Just pull books off the shelf and look at them. Find anything interesting?

→ Select a topic about which you have strong opinions and try arguing for the other side. Better yet, construct arguments for both sides and see if there's a possible middle ground or compromising point.

On a scale of 1 to 10, how would you rank your use of the flexible/adaptive mindset?

Never Use	1	2	3	4	5	6	7	8	9	10	Constantly Use

If you were going to tell an employer about your strength in this area, what example(s) would you use?

_____

_____

_____

_____

_____

MINDSET 10: THE PROBLEM-SOLVING MINDSET

The problem-solving mindset is closely aligned with action orientation and the positive mindset. True problem solvers are like dogs on bones—not content to stop until they are sure they've finished. Problem solvers actively seek solutions—and assume that they will find them. They gain their energy by keeping their focus on the outcome and looking for ways to influence it positively.

An entire counseling system is built around problem solving, aptly titled Solution-Focused Brief Therapy (SFBT). Practitioners of this type of therapy are active problem solvers and use several techniques with their clients. One technique is simply refusing to buy the problem. If you think about it, most people who have problems spend a lot of energy convincing you that they have a problem. What if you refused to buy it? What if you simply said, "I'm not buying the problem; I'm going to find a solution." Another problem-solving technique in SFBT is to empower the person while disempowering the problem. So to help solve a problem, you might focus on times when you didn't have the problem and try to replicate the behavior present at that moment. For instance, if you have a problem with procrastination, it's likely that you are more aware of the times when you procrastinate. What if you focused on the times when you didn't procrastinate and see if you can identify the characteristics of that situation? You might find a solution in your own behavior. SFBT focuses on past successes and, like chaos theory, encourages you to maintain a state of not-knowing. Not-knowing will keep you open-minded to new solutions.

Why Would an Employer Care About a Problem-Solving Mindset?

➔ Consultants are paid a lot of money to be problem solvers. Problem solving is an everyday skill in the work setting.

➔ Good problem solvers know how to ask the right questions to find the solution. They are willing to take risks and use an action approach. Problem solving is not a passive activity.

➔ The problem-solving mindset dovetails with the positive mindset. Problem solvers seldom hear the word *no*.

➔ Problem solvers focus on potential and planning, always helping the organization move forward and preventing it from getting stuck.

How You Can Develop or Use the Problem-Solving Mindset

➔ Come up with creative solutions. Put yourself in someone else's shoes: how would you solve their problems? For instance, do you think you could come up with a better solution for alcohol problems on campus than your dean has devised? Do you think you have a better way to run a career center? If you've thought these problems through, consider meeting with the dean or the director of your career center and share your insights. After all, your thoughtful perspective as a student might just be what they need to create a successful program that would benefit many students.

→ Refuse to hear the word *no*. See if you can find another way around the problem. Reframe it as simply a temporary impediment. Think about how you would handle it if you were working at your all-time best performance level.

→ Problem solving is closely related to decision making. Try using one of the many strategies designed by consultants and other professional problem solvers. Research problem-solving tools and techniques, such as decision trees, flow charts, SWOT charts, and so forth, to solve problems. You can search any of these terms on the Internet and find lots of examples and ways to use them.

→ For every problem you identify, see if you can come up with three different solutions.

→ Think over a time when a door closed, when you didn't get what you wanted. How did you handle it? What did you do instead?

On a scale of 1 to 10, how would you rank your use of the problem-solving mindset?

Never Use	1	2	3	4	5	6	7	8	9	10	Constantly Use

If you were going to tell an employer about your strength in this area, what example(s) would you use?

_____

_____

_____

_____

_____

Wow! That was a lot to think about. This may have been a difficult chapter for you to work through, but students who have taken the time to analyze their mindsets and actively develop them have found the results invaluable when interviewing for jobs. And if you haven't already, be sure to return to your Wandering Map and list the thinking skills you've honed over the years. We'll revisit the knowledge you've gained in this chapter when we cover interviewing in Chapter 11. In the meantime, keep thinking about the mindsets you're developing and using. They will come in handy very soon.

Take one more look through the ten mindsets and answer the following questions:

Which mindsets do I use the most?

_____

_____

_____

Do I see any potential problems with the patterns of my mindsets?

_____

_____

_____

Which mindsets would I like to develop?

_____

_____

_____

What actions can I take in the next twenty-four hours to start developing new mindsets?

_____

_____

_____

WISDOM BUILDERS

> ●

MAJORS AND MINDSETS

If you've already selected a major, take a minute to think about how it has influenced you. What mindsets do you use the most in your major? What topics do you tend to study? Do you look at situations or information differently from other majors?

Different majors emphasize different thinking skills. Some teach you to analyze and view things from a specific perspective; others teach you a variety of perspectives. Some emphasize the scientific model and are more rational and logical in their approach; others emphasize perception or creativity.

If you haven't selected a major, what major might fit the way you tend to think? Instead of selecting a major based on career options (because you now know that's not the best idea), have you considered selecting it based on the thinking skills you'd like to develop or strengthen?

Just as an experiment, let's take the movie *Good Will Hunting*. How might different majors perceive that film? What aspects might they notice?

Here are some possibilities:

- Psychology majors might focus on the therapeutic interactions between Will and his psychologist or the diagnosis of his condition.

- Economics majors might take notice of the class structure of Boston and the economic challenges for the working class to acquire a college education.

- English majors might focus on the story structure, the plot, or the character development.

- Anthropology majors might want to analyze the different subcultures that make up Boston: the clothing they wear; their different speech patterns, their relative acceptance into society.

- Math majors might be interested in the formulas and problems Will is solving.

How is your major your mindset? What do you notice about current events or other subjects that reflect the major you've studied?

WORDS CREATE WORLDS

Did you know that changing your vocabulary can change your thinking? The language you use in any situation has the power to affect your perception of a situation. Imagine you are describing something as "a complete disaster." What do you picture in your mind? Now, describe the same situation as "annoying." Big difference, huh?

We often use language that inflates or exaggerates to make something more interesting than it really is. We describe everyday things as "amazing" or small events as "miracles." While those words won't likely hurt your everyday experiences, changing some words can help you clarify your feelings about a situation. For instance, the word *should*. How often do you use that word, particularly in relation to the job search—as in "I should go to medical school"?

Here's an experiment: every time you would normally say "should," change it to "want to." So now you say, "I want to go to medical school." That's a very different sentence and much more powerful. It allows you to stop and think: do I really want to go to medical school? And if you do, you may feel more motivated now because it's something you want, not something you have to do. Conversely, maybe when you word the sentence that way, you don't actually want to go to medical school.

Here are some other changes to try:

- Change *can't* to *won't*. Instead of saying, "I'd like to look for a job, but I can't do it right now," try saying "I'd like to look for a job, but I won't do it right now." This may be a little harder to acknowledge, but it's honest, and you can decide if you really are choosing not to do something.

- Change *but* to *and*. Maybe you've said, "I'd like to look for a job, but I'm taking a really heavy course load right now." This sounds reasonable, doesn't it—after all, you're very busy. It's a good excuse. But let's reframe the statement with one simple change: "I'd like to look for a job, and I'm taking a really heavy course load right now." Do you see how that simple use of the word *and* opens up the statement to possible solutions? The first statement closes off any chance of change or problem solving. It also draws into question whether it's really true that you'd like to look for a job or if you're looking for excuses. The second one accepts that you'd like to look for a job and you also have a challenge. You can then start thinking about ways to solve that problem.

- Take a moment to use your reflective thinking skills and examine how often you have connected the words *should, but, can't,* and *must* to your job search.

CHAPTER 4

WANDERING BEYOND MAJORS AND MINORS

MAKE YOUR EDUCATION RELEVANT TO ANY EMPLOYER

You know, I have this crazy philosophy that your grades should represent your grasp of the material and not your negotiating skills, which are amazing, by the way.

—GREG KINNEAR AS PROFESSOR ALCOTT IN *LOSER*

id you know that your love of learning could make you a valuable employee? Wise college students are curious—always seeking new information, new ideas, and answers to questions. Employees who value learning will read more about the field in which they are working, will attend and present at conferences, will develop new ideas, and will create value for their employers throughout their careers. Remember the "don't make me think" philosophy from Chapter 3? Do you feel as if you have absorbed a lot of knowledge and information about obscure topics and still aren't sure of their value? On the contrary, your academic experiences (regardless of your major) are at the core of your career planning and development. In the classroom you have had the opportunity to acquire knowledge, connect with professors, learn valuable skills, and become exposed to new ideas and experiences you haven't even considered. *Your major is not your end goal; it's a series of classes that will help you accomplish your goal.*

Once again, this chapter might seem unusual for a career book.

If you're tempted to skip it because you've finished your education, don't. This chapter is designed to assist you with making sense of and getting the most from your education whether you are in your first semester of college, your last, or even if you've graduated. Considering that classes are the primary source of a college education, it's ironic that they are disposed of so easily in the career-advising process. In this chapter we're going to do an in-depth analysis of your classroom experience and examine the skills and knowledge you have acquired from classes so far and the classes you would like to take prior to graduation.

Your classes represent the classic point attractors in chaos theory. They have captured your attention, generated excitement, and are interesting, but they can also be distracting—particularly if you're not quite sure what you can do with them. Many college students dismiss their education for its presumed lack of marketability. They begin their sentences with apologies, such as "Although I'm not a business major, . . ." or "Even though I haven't taken any courses in. . . ." This approach virtually guarantees that you will not be taken seriously in the job market and that your potential will never be fully realized. You must have absolute confidence in your degree and your ability to apply it to the marketplace if you're going to persuade employers to hire you. So as we start examining your education, one rule is required: *no apologies, no regrets, no "if only's," and no "I should haves"* when it comes to your education.

Students select their majors for all sorts of reasons. Why did you select yours? At best it was because you enjoyed the professors and what you were learning, but life isn't always that simple. You might have been prevented from pursuing your desired major because it was overcrowded, or your grades weren't strong enough. Maybe you wanted to pursue a particular major but were turned off by its requirements—foreign language or math courses, for example. But now you're starting to wish you had bitten the bullet and taken those tough classes so you could be in a more competitive position for a job. Perhaps you selected a major that doesn't seem to have a direct career plan or one where the job market is saturated. Maybe you're looking at the list of recruiters coming to your career center and all you see are employers seeking a major you didn't take.

None of that matters. Remember chaos theory: assess what you currently know, what you don't know, and what you can learn. After all, you are where you are. Instead of focusing on what you didn't get, what knowledge/learning have you acquired? What else would you like to learn before you leave college? And just because you've already graduated doesn't mean you can't mine your classes for what you learned as well as find new opportunities to learn. And you don't have to learn everything through your classes. Chapter 8 will help you find ways to develop even more knowledge outside the classroom.

When taking classes, most students focus on the present moment—a "what do I need to know to pass the class" approach. You're focusing on the subject matter to pass a test or write a paper and likely not thinking beyond that. You don't see a connection between what you're learning and how that knowledge might be used. You may have even discovered that because your major isn't immediately understood by relatives or friends who took more "practical" subjects in college, it's ridiculed. Liberal arts majors in particular have become the ninety-eight-pound weaklings of the education field, beaten up by the public and media.

> But then, last time I checked, this "bracketology" business wasn't easy for anyone. I read the other day that there were 18,446,744, 073,709,551,616 possible combinations for filling out a 64-team bracket. For the liberal-arts majors in the crowd, that's, like, a lot.
> —**JIM ARMSTRONG,** *DENVER POST*

Students in preprofessional majors like accounting are told from day one that their education is relevant to the workplace and are encouraged to think accordingly—constantly applying their theories and knowledge to the workplace. If you took a less career-oriented major, you have not received this same encouragement. In fact, your professors may never have said a word about what you could actually do with the knowledge you were acquiring. If that's your situation, you have some catching up to do. Conversely, those of you who took preprofessional majors like advertising or marketing may be find-ing that there aren't enough jobs in the field to support the number of majors. When the first question you're asked in an interview for a position in banking is "You're an advertising major. Why aren't you interviewing for an advertising job?" suddenly your "practical" major seems like a liability. Even management majors can struggle in the job search if they feel they're always competing with finance or accounting majors. In many ways, a management major could be considered the liberal arts of the business school.

Getting the most out of your academic experience isn't just about attending classes, writing papers, and taking exams. It's about delving into fields of study that will expand your mind and help you develop new connections. Your classroom experience can be the start of a new world and open up career opportunities you didn't even know existed. In the rest of this chapter, we're going to mine your major and your classes for all the valuable knowledge and practical learning you've been acquiring whether you know it or not.

English at Work:

WHAT MOBY DICK AND ESPN HAVE IN COMMON

Are you sitting in English class wondering why the professor is making such a big deal out of *Moby Dick*? It's just a story. And how about that film professor who spends hours analyzing *Citizen Kane*? It's just a movie. We spend so much time and energy analyzing works of art, music, films, and books because analyzing them enriches our experience and understanding. We learn new information. We have a deeper understanding of the author or story and what happened. We learn to pay attention, notice details, find meaning, and maybe even understand ourselves better. So if you're thinking it's a waste of time to analyze works of literature, consider this: how many hours are spent on ESPN analyzing a football game? What about all those pregame and postgame shows? The commentators who pick apart the game, analyze the players and their moves, and how a mistake likely happened because a rookie was playing? It's just a football game, right? Right. And that's why English, film studies, and other courses could prepare you for a great career in sports broadcasting. Or analyzing world events for CNN.

Before we move forward, though, let's pause for a quick discussion of a common concern for students: grades. Never confuse grades and learning. Yes, it's easy to make a superficial argument that you learned more in a course where you received an A than in a course where you received a C. But as you have probably know, it's not that simple, as Angelo discovered:

I had to take a science class and I wasn't very good at science in high school. I thought I had hit the jackpot when I learned that a particular anthropology class counted for the science requirement. I knew I could handle anthropology. Well, within two weeks I was in over my head. It was fascinating—kind of like the CSI stuff on TV—and I was learning a lot, but it was all so foreign to me. For my final exam, I had to enter a room that contained nothing but old—and I mean old—bones laid out on several tables. I had to identify whether they were animal or human, their gender, their age, and so forth. I have never worked so hard in my life. I got a B minus and it was the hardest grade I ever earned. I'm more proud of that grade than the A's I had in other courses. When employers ask me if I can handle challenges, I tell them about the feeling I had when I walked into that room full of bones. They always laugh and tell me they admire my perseverance. And then we talk about the differences between anthropological reality and what's on TV.

Most studies reveal that ultimately there is little correlation between your college grade point average (GPA) and the salary you receive or how successful you are in your career. And once you're in the workplace, your GPA will continue to have less impact, except perhaps for highly academic employers such as institutions of higher education or think tanks. But it is also true that the higher your grade point average, the more opportunities will be available to you. Many prestigious programs, including White House internships, FBI programs, pharmaceutical sales positions, Wall Street jobs, and so on, screen candidates by GPA. And obviously, the better your grades, the better the graduate or professional school you will be able to attend. Good grades give you more freedom to select opportunities.

Does this mean if you don't have a perfect GPA. you're sunk? Of course not. There are numerous examples of successful people who had poor grades or even dropped out of college. Your GPA is just one factor in the employment and graduate school process and there are lots of ways to compensate. It still makes sense to go for the best grades you can within reason, but you are in college to learn, so don't avoid classes just because you might not get the best grade.

You've been working hard in your classes—studying, writing papers, taking tests, and so on. Isn't it time your courses did something for *you*? Let's look at strategies that will help you improve your grades, if needed, as well as present your education in the best possible light to employers.

MAKING YOUR CLASSES WORK FOR YOU

You already know from your Wandering Map and your analysis of your mindsets that you possess a unique set of talents, skills, knowledge, and experiences. Contrary to some people's thinking, you are not taking refuge from the workplace during your years as a student. You are actively acquiring knowledge and information that will serve you later on, so consider keeping your projects, papers, books, and other records of your learning to create a portfolio for future employers.

If you believe that your courses are not relevant to your life post-college, you are wrong. Even if the specific information from the courses isn't directly relevant, you are acquiring metaknowledge: knowledge that teaches you a framework for thinking about a situation. For example, most of us are seldom called upon to solve an algebra problem. But we developed logical thinking and problem-solving skills from working those formulas and we use that knowledge daily. Most courses contain metaknowledge that can be extrapolated and applied to workplace settings. So take some time to examine those courses you think don't apply to your future endeavors. Are you sure they are "useless"? How could you challenge an employer's assumption about your classes? How could you sell your potential based on your education? Did you take a class where you knew nothing about the subject but by the end of the semester were practically an expert? How could that skill apply in a job setting?

The concept of deriving skills from majors is hardly new. Career counselor and writer Dr. Howard Figler offered groundbreaking advice by identifying the importance of deriving skills from majors more than twenty years ago. But unfortunately, his brilliant ideas have been turned into trite lists of commonsense skills from majors: for example, English majors are great writers, history majors are great researchers, and so on. You need to get beyond identifying basic skills such as communication and thinking because it's all too easy to apply them to any major. Business majors can be just as good at writing as English majors, depending on the individual. It's more important to focus on what *you* learned and what skills *you* have developed from your classes and your major, rather than accept a few stereotypes (which every interviewer has heard a million times from other students, by the way). Here are just a few examples of what you could derive from some classes you might have taken:

English

→ What books did you read? Did any book stand out for you? Why?

→ Were the books written from a particular ethnic, cultural, or other unique perspective? What did you learn from that perspective? How could your knowledge apply to the increasingly diverse workplace?

→ What characters did you analyze? What did you learn about those characters? Into what situations were they placed? How did they respond? What motivated them?

- Atticus Finch in *To Kill a Mockingbird* has inspired many students to become lawyers.

- Langston Hughes's poetry often speaks to the hard work of the laborer and would help managers better appreciate the life challenges of the people who work for them.

- Arthur Miller's play *Death of a Salesman* is an interesting study of the role of the salesperson in a company, and the need for strong training and human resource services.

Sociology

- ❯ Did you study the concept of social Darwinism? How could that theory be applied to a workplace? Why and how do certain organizations survive while others fail?

- ❯ What about structural functionalism? What structures exist in a company because they serve a purpose? What structures have outlived their purpose? Is the company able to see this? If so, how does it go about changing the situation?

- ❯ How does self-fulfilling prophecy apply to the stock market?

Biology

- ❯ How would you apply the scientific method in the workplace?

- ❯ Why is it important to follow a logical thinking process?

- ❯ How do you analyze a situation?

- ❯ When decisions are made, are they based on sound research or on hypotheses, beliefs, or guesses?

Economics

- ❯ How does Pareto's 80/20 rule apply to the workplace? What could it say about productivity in the workplace?

- ❯ How does the concept of supply and demand apply to the career field you're pursuing?

Anthropology

- ❯ How do cultures operate in a workplace?

- ❯ Have you ever worked for an organization that has a union? Did you notice a cultural difference between the union workers and the management? Did any communication difficulties arise? How were they handled? Was each culture appropriately validated or did you perceive a power struggle?

Psychology

- ❯ What do you know about motivation?

- ❯ What factors influence an individual's behavior?

- How might the concept of extinction apply in the workplace?

- How could cognitive behavioral techniques be applied in the workplace?

- How could your knowledge of psychology help you reduce stress in your employees?

History

- What period did you study? What significant events and changes occurred during that time period? How did it influence today's situations? What did society learn from the events?

- Who were the leaders during the period? Were they strong, weak, charismatic, memorable, egocentric? How did their leadership style affect the events of the time?

- History teaches us to pay attention to who's in charge and the scope of their influence. The same holds true in the workplace. Who's in charge and how do they lead? What language do they use?

- Studying Martin Luther King's speeches, for instance, can teach you a lot about charismatic leadership and its role in rallying individuals to a cause or mission. You can even learn about the value of rhetoric and inspired communication. For instance, what if, instead of saying "I have a dream," Dr. King had said, "I have a thought." Notice how the impact of his speech would have been greatly reduced.

MAPPING YOUR MAJOR: MAKING YOUR MAJOR WORK FOR YOU IN THE WORKPLACE

Regardless of your major's relevance to your future, it contains a vast amount of information ready to be mined. And you're well skilled at mining by now. All you have to do is make another map. Even if you have selected a preprofessional major and you plan to work in that field, you still need to know what's special about your pursuit of the major and what you learned from it so you can set yourself apart from your classmates. So get out that blank piece of paper and your pencils or crayons: it's time to analyze your major.

STEP 1:

In the center of your paper write the name of your major and draw a circle around it.

STEP 2:

Scatter the following words on your paper, drawing a circle around each one:

- ❯ Courses
- ❯ Skills
- ❯ Theories or ideas
- ❯ Interesting items
- ❯ Knowledge
- ❯ Related courses from other departments

Add extra circles if a category hasn't been mentioned above.

STEP 3:

Jot down ideas related to each of the categories and draw circles around them as well. Write as much as you can, filling in everything you know about your major.

STEP 4:

If you're stuck, consider doing this exercise with other students in your major. Sometimes your classmates will think of things you forgot or didn't consider important.

STEP 5:

When you're done, take a step back and look at your map.

- ❯ What pops out for you?
- ❯ What is the most interesting part of the map? What "speaks" to you?

⦿ How have you done something unique with your major?

- How have you tailored it to fit your interests?

- Did you take a series of courses that focused on a particular aspect of the major? Why? What did you enjoy about them?

- What skills did you learn?

STEP 6:

Pull your thoughts together. What are the most important aspects of your major? If you had to identify three characteristics you've developed or acquired from your major, what would they be?

1. _____

2. _____

3. _____

A sample Major Map for a psychology major can be found on pages 94–95.

After doing several Major Maps, students have made some interesting observations:

⦿ History majors found that a key element for them was a never-ending search for "the truth." They found it was also imperative to be keenly curious about everything. They could spend hours of intense focus on one project if necessary.

⦿ English majors found that their major was extremely relevant and valuable to both work and life. They noted that to be a good English major you needed to be both classical and progressive. You needed to know where writing had been (that there is much to learn from the classics) and where writing is going (blogs, for example). They would be especially good in a multicultural workplace where appreciating and understand different cultures is imperative.

⦿ Economics majors noted its far-reaching stance in business, politics, and solving social problems. They discovered that economics majors needed to embrace complexity, be very good at math, and be strong problem solvers. They also had to digest large amounts of information and distill it to the main points.

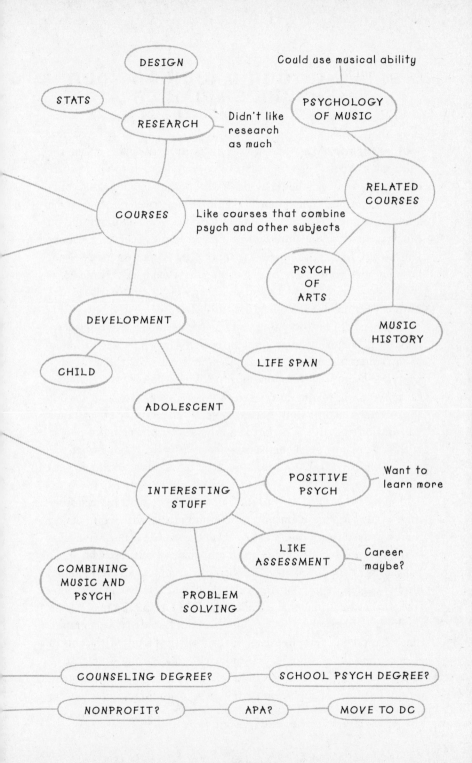

SELLING YOUR MAJOR TO YOUR FUTURE EMPLOYER

Now that you've analyzed your major and perhaps discovered new sources of knowledge and power in your experience, when the time comes you'll need to be able to communicate it to your future employers, whoever they may be. It will be important to put yourself in the mind of an employer—will the employer know as much about your major as you do? Not likely. The worst assumption you can make is that your interviewer already knows everything about your major. In fact, it's possible that not only is your interviewer not familiar with your major, but he or she may even harbor some negative or inaccurate views of it. So you need to become a star salesperson for your major and college degree.

A key piece of information you'll need to learn is your interviewer's college major. It's easy enough to discover: when you are about to say something about your major, simply ask, "By the way, what was your major?" and respond positively regardless of the response. Once you know the interviewer's major, you can adjust your approach in the interview. For example, if the recruiter understands your major (that is, she majored in it herself or hires a lot of people with your major), then emphasize what was special about what *you* studied or learned. What made you a better major than others who took the same subject?

On the other hand, if your interviewer majored in a subject other than yours, or doesn't usually hire individuals with your major, then you need to educate him or her on the value of your major. For example, some schools offer a geography major. For those who aren't familiar with the college-level study of geography, their last memory might be a geography class in grade school where they had to memorize all the states in alphabetical order. So their opinion may not be too high of a geography major. They may not know that a geography major has taken a very interdisciplinary course of study with roots in sciences and the social sciences, and usually has strong skills related to GPS tracking systems or would be a great urban planner. Or take a cognitive science major, a relatively new major. Many interviewers assume that it's the same as a psychology major. If you're a cognitive science major, then you know that's not a correct analysis, so be prepared to explain the key elements of your major *and* how they are valuable to the job you're applying for.

Even majors that are commonly known, such as English and history, are still going to require explanation to an employer who only took the one required English or history class in his or her academic career. In fact, he or she may have hated the course, so you're going to have to present what you found valuable about it.

Below are some steps you can take to prepare for questions about your major:

1. To better sell your major to your future interviewer, *what knowledge, mindsets, or approach would someone with your major bring to a workplace?* Don't worry if you don't know the kind of job you're applying these skills to yet; for the moment you can answer generically.

_____
_____
_____
_____
_____
_____

2. *Create stories related to your major and classes.*

Can you take advantage of your classroom experiences to create stories that will show your knowledge, ability to learn, mindsets, or other important factors? Try using what you learned in your classes (the actual subjects, the metalearning, the mindsets, or character traits such as perseverance) by answering these typical interview questions:

Why did you choose your major? It doesn't really relate to this job.

_____
_____
_____

Why didn't you major in _____ if you were going to apply for this job in _____?

_____

_____

_____

What skills beyond the traditional writing, research, and/or communication skills have you acquired as a function of your major?

_____

_____

_____

WISDOM BUILDERS: TEN ACADEMIC TRICKS AND TIPS TO IMPROVE YOUR GRADES AND LEARNING

1. ASK YOURSELF SOME KEY QUESTIONS

- When have you been at your best as a student?
  - How did you know you were at your best?
  - What did you do and what was the outcome?
  - How did you feel?
- Can you reproduce that behavior and the feelings?
- What would you like to do more as a student?
- What could you really excel at if you tried your best?

2. SHOW UP

Did you know that study after study confirms that classroom presence is the single most important factor in the grade you receive? And not only that, but because the most important parts of the class are the beginning and the end, it's important that you show up on time and not leave early.

And if you need another reason to show up, remember that you're paying good money to take each class. Consider your tuition the admission price for each lecture. Although your tuition dollars pay for much more than the hours in the classroom, let's focus on just the classroom for the moment. If a semester's tuition is $10,000 and you're taking four classes (a total of 180 hours of classroom time), you are paying approximately $55 for each class. That's a concert ticket or a seat at a sports event. So sit up because you actually paid for this lecture.

Here are some tips for getting the most out of your class time:

- Sit toward the front of the room. The better students do sit in the front, if only because sitting in the front forces you to pay attention and the professor is more likely to see you.

- Sit up. Don't slouch or look casual.

- Use your computer for taking notes only—professors can tell when you're e-mailing or instant-messaging.

- Look attentive and keep your eyes on the professor when you're not taking notes.

- Don't fall asleep. (A basic, yes, but you'd be surprised. . . .)

3. BE IN THE MOMENT

Remember in elementary school when your teacher would point at you and say "Pay attention!" What motivated her comment? What were you or your classmates doing that caused her to notice you? Let me ask you a question: Are you paying attention? Or is your behavior the same now?

You can take an active role even in a lecture-based class where you're basically expected just to sit and listen. Look around. Watch how everyone else sits. Are your fellow students taking notes or are they checking e-mail? Are they actively listening or does it look as if their thoughts are a million miles away?

Ask yourself questions throughout the lecture: Do I get this? Does it make sense? Can I put myself in the mind of the individual being described? For instance, if your history professor is talking about Lincoln's presidency, can you try to put yourself in the mindset of Lincoln? What was he feeling/thinking?

Notice and keep track of the skills you're developing in your classes. Are you learning to work on a team, writing more efficiently, or managing your time better?

And when it comes to reading your assignments, don't just passively read your textbook, looking to see when you can quit. Develop a relationship with what you're reading. Why are you reading the assignment? What are you learning from it? Does the knowledge you're gaining primarily comprise details and facts or concepts and ideas? Most textbooks help you find the important information by highlighting important material. Try to think beyond the text: Is what you're reading related to what you're learning in another class? And of course, how might you apply this to the workplace? How can you make an employer care that you're learning this?

4. FIND A RATIONALE FOR EVERY CLASS YOU TAKE

Unfortunately, you don't always get to pick your classes. Your curriculum has been designed to provide you with a depth and breadth of knowledge and experiences, which you may not be appreciating, particularly when you're sitting in a boring class you don't like. How many times have you said, "I'm just taking this because it's required"? Or "I don't really want to take this class; it just fit into the time slot I had available." It's time to change that attitude. Here are some strategies:

- Think about the Big Picture. Just because you don't think you need this class right now, are there ways it might help you in the future?

- Try not to take any classes just because they make your life convenient, that is, because they fit neatly into your schedule. Start by identifying the classes that are most important to you and fit your schedule to accommodate them.

- Try creating metaphors for classes you don't like. Chances are you've already come up with some choice adjectives to describe these classes: useless, boring, awful, wasteland, and so on. So could changing your metaphor change the way you approach the class? What if you called it a challenge you are determined to conquer? What if you referred to it as a game? Every game has a winner and the winner gets a prize. How will you define winning this game? Is it a particular grade? Surviving the class? Showing up every day? Completing all the assignments on time? Learning something in spite of the professor? And what is the prize you will give yourself for winning?

- Start developing your interview story about this class. Make it a lesson in survival—maybe even prevailing by getting an A despite the challenges.

- Try linking the class with something you enjoy doing, such as reading your assignments at your favorite coffeehouse. Or alternate your time preparing for the class with something you like to do, like watching a TV show or spending a few minutes on the computer. Just don't get so caught up in your fun activity that you don't get back to the assignment.

- Talk to students who are majoring in the topic you don't like. Find out what they like about it and get tips for succeeding in it. Maybe you'll pick up some of their enthusiasm.

- Could you consider the class a version of Facebook and see how many friends you can develop? Look around your classroom—any interesting people you'd like to meet? Maybe you could make it a goal to strike up a conversation after class with at least one different person each week—if nothing else, you could compare notes on how bad the class is. Or maybe they'll have a different perspective you could learn.

- Consider the results of an alumni survey conducted a few years ago. Alumni were asked to name their favorite "useless" course, that is, the course they thought they would never enjoy or never need. You wouldn't believe the enthusiastic replies. Here are some samples of classes they thought were useless and how they feel about them now:

  - Art history. "I now love going to museums." (Wall Street analyst)

  - Chemistry. "It's turned out to be helpful because I have developed a niche in medical writing and editing." (Freelance writer)

  - Biology. "I took it to satisfy the distribution requirement and I ended up majoring in it." (Pediatrician)

  - Ceramics. "I discovered an unknown talent and a lifelong stress-reducing hobby." (Attorney)

  - Comparative religions. "I was forever changed in my approach to life." (Orthopedic surgeon)

Remember, you have lots of opportunities to learn while you are in school, and you might just learn the most from that class you thought you didn't want or need. Take a few minutes to brainstorm some positive reasons for the classes you've taken.

Class: _____

Rationale/Possible Value:

_____

_____

Class: _____

Rationale/Possible Value:

_____

_____

Class:_____

Rationale/Possible Value:

_____

_____

OK, so you're never going to be wildly enthusiastic about every course you take. But that's no reason to let them slide and potentially mess up your GPA or just ruin your day.

5. USE VISUAL MAPS IN YOUR CLASSES

Throughout this book you've been developing your skill in creating visual maps. You've learned their value in helping you see the Big Picture and notice details or information you might have otherwise missed. Have you ever tried using maps to help you with your coursework or prepare for tests or papers? For instance, if you're writing a paper and finding it hard to make sense of all the research you've gathered, you can start by placing the main topic in the center of your paper. Then just start dumping all the chunks of information you've acquired. Once you've put it on the paper, take a step back and look. Do you see connections? Is there a logical order you could develop? If you're studying for a test, you might try dumping all the basic information on a piece of paper. What do you already know and what areas are hazy? Where should you focus your studying? Visual maps can help you with all aspects of your schoolwork if you enjoy using the technique.

6. WORK SMARTER, NOT HARDER

Some students try to read and learn everything. In general, the 80/20 rule can be applied to the material you read for a class. About 80 percent of important information will come from 20 percent of the material. Think about it: this means that if you have to read fifty pages, about ten pages of the information will actually be important. Take special note of the beginnings and endings of each chapter. Note what concepts your professor chooses to focus on. Look for charts and other illustrations that usually highlight the most important information.

7. DON'T USE A HIGHLIGHTER

Highlighters are great: they provide visual proof that you read the chapter, right? Not really. Studies show that highlighting can actually detract from your understanding of the material and focus your attention on superficial concepts and words. Underlining or highlighting while you're reading something for the first time is distracting and does not help retention. A far better system is to take notes in the margins of your text after you've read the paragraph. Print summary phrases or keywords (in your own words) in the margins so you can scan them later when studying. You can even quiz yourself before a test by turning your margin notes into questions.

8. USE THE CLOZE PROCEDURE TO ASCERTAIN THE DIFFICULTY OF YOUR TEXTBOOK

You probably haven't heard of it, but the Cloze procedure is a quick system for determining whether a text is written at a level you can easily grasp. If you're having difficulty understanding your textbook, it may be written in a style that is hard to read or it may be beyond your current level of knowledge. Get a roommate or friend to help you set up this little test to help you discover how well you comprehend the material in your textbook:

1. Ask your roommate or a friend to select a passage from your textbook. Two or three paragraphs will be enough.

2. Have them photocopy the passage.

3. Tell them to leave the first sentence alone but black out every fifth word so it can't be seen.

4. Now, you read the passage and guess what words belong in the blackened spaces. Write them down.

5. Compare your guesses with the actual words in the text.

6. Score your results, giving yourself one point for each correct answer. (Give yourself credit for synonyms or closely related words.)

What percentage of the total blacked out words did you answer correctly?

*   At least 61 percent correct? Then you can read the material fairly easily.

*   Were 41 to 60 percent correct? The text is challenging and instructional. You'll have to concentrate, but you can do it. Set aside more time to read the material than you normally would.

*   Below 40 percent? This text will be frustrating and you may find that you aren't getting the necessary information. In this case, you might want to look for an alternate text or study guide. Sometimes just finding a text that explains the topic in a different style will help you understand it better. Some students have even found a high school text in the same subject helpful. Check a used-books store or secondhand textbook store to get a book you do understand at a cheaper price. Your school library probably has other textbooks for the same subject as well. Just remember that when you find the text challenging, you need to pay extra attention to the lectures so that you can glean as much information from them as possible.

9. USE A PLANNING SYSTEM

You're busy. Overcommitted. Perhaps you forget important events or even sleep through classes. If you don't have one already, it's time to develop a system for planning your time. Use what works for you: your computer likely has a calendar function (in Outlook or other software), or use a paper-based approach like a calendar or day planner. It doesn't matter what system you use: what matters is that you use a system. Your time is way too valuable and you have too many important events in your life not to have a system to record and organize them. And that includes parties, sports events, and other fun things. Because if you don't make room for the fun stuff, you won't stick to the work stuff.

10. GET TO KNOW YOUR PROFESSORS

Believe it or not, professors are people too. They have pressures and problems and personal lives and all the challenges that you face. Most professors genuinely like students and want to teach them and want to be appreciated. They also want to help you when they can. It's important to develop relationships with your professors: they can provide invaluable references for you when you seek a job or go to grad school. So, first and foremost, show some respect.

- If you have an issue to discuss, approach the professor as one adult to another in a calm voice—don't whine. Use a pleasant voice no matter how angry or upset you might be.

- Catch your professor after class rather than before.

- Take advantage of your professors' office hours—most students don't.

- Tell the truth. Professors have heard every excuse in the book, so bring proof if you are turning in a late assignment or missed a class. If you say your car broke down, bring the repair or towing receipt. If you were sick, bring a doctor's note. Not all professors will care, but the fact that you took the time to be diligent will be noted and you're likely to get more understanding and assistance.

Oh, and here are some examples of what *not* to say to a professor (which, unfortunately, are said all the time):

- "I couldn't come to class yesterday. Did I miss anything?" What is the professor supposed to say? That you missed nothing important?

- "Could you send me your teaching notes and PowerPoint from yesterday's class?" or "Would you summarize the lecture I missed?" Get the information you missed from classmates; ask the professor only if you absolutely can't get the information somewhere else. It's not your professor's responsibility to make up for your missed classes or assignments.

- "I can't come to class; I have to work during those hours." "I will be late for class every day because I have a scheduling conflict." "I have to leave class twenty minutes early each day." If you have a conflict, don't take the class. If you can't arrive on time and stay for the class, don't enroll unless you have received permission from the professor to arrive late/leave early or not show up at all. And don't wait until the first day of class to raise those questions.

- "Did you really mean what you said on the syllabus? I thought that was just a possibility." Professors know that syllabi are quasi-legal documents. They represent a form of contract and they don't put assignments or other class requirements on the syllabus if they don't expect you to follow them.

Now that you've completed the first four chapters of this book, you should have a much more concrete and positive view of your education and a steadily improving ability to articulate it to an employer or graduate program. You have learned to identify your key mindsets, and even some classroom tricks to improve your grades so that you'll be eligible for even more interesting job opportunities.

But of course **THE QUESTION** still haunts: What are you going to *do* with it? Don't worry: the answer awaits in the next chapter. But before we leave this chapter, take a moment to answer the following questions:

On a scale of 1 to 10, how *important* do you think it is to be able to explain and articulate the value of your education and/or classes to an employer?

Not important at all	1	2	3	4	5	6	7	8	9	10	Imperative: it's key to my success

And again on a scale of 1 to 10, how would you rate your ability to explain the value of your major and/or classes to an employer?

Can't explain the value	1	2	3	4	5	6	7	8	9	10	Well prepared and highly confident

Is there a gap between how important you think it is to articulate the value of your education and how you rank your ability to do so?

What could you do in the next twenty-four hours that would help you move your ability score up by one point?

_____

_____

_____

And finally, is there a class you've been secretly wanting to take, but are concerned that you might not do well in it? If you knew you couldn't fail, what would you do?

_____

_____

_____

CHAPTER 5

WHY SETTLE FOR ONE CAREER WHEN YOU CAN HAVE TEN?

THE WISE WANDERER EXPLORES THE FUTURE

> The chalk outline guy's got a good job. Not too dangerous—the criminals are long gone. I guess these are people who wanted to be sketch artists but they couldn't draw very well. "Uh, listen, John, forget the sketches, do you think if we left the dead body right there on the sidewalk you could manage to trace around it?"
>
> —**JERRY SEINFELD,** *SEINFELD,* FROM THE OPENING MONOLOGUE EPISODE 42, "THE TRIP"

It's time to revisit **THE QUESTION**. You've been wandering for a while now uncovering and developing your talents, and you've discovered that your major is just one element of your future plans. But even if you've told everyone to stop asking you what you're going to do with it, you're probably still running headlong into the condensed version of **THE QUESTION**: "What are you going to *do*?" And that one is almost as bad if you don't have an immediate answer.

What do you find challenging about that question? Is it that you have absolutely no idea what you'd like to do? Or maybe you were interested in one career but something changed, so now you're not so sure. Or you have a career dream you'd like to pursue, but everyone has warned you about how few people succeed in the field, so you prefer to keep it a secret. Or maybe, just maybe, you're like a lot of students who don't have *one* idea about what they'd like to do because they have *ten* ideas. And it's starting to look like career chaos again.

And the chaos expands geometrically when you add in noncareer ideas you're considering, such as taking a year off after school to volunteer, travel, or pursue hobbies. Sometimes it feels as if the only way to bring order to the chaos is to select one choice and go for it. After all, isn't that what most people do? But that's a lot of pressure. It's like staring at a candy machine with twenty interesting options, and you just can't make up your mind. But you know you have to pick one and only one. So there you stand in career paralysis, a state where you either wait for the aha moment of career inspiration, or where you just avoid thinking about it at all. Or worse yet, you just choose something because you're "supposed to."

Well, you can relax: life is not a candy machine. That metaphor won't work for you. Because the candy machine approach to careers is very linear, and we've already established that you are not a linear person. Forrest Gump may be right: life is much more like a box of chocolates. It's your box of chocolates and you get to select them all in the order you want, and in the form you want. And chaos theory tells you that some new chocolates will emerge that aren't even in your box yet. But since you can't sit around and wait for them to emerge, how do you move forward when you don't know where you're going?

Sounds like a good time to create another map to clear up the chaos. Remember the attractors from chaos theory in Chapter 2? Just like a point attractor, one career idea can pull you in a particular direction and become your focus. Pendulum attractors can have you bouncing between two disparate choices, like becoming a golf pro or working in advertising. The Bureau of Labor Statistics reports that between the ages of eighteen and thirty-five, the average person will change jobs about nine times. Some individuals change jobs as many as fifteen times during that time period, so instead of forcing yourself to select one point attractor, maybe you need to find several. Instead of swinging back and forth between two choices, choose them both. Back in 1988, researchers coined the phrase "possible selves," which referred to the multiple potential selves you could try on to design your future. Let's call your potential choices Possible Lives, and in this chapter you're going to map, mine, and design them.

So take a moment to assess where you are in your future planning process:

> ⇒ Do you have a point attractor; that is, is there one job, field of work, or activity that seems to call to you?

> ⇒ Do you have a bunch of attractors—so many interesting options out there that you don't even know where to start?

> ⇒ Do you have no attractors—nothing interests you because you don't even know what's out there? That can be particularly scary and stressful because it seems as if everyone else has a plan.

> ⇒ Is your attractor something that seems unattainable? Why?

> ⇒ Are you being "advised" by your parents, professors, or others to pursue a particular path? Do you agree with them? Is it *your* attractor or theirs?

> ⇒ Do you have those pesky pendulum attractors pulling you in disparate directions with no middle ground to be seen?

Whatever your situation, Possible Lives planning will help you start finding the sense in this seeming chaos of your future. You already know from chaos theory that it's pretty dangerous to assume that you will know exactly where you will be in five or ten years. But as you also recall from chaos theory, it is possible to make some general assumptions, and it's also possible to make better predictions about the near future. So that's what we're going to do: we're going to examine all those ideas you have right now to see if we can turn them from a chaotic jumble of thoughts, hopes, dreams, and fantasies about the distant future to form a plan for the immediate future.

You will start by identifying your Possible Lives: all the different careers or future plans you've considered in the last few years, no matter how wild, crazy, or seemingly impossible. If you want to, you can even list that firefighter job you wanted when you were five years old. We're going to focus on where you *might* go, not where you have to go. And not necessarily even where you *will* go (don't forget that the butterfly hovers nearby). In just a few minutes you're going to create a Possible Lives Map that will help you identify and organize some future plans while still keeping the door open to lots of new ideas. You don't need to know what one thing you're going to *do:* you're going to *do* many things throughout your life. The Possible Lives Map just helps you get your ideas down in one place so you can see them more clearly.

IDENTIFYING YOUR POSSIBLE LIVES

Possible Lives planning starts with you and where you are right now. So take a moment to consider your position. What year are you in school? What knowledge have you mined from your courses, your major, and other experiences? Or have you graduated and are working at your first real job? Are you in a job or field you like? What strengths and themes have you identified?

As you reflect on your current status, it's not unusual to start thinking about regrets. Maybe when you look at where you are, you find yourself frustrated or unhappy. Maybe you wish you had pursued a different major. Maybe you wish your grades were higher. Maybe you . . . *it doesn't matter.* That's "if only . . ." and "should" thinking and if you recall the positive mindset in Chapter 3, you know that that kind of thinking isn't going to help, so stop right now. *You are where you are* and you are just fine. It has to be fine—you can't change it, right? The Possible Lives Map is about hope and possibility, not regret or blame. So pull out your Wandering Map and any lists you've created so far, and remind yourself of your strengths and interests. Think about Possible Lives you'd like to live. What careers or other ideas about the future have you considered?

Here are some Possible Lives other college students are considering:

Actor	Advertiser	Ambassador	Architect
Art Critic	Attorney	Ballerina	Bar Owner
Cancer Researcher	Chef	Clothing Designer	Coach
Congresswoman	Conservationist	Consultant	Counselor/ Therapist
Cultural Anthropologist	Doctors Without Borders	Economist	Editor or Publisher
English Teacher, Abroad	Event Planner	FBI Agent	Filmmaker
Freelance Journalist	Gay Rights Activist	Geologist	Graphic Designer
Human Resources Manager	Investigative Reporter	Investment Banker	Latin Ballroom Dancer
Military Officer	Model	Museum Curator	Nutritionist
Policy Analyst	Professor	Psychologist	Public Relations
Rapper	Real Estate Agent	Small Business Owner	Social Worker
Sports Agent	Stockbroker	Tech Blogger	Traveler to India
Urban Planner	Vegan Restaurant Owner	Veterinarian	Writer
Zen Garden Designer	Zookeeper		

Are you getting some ideas from this list? Are these interesting futures appealing to you? Notice that not all of them are jobs, certainly not those traditional linear jobs you'd expect from a particular major.

Want some more ideas? The chart on the next page shows common career fields that represent potential areas for your Possible Lives. Dozens of job titles can fit under each field.

For example, jobs under the Publishing category could include editor, researcher, technical writer, production assistant, marketing coordinator, agent, and sales representative. For the moment, just look at the chart and note any of the fields that sound interesting to you. You don't need to make any decisions.

Accounting	Acting/Drama	Advertising	Aerospace
Agriculture	Airlines	Animals	Architecture
Art	Arts Administration	Athletics	Automotive
Banking	Biological Sciences	Boating	Bookkeeping
Building Services	Chemical Sciences	Children's Services	Commercial Art
Communications	Computers	Construction	Consulting
Corrections	Counseling	Crafts	Criminology
Data and Statistics	Economics	Electronics	Elementary Education
Energy	Engineering	Entertainment	Entrepreneurial Enterprises
Environment	Family Services	Film	Finance
Fine Arts	Food	Forestry	Geriatrics
Government	Graphic Arts	Hazardous Material Management	Health Care
Higher Education	Hospital Administration	Hotel/Motel Management	Human Resources
Industrial Design	Information Services	Insurance	Interior Design
Investment Banking	Journalism	Languages	Law
Law Enforcement	Leisure	Lobbying	Management
Manufacturing	Marketing	Market Research	Mathematics
Medicine	Mental Health	Merchandising	Museum Work
Music	Nonprofit Organizations	Oceanography	Office Services
Parks and Recreation	Performing Arts	Personal Services	Photography
Physical Sciences	Politics	Preschool Education	Printing
Project Engineering	Public Relations	Publishing	Real Estate
Recycling	Religion	Repair Services	Research
Restaurant Management	Retailing	Sales/Sales Management	Sciences
Secondary Education	Social Entrepreneurship	Social Services	Speech Pathology
Sports Management	Systems Design	Technology	Telecommunications
Television and Video	Textiles	Toys and Computer Games	Trade
Transportation	Travel/Tourism	Union Operations	Urban/Regional Planning
Wellness	Writing		

Another way to tackle the brainstorming process is to think about the types of people you'd like to be around every day. The list below will help you start thinking of possible colleagues or clients. Part of designing your future involves knowing whom you'd like to work with. And you won't only be working with these people as colleagues—you may have lots of other roles with them. Would you like to teach them, consult with them, influence them, sell things to them, help them, support them? Can you identify careers that might help you do that?

Accountants/ Budget Planners	Adolescents	Artists or Musicians	Athletes/Coaches
Business Executives	Children	College Students	Computer Experts
Creative People	Doctors	Elderly People	Engineers
Entertainers or Actors	Environmentally Conscious People	Health Care Workers	Infants and Preschoolers
Investigators	Journalists	Lawyers	Low-Income People
Military Personnel	People from Other Countries/Cultures	People Who Have a Specific Hobby or Interest	People with Mental or Physical Disabilities
Police or Security Personnel	Politicians	Prisoners	Professors
Psychologists	Researchers	Salespeople	Scientists
Socially Conscious People	Stockbrokers/ Investors	Students	Teachers
Veterinarians	Volunteers	Wealthy People	Writers/Editors
Young Adults	Zoo or Habitat Workers		

This list is just a start. Add any additional people with whom you'd like to work:

1. _____

2. _____

3. _____

4. _____

5. _____

Ready to create your future? It's one blank piece of paper away.

MAPPING, MINING, AND DESIGNING YOUR POSSIBLE LIVES

The Possible Lives Map can be one of the most enlightening, helpful, and inspiring maps you create because it provides a chance to dream, fantasize, and examine your many thoughts, ideas, and plans for the future. Creating your Possible Lives Map is very similar to creating your Wandering Map in Chapter 2 except that instead of looking back, you're looking forward. You will include the jobs or careers you are considering or have considered in the past, but you might also want to include other important parts of your life, such as travel, volunteering, raising a family, and so on. And as with the Wandering Map, you will be able to mine it for lots of career gold. And also like the Wandering Map, it is a work in progress, not a final statement. You can keep adding to it anytime you want.

Now, at this point you might be thinking, "I don't need to do this map. I know what I want to do. I want to be a＿＿＿." That's a great plan, but heed the warnings of chaos theory. Be careful about predicting too far ahead. Your career plan may be a wonderful dream you should pursue with all your energy and commitment. But life has a way of intervening in our plans and you might find that a year from now you no longer want to pursue that career. For instance, taking organic chemistry often changes medical school plans. Doing an internship in a law firm can change your mind about going to law school. Spending an afternoon on the trading floor can change your mind about that career on Wall Street. Of course, all of those experiences might serve to cement your determination to pursue your chosen career, but because *you don't know what you don't know,* go ahead and play along. Do the Possible Lives Map and see what shows up. If nothing else, you will discover terrific Plan B career options so that if your first choice doesn't work out, you won't panic or become discouraged. You'll have another plan ready to go. So let's get started.

MAPPING YOUR POSSIBLE LIVES

1. Take out a blank piece of paper. In the center, briefly write your current status. Keep it simple. "Junior: Marketing Major." "Senior: Writing Theme." "Graduate: Working at coffee shop." "Theme: Helping others." "First job in journalism. Want to move up." Draw a circle around your status.

2. Start brainstorming and write down Possible Lives all over the paper in no particular order—everything you've ever thought about, fantasized about, or thought would be interesting or cool to do. Draw a circle around each one and then draw a line connecting each one back to the circle in the center (you).

> ⇢ List two to ten possible lives (or more, if you don't find it overwhelming).
>
> ⇢ Always include one blank circle for the yet undiscovered career.
>
> ⇢ Don't censor your ideas.
>
> > • No limitations other than basic laws of physics or physiology
> >
> > • Don't consider whether you have the education or talent
> >
> > • Don't consider the salary (or lack thereof)
> >
> > • Jot down your ideas even if you "know" they're unrealistic

A sample Possible Lives Map is shown on the next page.

MINING YOUR POSSIBLE LIVES

Now that you're done, step back and take a look at your map. Do any opportunities seem particularly exciting or interesting? Was it fun to just dream and write whatever you wanted? Did you uncover any new ideas or hidden wishes? Just as you did with the Wander-

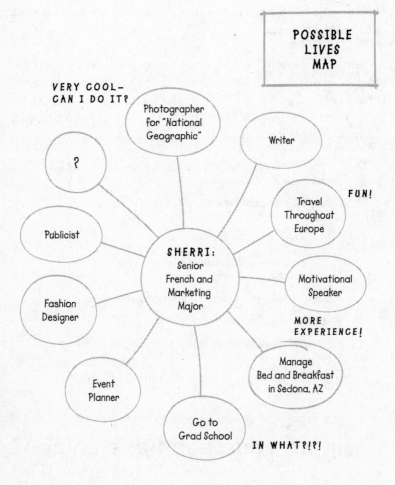

POSSIBLE LIVES MAP

VERY COOL—
CAN I DO IT?

Photographer for "National Geographic"

Writer

?

FUN!

Publicist

Travel Throughout Europe

Fashion Designer

SHERRI: Senior French and Marketing Major

Motivational Speaker

MORE EXPERIENCE!

Event Planner

Manage Bed and Breakfast in Sedona, AZ

Go to Grad School

IN WHAT?!?!

ing Map, you're going to analyze your Possible Lives Map for common themes or relationships among your different lives. Are many of your lives

- ❯ Artistic or creative?
- ❯ Athletic?
- ❯ Active?
- ❯ Thoughtful or quiet?
- ❯ People intensive?
- ❯ Serving or helping others?
- ❯ Related to money or status?
- ❯ Based on additional education such as graduate school?
- ❯ Based on a talent?

Notice your role or the setting you'd be in:

- ❯ Are you often in charge?
- ❯ Are you the center of attention?
- ❯ Are you in a medical, educational, business, or other setting?
- ❯ Are you performing in some way?
- ❯ What skills are you using?
- ❯ Are you in the United States or are you abroad?
- ❯ Are you in a permanent career or in something you'd do for just a year or so?

As you discover your themes, write them down on the back of your map. If you look at Sherri's map, you'll notice that a lot of her possible lives are creative or artistic in nature, or they are business or management oriented and require attention to detail, strong communication skills, and lots of energy. Notice too that she left one life blank to fill in later. She's leaving room for the butterfly.

As you continue reviewing your map, how many of these Possible Lives would you like to pursue seriously?

↪ **One?** As you look at your options, do you have one particular point attractor? Does something jump out at you as an obvious first choice? Then that's where you can begin your planning. On the line connecting your first choice to the circle in the center (you), list some steps you need to take before you can start doing that activity or job. Don't worry if you don't know every step; you'll develop a more detailed plan later. For instance, if Sherri had selected "event planner," she might write "Find internship at hotel" on the line.

↪ **Two or Three?** Draw an extra circle around your top choices or put a star next to them. Start thinking about how you could begin pursuing each of them now, and write those ideas on the lines connecting to the circle in the center.

- For instance, if each of the three options requires a college degree, then you're already on the way. You can keep doing what you're doing.

- If any of your choices requires a particular skill (like writing), then you can look for opportunities to improve that skill and develop a portfolio of writing samples.

- If you see them as opposing ideas (pendulum attractors), do they have to be? Can you think of a creative way to combine them? If you are interested in a career as a golf instructor but are also considering graduate study in architecture, could you find a graduate program at a university that has a great golf program as well? Maybe you could work at a golf resort while attending school. If you can't find an instructing job, there's always caddying or working in the store, playing in local tournaments, and so on. You'll learn a lot just being around the golfing atmosphere. Maybe you could even specialize in designing golf resorts by adding landscaping courses to your architectural degree.

↪ **More Than Three?** That's OK. Let's play with some ways you could handle all your choices. Remember that you don't have to choose; this is a box of chocolates, not a candy machine. Here are some ways to resolve the "I want all the candy in the box" feeling:

- Pick one at a time, fully enjoy it, and then move on to the next.

  - Maybe you want to teach English in Japan, travel throughout South America, and also start a career in human resources (HR) management. Knowing that once you start up the management ladder you might not be as free to travel, you might choose to take two years now and teach in Japan for one year and in South America the next, and then pursue the HR career when you return.

- Perhaps you would like to start a nonprofit organization to fund college education for traditionally underrepresented students, but you need to earn a lot of money first. You might want to work in a financial field for part of your career and then when you've saved the money you need to start your business (and developed some great connections), you can pursue your ultimate dream.

• Pick several and take a bite of each by pursuing several avenues at one time.

- The person above who wanted to teach abroad before starting her HR career could *do everything at once* perhaps by teaching English to workers in foreign corporations. She could contact their HR departments and perhaps be hired temporarily or be permitted to advertise her services in the company newsletter. She might get a taste of HR while she's exploring the world. Just think how that will look on her résumé when she returns to the United States.

- Maybe you listed "rock star" as one of your lives. And maybe you actually play in a band and have started playing in clubs. There's no reason you can't *explore one career on the weekends while you work at another job to cover your expenses.* And it's even better if you actually enjoy your day job. Then when that music career takes off and your travel interferes with your day job, you'll know which choice to make.

  One recent graduate pursued an accounting career, which he enjoyed, while pursuing his dream job, musician, which he loved, playing in clubs on weekends. When his music career picked up and he found an agent, he dropped his regular job to pursue the music career full time. The bonus: he knows accounting, so he can monitor his income and investments. But he also knows the fickle nature of the music business, and if his music career doesn't take off, he plans to start a financial management business for musicians in a few years.

• Bounce back and forth with one option remaining consistent and the other changing as you wish.

- Teaching, for example, gives you three months a year to sample different ideas. Some teachers save up for a trip each summer to teach English in Mexico, volunteer in Costa Rica, research a special interest, or work at archaeological digs. Others devote their time off to a creative project, such as writing a book or composing a symphony. Many teachers supplement their income and find variety by pursuing extra careers as travel agents or entrepreneurial tutors or other business roles. If you have always had an interest in space travel, NASA offers a special summer program just for teachers.

- You can use this approach to *pursue grad school on a part-time basis while you work at your regular job.* Your employer might even pay for grad school.

- *You can incorporate your different career ideas and themes into one job.* It's a little like taking several pieces of candy and mixing them together. It might be hard to see while you're a student, but it is possible to incorporate your interests into your job. Even though I've managed career centers for the bulk of my career, I've added lots of extras to my job, including taking students to Ireland to explore internship opportunities, teaching film courses such as Psychology and Cinema, training college professors in Italy, and even doing art projects (a hobby) with students and staff.

- You can *choose to pursue one or more areas as a hobby or volunteer opportunity.* You don't have to abandon your dreams just because you can't make a living from them. Pursue a living you enjoy while continuing to play the French horn, take photographs, create a blog, write in your journal, and so on. If you love opera but can't even sing in the shower, you could volunteer for your local opera society and be surrounded by people who love the same thing you do. You can channel your creativity or other themes and skills into jobs that on the surface don't seem related. If you have strong creative talents, you're probably also an idea person, and you might like a job where you would use your imagination and creative thinking skills. Have you considered consulting firms that design creative training programs for large corporations? If you're a writer, you might want to look at technical writing where you can craft the best how-to manuals for the nontechnical people among us. You might want to teach in a public or private school where you can design unique lesson plans and teach courses related to your interests.

➔ **None?** What if you are still staring at a blank piece of paper? If you are, you might feel like quitting. Don't. There's no reason to. All the blank piece of paper is saying is that you don't have an idea right now. Remember chaos theory: figure out what you know, what you don't know, and what you need to learn. And you have done just that: you know what you don't know.

- In a recent talk based on his book *The Power of Intention,* Dr. Wayne Dyer said that if you don't know your purpose in life, then that's your purpose in life: to find your purpose in life. Well, if you don't know what your Possible Lives might be, then you have a mission: to find some Possible Lives that might interest you.

- In the same way that other readers with career ideas are going to be encouraged to make plans, set goals and intentions, and start experimenting—so are you. Just keep going. The answer is inside you; for a variety of reasons, it's just not ready to come out.

- Be honest with yourself, though: is it true that you have no ideas or is there another issue at work here? Do you have a dream, but you're too afraid to write it down because of what others might think? Do you just not have the energy or interest? Is there something blocking you? If so, you might want to take your Wandering Map and the other exercises you've done to a counselor and get some assistance sorting it out. Often other people can see what we can't see about ourselves.

Jillian created a very lackluster Possible Lives Map. She wrote down a few ideas halfheartedly and stared at her paper. "I just don't have any ideas. I'm majoring in sociology and I don't think I can do anything, I guess. At least nothing I can think of." We talked for a few moments and she told me that she was the first person in her family to go to college. She felt this huge burden to be "special" and fulfill everyone's dreams for her. "I feel like a bug stuck on a pin. I can't move anywhere." I told her to close her eyes for a minute and just breathe. She didn't have to go anywhere—at least not this minute. When she relaxed a little, I said, "I want you to pretend that it's tomorrow morning and you wake up and you know exactly what you want to do. Quickly now, what is it?" She opened her eyes looked at me and said, "Nanotechnology." We looked at each other in shock and both of us burst out laughing. Where did that come from? How did she go from "I don't know what to do" to "Nanotechnology" in one minute? "I like reading about nanotechnology," she said. "I know that sounds weird, but I heard about it on TV about a year ago, and I've been reading about it ever since: books, magazines, research. But I don't have any formal training. It's stupid to even think I could work in that field." Within a week, Jillian had made a connection with a woman who had a liberal arts degree and was working at a nanotechnology research company. She invited her to intern in the summer.

Whatever you do, don't stop. There's a simple formula for moving forward in the chaos: Left foot. Right foot. Breathe. Repeat. And just keep wandering.

DESIGNING YOUR POSSIBLE LIVES

In Chapter 6 you'll start developing a strategic plan for living your Possible Lives. But before you move on, you have one more step to complete: creating a Possible Lives scenario plan. Creating scenarios for your Possible Lives will serve four purposes:

1. See how clear your vision is of your Possible Lives

2. See what you know and don't know about each Possible Life

3. Confirm your genuine interest in the Possible Life

4. Help you determine which Possible Lives to focus on first

It will be easier to set your goals and intentions in the next chapter if you can picture your Possible Lives clearly.

So take one more look at your Possible Lives Map and determine how many of your Possible Lives you'd like to proceed with. Then get out a piece of paper for each one you want to consider. (If you don't have any Possible Lives, get out one piece of paper and jot down what you think the next month or two are going to look like. What classes will you be taking or what experiences will you be having? What would you like to happen in the next month or two? What could you do during the next month or two to start developing some ideas?)

Label each page with one of your Possible Lives. Now, take a few minutes to flesh out your vision. Create a short description or story about your Possible Life. You can do this by writing a paragraph or two, a list of words, or even drawing some pictures about each of your Possible Lives. Work quickly; don't make this an interminable process. Set a timer and only allow yourself about ten to fifteen minutes to complete the task. Just as a filmmaker creates a scenario, you're the director of these scenarios, so make them look as concrete as possible. How do you think your life will look if you choose this option?

- ⇥ Can you picture yourself living this Possible Life?
- ⇥ What is it like?
- ⇥ Where are you?
- ⇥ What are you doing?
- ⇥ What do your surroundings look like?
- ⇥ How vivid are your images? Crystal clear or gauzelike?
- ⇥ Have you already started taking actions toward one or more of these scenarios?

Go as far into the future as you can. For some, the furthest they can see is the end of the semester. Others can see years ahead. A common phrase in scenario planning is "long fuse/big bang." This refers to Possible Lives that are going to take awhile to develop, but will be life changing when they finally occur. For instance, if you're a freshman and planning to become a doctor, you have a long fuse/big bang scenario that will require years of determination.

Usually, people who have selected just one or two Possible Lives have a fairly clear picture of what their future might look like. For instance, if you're planning to become a lawyer, you can probably picture yourself finishing college and then going to law school and ultimately starting your job at a law firm. Try listing some possible law schools or some of the classes you might take before you get to law school. If you have an idea of what kind of law you might practice, write about that. Who are your clients? How are you spending a typical day? Are you in a courtroom? Are you writing unbreakable contracts?

When you're done, take a look at all your scenarios.

⇥ Which ones are the strongest?

⇥ Which were the most fun to dream about and create?

⇥ Can you visualize yourself in all the roles?

⇥ How does it feel to picture yourself doing your Possible Life?

⇥ Is one scenario easier to follow than another?

⇥ Do any of them make you a little anxious or uncomfortable? Why?

⇥ Are any of them risky? And is the risk worth the possible outcome?

⇥ Which ones give you energy and which ones (if any) take away your energy?

⇥ Can you see any of them blending together in any way?

⇥ Does one scenario stand out as a starting point with other scenarios following later?

Remember, these scenarios are not predictors of the future. They are only ideas that you have right now and they just represent different options for your life. You can keep developing them as much as you wish. Fleshing them out just helps you gain perspective. You can also abandon them if you find yourself less intrigued as you consider the details. Some people find that within seconds of starting to describe their Possible Life they're already bored. It would be a good idea to remove that life immediately. You will quickly see where you have clear thoughts and where you need to learn more about your ideas. Don't reject an idea just because you don't know much about it or how you're going to do it. If it still sounds intriguing, keep the idea.

That's it. You're done with your Possible Lives, at least for the moment. If you've completed the Possible Lives Map and analyzed it, you have really come a long way toward finding your future. Be sure to take a moment to reflect on all that you've accomplished since reading this chapter.

WISDOM BUILDERS

. . . . →

I. ARE YOU CONSIDERING A CAREER IN THE ARTS?

It's not unusual to discover lots of creative interests on Possible Lives Maps. Most people have creative interests or pursuits and you may too. But do you have the talent or drive needed to pursue the creative field as a primary interest? This is always a dicey area: Who gets to make that decision? In theory, you should make the decision. But on the other hand, if you've watched *American Idol* tryouts, you have seen the, shall we say, misguided dreams of those who think they have talent. If you're considering a professional career in the arts, you might want to assemble your own *American Idol* panel of judges just like the original panel. You need to find someone like Randy: a talented artist/producer who knows the business thoroughly and has managed careers of other people with talent like yours. Then, of course, you need a Paula. Someone who will be kind, encouraging, and tell you how genuine you are while offering fashion advice and motivation. Finally, you really do need a Simon. Someone who will look you in the eye and give you the most honest (if blunt) opinion of your work. It may be painful to hear, but if it's a positive verdict, then you really know you have the talent you need.

Start thinking about who could serve those roles in your creative ventures: Your professors? Professionals in the field? If you're considering a performing art, an audience can help—they applaud, laugh, boo, walk out, or give you a standing ovation. Whatever they do, you will have feedback. If your art is visual or written, you can post it on your Web site and actively seek feedback. Ignore the Internet crazies who always respond with ridiculous comments and non sequiturs. Look for the general audience reaction and then make your decision. Or consider asking a local store or library to display your paintings, photos, or visual pieces. Label each piece carefully with its name, your name, and even a price, if you'd like to sell it. Money talks, as they say. Or leave a clipboard with a pen attached and ask people to join your mailing list for future showings, and invite them to leave comments about your work. By the way, a negative audience reaction doesn't always mean you should stop. It might mean that you work harder or you try new approaches. But you keep going as long as you want and are able to keep going.

Wandering Off:
WHEN A HOBBY SHOULD STAY A HOBBY

It always seems like a dream to be able to pursue something you love as a career. But some people find that turning their hobby into a career is no dream.

Alexis loved making cards and paper craft products. Everyone told her she should turn it into a business—her work was so professional. Alexis envisioned a wonderful life where she could make money crafting all day. What could be better? So she contacted a local craft store and arranged to teach several classes, and she advertised her services to make scrapbooks and other projects for customers.

She quickly learned that preparing art classes was a lot of work. She had to do the boring prep work of cutting the paper, setting up the kits, gathering the materials, writing the instructions, and then teach the class—something she found very frustrating when not everyone worked at the same pace or followed her instructions. She also learned that it wasn't nearly as much fun to put together a project for someone else—she had to abide by their wishes, which stifled her creativity.

Alexis happily returned to crafting for fun, not for profit, doing projects as she pleased.

2. AVOID THE THREE TOP EXCUSES FOR NOT PURSUING YOUR PLANS: AGE, EDUCATION, AND MONEY

- **Age:** Age is a state of mind. Years ago, someone wrote advice columnist Ann Landers about whether to pursue a college degree at age 40. The person commented that it might take eight years because he'd have to pursue it part time. He worried that he would be 48 by the time he finished. Her reply: "How old will you be in 8 years if you don't pursue the degree?" So you have a choice. You're going to be whatever age you're going to be. The only question is do you want to be that age having achieved your dream or not? You might also think you're too young to do something. Unless you're running into a law or unbending rule (such as having to wait until you're 35 to become the president of the United States), chances are you're never too young to do what you have a passion to do.

- **Education** is another roadblock for some. It works both ways: sometimes people feel they must pursue a particular career because they have a degree in that field; others think they can't pursue a particular career because they don't have a degree in that field. Just because you're getting a law degree doesn't mean you need to practice law. And if you want to work with lawyers but don't want a law degree, there are lots of ways to acquire the knowledge and skills you need to enter the legal field in another capacity.

- **Money.** Don't let the potential salary in a field keep you from pursuing it. Consider pursuing it for just a year or two, or get additional education or certification that will give you a higher salary in the same field. There are often entrepreneurial ways to make money in almost any field. Most experts would tell you there's no money in early childhood education; after all, home day-care operators seldom get rich. But don't tell that to Julie Aigner-Clark, who created some preschool videos from her home and developed them into a multimillion-dollar business called Baby Einstein. So don't assume that you can't make money. The reverse is also true: don't assume that a field that pays a lot of money will make you happy. The more a job pays, the more likely you will earn that pay in terms of the hours you'll be expected to work and the intensity of the work. It's not a perfect linear relationship, but if you're not enjoying your life, the money will lose its cachet.

TWO FINAL QUESTIONS

What could you do in the next twenty-four hours to move one step closer to your Possible Life or to become a stronger candidate for it?

_____

_____

_____

As you look over all the Possible Lives you placed on your map, if you knew you couldn't fail, which one would you choose?

_____

_____

_____

Ponder that for a while. And then it's time to move into goal setting chaos-style.

CHAPTER 6

EVEN WANDERERS MAKE PLANS

WHERE ARE YOU NOW AND WHERE DO YOU WANT TO GO?

[It's] like driving at night in the fog. You can only see as far as your headlights, but you can make the whole trip that way.
—**E. L. DOCTOROW,** QUOTED IN *WRITERS AT WORK*
BY GEORGE PLIMPTON, EDITOR, 8TH EDITION, 1988

In Chapter 5 you started creating images of your future—the Possible Lives you might lead. The ideas you developed are not necessarily predictions of what will happen, but rather are probable or possible glimpses into the future based on what you currently know. The quote above from novelist E. L. Doctorow was taken from an interview where he was asked if he plotted out his stories ahead of time. As you can tell, he was content to let the story develop as he wrote. You can plan your life the same way. As you start developing your plans, keep the pressure off and your anxiety level down by remembering a key tenet of chaos theory: the further into the future you're trying to plan, the less accurate your plan will likely be. So in this chapter you're going to plan only as far as your headlights will permit, organizing and reducing the chaos. And even better, by the end of this chapter, no matter where you are right now, you will have an amazing answer to **THE QUESTION**.

Planning your future isn't a once in a lifetime activity. It's a series of decisions and experiments you'll be crafting throughout your life. The plans you're about to develop are designed to help you be focused as well as flexible, not only about your career but also about any other aspects of your life you'd like to change. You will learn to set up your environment to make achieving your goals natural and easy. Through this approach to planning you'll be able to take advantage of, and be resilient to, any changes.

In order to set up your plan, you need to know two things: *where you are* and *where you're going*. In this chapter we're going to assess both. The metaphor I like to use involves a GPS tracking system. Maybe you have one in your car. You enter your starting point and your destination, and the computer guides you all the way. Even if you ignore it and make a turn that's not in the original plan (notice I'm being very careful here not to say "wrong turn," because there are no wrong turns), the GPS tracker just resets the plan to get you back on track to your destination. If you change your mind and want to go somewhere else, it will show you how to do that as well. The first section of this chapter focuses on where you are. In this section you're going to take stock of all the knowledge and information you've accumulated up to this point: what you've acquired by doing the exercises in the first four chapters.

In the second portion of this chapter, you're going to examine where you're going by looking at the Possible Lives you've created and mapping out your plan to get to them. If you've ever avoided goal planning because it is usually presented in a boring and linear manner with lots of rules, you will find possibility planning and intention setting much more interesting. Maybe even fun. After all, goal setting is not a one-size-fits-all activity. Your experiences are too unique for that. The plan you develop will fit your style, not someone else's. There are so many ways to get from where you are to where you want to go that it only makes sense to pick a way that you'll enjoy and will work for you.

Any type of goal-setting system has built-in roadblocks, so before you set the course for your goals, let's consider some of the roadblocks that can wreck your plans before you even start. The chart below illustrates the most common goal-setting challenges and some quick ways to avoid or overcome them.

PROBLEM GOAL	SOLUTION
Too large and grandiose: Some planners call this the "big hairy audacious goal." *I plan to become a Supreme Court Justice.*	Dreaming big is fine. But when you try to move toward the big goal, it seems so big you quickly become overwhelmed and lose energy. *Break your goal into smaller bites where you can see results quickly.*
Too many goals: *I want to become an Olympic swimmer, write the next great American novel, get married, and raise six children.*	Having lots of dreams is fine. But you probably can't do them at the same time or perhaps at the level of perfection you're describing. *Prioritize and move toward the one that is most appealing and then see what happens.*
Too distant goals: *In twelve years I want to be a heart surgeon.*	This is a wonderful goal and very attainable for the right person. But it's a long fuse/big bang goal, so once again you need to *break it down into specific actions you can take now that will lead you to the goal.*
Problem-oriented goals: These goals are created to make your anxiety go away. *I just want to secure a job now so I can relax and do nothing the rest of my senior year.*	There is no energy or enthusiasm toward this goal so you're more likely to grab "whatever" so you can achieve your real goal of relaxation. Instead, *develop an interesting plan that moves you toward a desirable goal and makes you less anxious about the job search.*
Media-influenced goals: *It would be so cool to be a CSI.*	Being a CSI is a great career for the right person. You just need to make sure you're the right person. *Do your research. Learn the reality rather than the image.*
Parent-influenced goals: *My mom would be really pleased if I joined her law firm.*	Your parents can be a wonderful source of inspiration and support. But it's your life, not theirs, so be sure you're pursuing a career because you want it also. Law school is an investment of money and three years of your life. And then you're a lawyer. Hmm. Still sound good? Then go for it.
Money-focused goals: *My goal is to make $50,000 in my first job out of school.*	This is a fine goal and achievable in certain fields of employment. But by setting such an arbitrary figure, you're limiting yourself to the opportunities you can explore. *Consider how flexible you can be about the money.*

Baby steps get on the elevator . . . baby steps get on the elevator. . . .
Ah, I'm on the elevator.

—**BILL MURRAY** AS BOB WILEY IN *WHAT ABOUT BOB?* (1991)

WHERE ARE YOU?
ASSESSING THE PRESENT

It's time to compile all the information you've acquired so far. You have at least four main sources to consider:

1. Your **Wandering Map** categories, themes, and threads (from Chapter 2)

2. Your **key mindsets,** including the ones that are your strengths and the ones you want to build (Chapter 3)

3. The **strengths, skills, knowledge, and mindsets** acquired through your major, your additional coursework, and your experiences (Chapter 4)

4. The **Possible Lives** you'd like to lead (Chapter 5)

This information is your gold mine; it contains the unique strengths you possess that will interest employers and graduate schools. You will want to keep your gold mine in mind as you go through the rest of the book to arrive at your final destination.

On the next page you will find a form to help you gather the information you've acquired in one place. You can fill in the form or create a similar list in your notebook. Note: If you've skipped some of the chapters or exercises, this would be a good time to go back and complete them so you'll have the best information as you start making your plans.

WANDERING MAP SUMMARY

Categories:

_____
_____
_____
_____
_____

Themes/Threads:

_____
_____
_____
_____
_____

Key Strengths, Skills, Knowledge, and Mindsets Acquired Through Major:

_____
_____
_____
_____
_____

Key Strengths, Skills, Knowledge, and Mindsets Acquired Through Experiences:

_____
_____
_____
_____
_____
_____

KEY MINDSETS

Strengths:

_____
_____
_____
_____
_____

Want to Develop:

_____
_____
_____
_____
_____

Key Strengths, Skills, Knowledge, and Mindsets Acquired Through Other Coursework:

_____
_____
_____
_____
_____

Any Additional Information Helpful to the Job Search Process:

_____
_____
_____
_____
_____
_____

WHERE DO YOU WANT TO GO? CHOOSING YOUR FUTURE

"Ghost of the Future," he exclaimed, "I fear you more than any spectre I have seen."—**CHARLES DICKENS,** *A CHRISTMAS CAROL*

The Wise Wanderings system offers three approaches to planning your future based on the clarity of your vision. One way to determine which system will work best for you is to simply read all three approaches and then select the one you prefer. Or you can base your selection on your response to the following question:

What would you like to do after you graduate?

If you honed in on one Possible Life in Chapter 5, and your answer is something like one of these:

⇒ I am going to law school.

⇒ I want to be an investment banker in New York City.

⇒ I'm going to teach history to high school students.

⇒ I'm going to get my Ph.D. in economics and become a college professor.

⇒ I'm going to medical school.

⇒ I want to work in retail merchandising.

⇒ I'm going to teach English in Japan.

⇒ I want to work with adolescents in a nonprofit center.

then you have developed a clear and reasonably certain goal and can move forward with the Probability Planning (Wandering Strategy 1) opposite.

If your answer is more like the following:

⇒ I've got two ideas but they have nothing in common (pendulum attractors).

→ I'm going to teach English abroad or maybe work in a kibbutz or do something in the nonprofit area.

→ I selected several Possible Lives but I'm not sure which to follow first.

→ I want to go to graduate school but I'm also interested in several different jobs.

→ I have several career ideas but I want to do something interesting first, such as traveling to South America.

then you will want to try Possibility Planning (Wandering Strategy 2), which starts on page 146.

Finally, if your answer is general or nonspecific, such as one of these:

→ I have no idea what I want to do

→ I want to work with people.

→ I want to work in business.

→ I'd like to work internationally.

→ I want to work in a nonprofit setting.

then you will want to try Seeking the Butterfly (Wandering Strategy 3) described on page 152.

PROBABILITY PLANNING (WANDERING STRATEGY 1)

Probability Planning is traditional goal-setting planning with a chaos theory twist. Chaos theory tells you that even though your goal may seem etched in stone, as you move toward it you will learn new information and it may change. Probability Planning means you focus on that one option ("I will be at Harvard Law School in three years"), but as you move toward that option, you broaden your search to include other related options. After all, in most decisions or choices, you aren't completely in control. If you could just will yourself into Harvard Law, then it would likely happen. But chaos theory reminds us of the complexity of the admissions process: how many other students are applying this year to Harvard, their grade point averages, the type of student Harvard is seeking (and are you their type?), the average LSAT score for admission, and so on. You don't have control over all the variables, and since you don't have 100 percent control, you will want to develop some secondary options. In this example, specifically, you will want to identify other law schools you're willing to attend. If you're determined to attend Harvard and no other law school, then what would Plan B look like? Perhaps a year off after graduation to build experience?

Because here's an even wilder option: suppose senior year comes along and you suddenly realize you don't want to be a lawyer? Oops. Now what do you do? No problem. Possibility Planning (in the next section) has you covered. But for the moment you are fairly certain about your decision, so use the Probability Planning method. You can always use a different system if new information or knowledge emerges.

On pages 142–143, you will find a Probability Plan Worksheet that you can adjust to fit your needs. While at first it looks a little complicated, it's actually very simple to use and easy to follow.

1. Start by brainstorming the key steps you need to take to attain your goal. If you're having trouble with this step, you probably don't know enough about the subject. It's time to research or speak with someone who can help you.

2. Write the steps in the first part of the chart below (or on a separate piece of paper). At this point, don't try to put them in any particular order. Just write them down as you think of them. The chart has an arbitrary number of twenty steps—you may have more or less, so adjust it as needed.

3. Determine the time frame from now until you plan to achieve your goal. For instance, if you goal is to work for the Peace Corps after graduation and you just finished your sophomore year, you have approximately two years before you will get there. That gives you a lot of time to prepare to be the best candidate for the job. On the other hand, if you're a first semester senior and your goal is to join the Peace Corps, you only have a few months, so you will need to work quickly to become the best candidate.

4. Review your steps to achieve the goal and renumber them beginning with the first step to the last step. Break the steps into small groupings on the chart and write in a specific deadline when you will achieve the various steps. Again, the grouping of five steps is arbitrary. Only use what you need, or add more if needed. You can start from where you are now and go forward to your goal, or you can start with the goal and work backward on your planning sheet, whichever you prefer.

As you set up your plans, keep your academic calendar in mind—don't schedule steps toward your career during exam week or when papers are due. Don't try to crowd too many deadlines into one time period. And don't set goals for Saturday night (unless they're fun, of course). You can assume obstacles will come up. Walk around them. You can also assume that you might change your goal, in which case you just go back to pages 138–139, determine where you are, and use the system that best applies to your new thinking about the future.

You know what the best part of Probability Planning is? When you're asked **THE QUESTION**, *you'll have no trouble saying, "I plan to ____ and I've outlined my plan to get there.*

After the Probability Plan work sheet, you'll find a sample plan developed by Madison, a sophomore who will be graduating in May 2011. She wants to become a lawyer, but hasn't decided which school she'd like to attend or what area of law to pursue. She has identified ten steps, so that's where she's starting, but she may add more later as she learns more about the process.

PROBABILITY PLAN

GOAL: _____

CURRENT DATE: _____

DATE TO ACHIEVE GOAL:_____

TIME REMAINING: _____

List of steps to attain goal:

1. _____
2. _____
3. _____
4. _____
5. _____
6. _____
7. _____
8. _____
9. _____
10. _____
11. _____
12. _____
13. _____
14. _____
15. _____
16. _____
17. _____
18. _____
19. _____
20. _____

Breakdown of time line to achieve goal:

BY _____ (INSERT DATE) I WILL HAVE COMPLETED
THE FOLLOWING STEPS:

1. _____
2. _____
3. _____
4. _____
5. _____

BY _____ (INSERT DATE) I WILL HAVE COMPLETED
THE FOLLOWING STEPS:

1. _____
2. _____
3. _____
4. _____
5. _____

BY _____ (INSERT DATE) I WILL HAVE COMPLETED
THE FOLLOWING STEPS:

1. _____
2. _____
3. _____
4. _____
5. _____

BY _____(INSERT DATE) I WILL HAVE COMPLETED
THE FOLLOWING STEPS:

1. _____
2. _____
3. _____
4. _____
5. _____

PROBABILITY PLAN

GOAL: Attend law school
CURRENT DATE: May 2009
DATE TO ACHIEVE GOAL: September 2011
TIME REMAINING: 2 years, 4 months

List of Steps to Attain Goal (in any order)

1. Take LSAT
2. Prep for LSAT
3. Review law school info—needed GPA, LSAT score, etc.
4. Get references
5. Keep grades up
6. Review online applications
7. Prepare essays
8. Do internship or find summer job in law firm
9. Research interest in criminal law
10. Research interest in public law

Breakdown of Timeline to Achieve Goal:

BY December 2010, **I WILL HAVE COMPLETED THE FOLLOWING STEPS:**

1. Submitted all materials to Law School Data Assembly Service (LSDAS) to be forwarded to my schools
2. Submitted specific applications to law schools as needed

BY October 2010, **I WILL HAVE COMPLETED THE FOLLOWING STEPS:**

1. Finished final draft of all essays
2. Shared essay with prelaw adviser for advice
3. Read essays to friends for their reactions

BY September 2010, **I WILL HAVE COMPLETED THE FOLLOWING STEPS:**

1. Asked professors and others for letters of recommendation
2. Given LSDAS info to my references
3. Given my references a copy of my résumé to remind them about my background

BY August 2010, **I WILL HAVE COMPLETED THE FOLLOWING STEPS:**

1. Collected all admissions information from schools I'm interested in
2. Researched all the schools to determine their specialties
3. Started drafting my essays, taking into account the advice of admissions office

BY Summer 2010, **I WILL HAVE COMPLETED THE FOLLOWING STEPS:**

1. An internship or summer job with a local law firm
2. Researched the specifics of criminal law
3. Contacted alumni practicing different types of law
4. Registered for LSAT

BY December 2009, **I WILL HAVE COMPLETED THE FOLLOWING STEPS:**

1. Researched law careers in general
2. Learned typical salaries and best firms to consider for internship or summer job
3. Met with prelaw adviser to confirm that I'm on the right track
4. Begun creating a list of alumni who are lawyers
5. Researched best way to prepare for LSAT

Notice how Madison's plans get more specific the closer she gets to deadline dates. Also, notice that she was flexible in her designation of dates. She didn't lock herself into a specific date at first, but rather chose to use general terms like "summer." You may find you prefer a general date, or you may respond better to specific dates. It's your plan, so develop it according to what works for you.

Here are some questions to ask yourself as you set up and work through your goals:

⇢ How will I know that I'm on the right track? Which of the steps are particularly important?

⇢ Am I already pursuing this plan? Is any part of this plan already occurring?

⇢ What do I need to change or do differently to make this plan succeed?

⇥ Are there any requirements I must meet to make this plan succeed?

⇥ Who could help me with various steps of this plan?

⇥ What is my backup plan and how can I incorporate it into these steps?

POSSIBILITY PLANNING
(WANDERING STRATEGY 2)

Possible Lives are all about dreaming, and Possibility Planning will help you organize your dreams and give you a more flexible and creative approach than Probability Planning. In their book, *Creative Decision Making,* H. P. and Carol Gelatt call this type of decision making the "shift from 'either/or' to 'both and more'" kind of thinking. Instead of having to choose between appealing futures (pendulum attractors), you get to plan as many as you want while you learn more about each one.

For this type of planning, you will need two tools that you can buy at your college bookstore or almost any grocery, drugstore, Target, or Walmart: a large piece of poster board (so you'll have enough room to work) and a pack of small Post-it notes (sticky tabs). The poster board can be white or any color you choose, as long as the sticky tabs are in a contrasting color so you can read them easily.

Review your Possible Lives Map from Chapter 5 and make any additions or deletions you want based on where you are now. Decide which ones you want to continue considering. Don't worry about how disparate they are. They don't have to be in agreement. As you work through this process, you'll start to figure out how you might resolve any tensions or differences. Write each of the Possible Lives you're considering on a sticky tab and place them in a line at the top of your poster board.

Review what you wrote in the Where Are You? section of this chapter. How do your particular strengths or themes relate to any of your Possible Lives? Write some of those key strengths or themes on sticky tabs and place them near the Possible Lives they apply to. This will remind you of why you are pursuing this area.

Take a look at each Possible Life and think about what you need to do before you can do that job or activity. One way to think about this is "Could I start this career (or experience) on Monday?" If the answer is yes, then you probably just have a few things to do. If it's no, then brainstorm what events or actions would need to occur to get you there. At this point, you probably won't know every step until you've done more research, but fill in the likely steps you'll need to take, given your current knowledge about the field. Write each step you identify on a sticky tab and start placing them below the Possible Life. They don't necessarily have to go in order. As usual, don't worry about making your board perfect. The advantage of the sticky tab system is its complete flexibility. You can move lives around, reorder the steps, remove steps, and add new ones as often as you like. Your planning strategy keeps up with your life and with what you learn as you go along. Just to get you started, here are some typical general steps needed for most experiences (whether in the workplace or graduate school):

- Write résumé
- Write cover letter
- Search Web sites for more information
- Identify books that might provide helpful information
- Get application and apply for admission
- Acquire more education
- Take GRE or other exams
- Find a related internship or other experience
- Talk with people in field
- Identify who can help you
- Raise money to afford your plan
- Note trends in your areas of interest—is it a hot field with lots of opportunities?

You will want to modify this list based on your specific needs and what you learn as you start experimenting, which we'll get to in Chapter 7. Take the generic terms above and adapt them to your situation. For instance, you might adapt "get education" to "get an M.S.W. degree" or "get certification in massage therapy." Keep creating the steps for each of the Possible Lives you've listed. Once you're done, step back and take a look:

- ❧ Which of your strengths and skills enhance your ability to do each one of these Possible Lives?
- ❧ As you started identifying the steps to your Possible Lives, did any particular thoughts come to you?
- ❧ Did you find it easier to fill out the steps to one life than another? Why?
- ❧ Does one life seem more doable at the moment? Why?
- ❧ Does one life seem more appealing or motivating than the others? Why?
- ❧ Is one life more challenging than another? Does this make you less inclined or more inclined to pursue it?
- ❧ Are you excited about a choice but resisting it for some reason?
- ❧ What are the pros or cons of your possible lives? Are any choices particularly risky? In what way?
- ❧ What evidence are you using to make your decisions? Do you need to do more research before you can answer these questions?
- ❧ Is there a point where you'll need to make a decision or choose between two or more possible lives? When will that likely occur?
- ❧ Who could help you move forward with your ideas?

Based on your findings so far, would you like to eliminate or change any of your Possible Lives? If so, just remove it and the sticky tabs associated with it. Now, take a look at what's left. Can you picture yourself in each of these roles? How does it look? How do you feel?

Do you have any duplicate steps in your lists? For instance, maybe all of your Possible Lives require a résumé. In that case, take the "Write résumé" sticky tab away from each list and put it at the top of a new list. Now, write out the steps to doing your résumé on sticky tabs below the "Write résumé" sticky tab. (Hint: Read Chapter 8 if this is the first time you've written a résumé.) If each life has several steps in common, then you can easily pursue all of your Possible

Lives simultaneously without having to eliminate anything for the moment.

Do your Possible Lives have no steps in common? How would you like to proceed with them? You could start by pursuing the steps that sound most appealing to you, regardless of which life they lead to. Then, as you learn more, see if one Possible Life jumps forward. If it does, switch to the Probability Planning approach. Otherwise, use the ideas in Chapter 7 to help design experiments to learn more.

Whatever you decide, put your poster board up on a wall near your desk or transfer your sticky tab lists to pages in your notebook. They're all in one place, and you can change them as needed. The more visible your various plans are, and the more you see them, the more likely you are to move forward in one or more of the directions. By doing this, you will quickly learn which ones are most appealing to you (for whatever reason) and help clear the chaos and confusion of too many lives.

Emily is a sociology major and created her possible lives chart as seen on page 150.

After studying her chart, Emily decided that she was most interested in pursuing three options for now: writer, comic, and social worker. She is still interested in urban planning, but she thinks that she might look into serving on a city council or something like that after she's worked as a social worker first. She believes that her knowledge of some of the problems in the community might help her see a bigger picture of the needs of the city. She also knows she doesn't have the commitment to being an actress right now—that's more of a dream. But becoming a comic sounds like fun and right up her alley, because everyone always tells her how funny she is. She would like to be a writer also, but has no idea how to start that career. After doing a very quick search on the Web (by Googling "writing career," "comic career," and "social worker career"), she was able to quickly learn some basic steps to getting started in all those fields. She used her sticky tabs and poster board to create the plan shown on page 151.

Several of Emily's tasks overlap, including preparing a résumé and cover letter (which can be included in her publicity packet as well) and using a notebook to record ideas and inspirations. Emily may choose to start with those steps. Also, several of the steps can be combined: most comedy clubs operate in the evening, while most social work activities occur during the day, so Emily will be able to

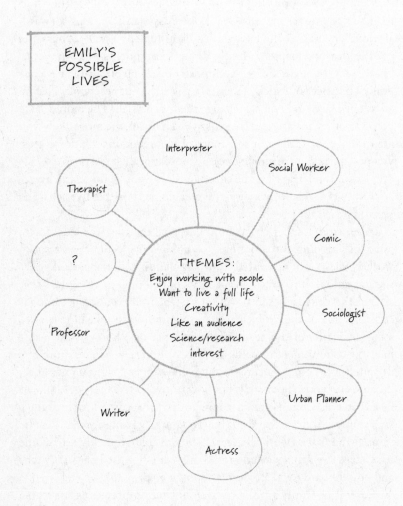

Writer	Social Worker	Comic	
decide on type of writing	volunteer for local agency	prepare a 5-minute set	
create portfolio	look for summer experience	try out routines on friends	
carry notebook and pen	do short exp with differ-ent clients	visit local comedy club	
join writer's group	research MSW programs	study favorite comedians on TV	
add writing to Facebook page	take more Spanish classes	do an open mic	
research likely employers	write résumé and cover letter	carry notebook to catch ideas	
who would buy my writing?		put video on YouTube	
write résumé and cover letter		prepare publicity packet	

proceed with finding an internship or summer job related to social work while pursuing her comedy career plans at night. And writing can be done almost anywhere and anytime, so Emily will be able to find some time to write every day if she wants—carrying a notebook or journal will definitely increase the probability that she will write. Emily can pursue her three dreams all at once for the moment; if she changes her mind, she can simply adapt her plans accordingly.

Remember, singling out your top choices doesn't mean you have to completely forget about your other choices. If you choose for the moment to seek a career in advertising, it doesn't mean you can't later investigate teaching or consulting. You might want to try thinking about your decision in phases: "For my *first* career, I'd like to pursue_____." This keeps the door open to other opportunities.

> *But regardless of how many Possible Lives you're pursuing, you now have a wonderful answer to* **THE QUESTION**: *"I'm actively pursuing several exciting plans at the moment. I'll let you know where I end up."*

SEEKING THE BUTTERFLY (WANDERING STRATEGY 3)

The only thing we know about the future is that it will be different.
—PETER DRUCKER

So you don't know what you want to do. Join the crowd. You probably thought you were off the hook here. After all, because you don't know what you want to do, how can you plan? There's actually a lot you can do—every action you take will reduce your anxiety about the future and because you're so open-minded, you're the most likely candidate for the butterfly effect. You just need to do a few things to increase your odds of finding the butterfly.

Seeking the Butterfly is a planning system for nonplanners that uses intentions instead of goals. It works just as well as, and sometimes even better than, any traditional goal-setting linear plan. Want to know a secret? It's my favorite planning method. I have used intention setting for everything—with it I have found my jobs, my agent, written this book, and discovered lots of other opportunities in my life.

There are lots of hypotheses about the reasons some people don't make a clear career decision. Journal and magazine articles about career indecision cite lots of psychological explanations: perfectionism, anxiety, low self-esteem, fear of commitment, depression, lack of motivation, procrastination, and so on. Some students get angry and blame themselves and everyone else, including their career centers, for not finding them a job. For the most part, I have found that it's more likely that you simply don't have the information you need about your strengths and skills and how to use them in the workplace, and perhaps you don't have enough knowledge about what's out there. So then you get bogged down and feel ashamed, angry, or anxious because you don't have a plan, particularly when it feels as if everyone else does. But the bottom line is it doesn't matter why you're undecided, because we're going to focus on the solution, not the problem. We already know that chaos theory supports you— there are no believers in chaos theory who would be silly enough to say that they know exactly where they'll be in ten years. So instead of viewing yourself as undecided (or clueless) consider yourself open-minded. And you do have a plan: *your plan is to find something that interests you.* To paraphrase the earlier quote by Dr. Wayne Dyer (p.123), if you don't have a career goal in mind, then your goal is to identify a career. And it may be that you're just thinking too hard instead of *doing.* In Chapter 8 you will find lots of ideas and actions you can take to help you find the butterfly and develop your career options without making any long-term commitments.

One concern often expressed about this type of planning is that it's too risky—aren't you just casting your fate to the wind? Also, isn't it just an excuse for doing nothing? Actually, this system is quite the opposite. You're doing a lot of work: focusing, noticing and evaluating opportunities (maybe for the first time), and moving forward with your ideas and interests.

So let's get started. Review the information you collected about yourself in the Where Are You? section of this chapter. Are there any themes, strengths, or threads you'd like to continue in your life? For instance, maybe you have a thread of "writer," but no careers are coming to mind. Or maybe you have a strength in "athletics," but you know you can't be a professional athlete and don't want to coach but don't know what else to do. Why not use one of your threads or themes as your starting point? And then, because the destination is still a question mark, you can develop some intentions (instead of goals) that might help you map out your direction.

Intentions are statements that invite an as yet unknown answer. They are less concrete and specific than goals. By creating an intention and *reminding yourself of it on a regular basis,* you encourage the likelihood of bringing it about. It all goes back to what you think about, you bring about; when you believe it, you will see it; and you see what you want to see. Psychologists have a fancy term for this: *selective perception.* I like to call it the MINI Cooper effect. You see, a few years ago one of my friends started talking about a great car called the MINI Cooper. She desperately wanted to buy one and had even created her ideal MINI Cooper on their Web site. I kept telling her I didn't know what she was talking about, which she found very frustrating. Finally, she took me to their Web site and showed me the car. The next day as I was driving to work, I saw at least ten MINI Coopers on the road. Not only that, my next-door neighbor owned one! MINI Coopers were around me all the time, but my mind wasn't on them so I didn't "see" them. Your future is like the MINI Cooper: it's out there; you're just not seeing it yet. As soon as you start focusing on it, it will appear and appear and appear. That's where intention setting comes in. You set an intention and focus on finding an interesting summer job, or an interesting internship, or meeting someone who will help you find your career and you'll start seeing a way to make these things happen.

All you need is to identify what you want and be ready for it to happen. When you create your intentions, make them as specific as you can, based on what you currently know. Here are some sample intentions to get you started:

→ I intend to find a great summer experience.

→ I am creating an amazing career plan.

→ My intention is to go calmly through the job search process, honing my skills.

→ My intention is to attract helpful people who can assist me with my career plans.

→ I'm creating an interesting future for myself.

→ I intend to find an interesting international opportunity.

→ I'm collecting all the information I need.

→ I am in the process of finding a great opportunity in nonprofit services.

→ I am developing a writing career.

→ My intention is to attract a great job in the advertising field that allows me to use my talents and skills.

→ I'm going to find a way to work with special needs children this summer.

→ I'm excited at the thought of finding my career direction.

Now it's time to create your own intentions. You can fill them in below or write them down in your notebook.

I intend to _____.
I am seeking _____.
I am developing _____.
I am creating _____.
I'm in the process of _____.

To succeed in this approach, you must keep your intentions in mind and be ready to take action when opportunities appear. You have so many distractions in your life, it would be easy to set some intentions and then forget all about them, like last year's New Year's resolutions. Visual reminders are one of the best ways to keep your focus on what you really want. You could write your intentions on your class notebooks so you'll see them every time you go to class. Or place them on an index card on your mirror or at your bedside. You can even create a special notebook or collage, or make a box to keep reminders of your intentions or things you'd like to have in your life. Doing this is a great way to make your vision of the future more tangible.

To create a simple intention box, just get a box (plain or fancy—any size you want), and when you see something that interests you in a newspaper, magazine, or elsewhere, cut it out and place it in your intention box. Collect pictures of what you'd like to attract into your life. You can keep the focus on career-related items, or you can include anything you'd like in your life—from a car to a house to a relationship. You can put in pictures of places you'd like to visit or live in, articles about someone living a life you'd like to live, favorite quotes, and so on. If an idea comes to mind of something you'd like to do, write it out and place it in the box. Take some time every now and then to go through your box and remind yourself of what you want. Remove the items or experiences that you've already acquired (it will happen) or anything you decide you no longer want. You can even make a "digital" intention box by setting up a bookmark folder called Intentions and bookmark interesting Web sites and online blogs or other inspiring items from the Web. While this may sound trivial or even silly, the act of collecting these interesting items helps you focus and encourages you to look for clues that might lead you to your future.

Now that you have set your intentions, are keeping them in mind and actively seeking the butterfly, you have a great response to **THE QUESTION**. *Just say (with complete confidence and pride): "I am in the process of designing an amazing career."*

WISDOM BUILDERS

. . . . >

I. DESIGNING EACH DAY: ARRANGING YOUR LIFE TO FIT YOUR DREAMS ONE DAY AT A TIME

Your future arrives one day at a time. And we know from chaos theory that it's a lot easier to plan in a controlled environment, such as a twenty-four-hour period rather than five years out. How you create each day will go a long way toward how you create your future.

Every day you make choices. (Getting out of bed in time for that eight o'clock class is a choice.) And it's not so much about whether each is a good choice or a bad choice but rather what will be the effect of your choice. Is it going to move you (and your life) forward in some way or is it going to hold you back or keep you further away from your dream? What will happen to you today because of your choices? How will the choices you make today affect you at the end of the semester or in a year? Remember, the butterfly requires almost no time to do her work: one day in your life can be life changing.

➔ Have you placed the job search in the background? Do you think or fantasize about it occasionally, but then go back to your friends, your activities, or your classes, thinking "I'll work on it when I have time"? Do you find yourself saying, "I have a life. I don't have time to worry about this now." In his book *On Writing,* Stephen King explains how he was able to write profusely even before he was paid for it. He, too, had a job, a family, and a life. But he found, and continues to find, a way to write every day. Before or after work, during his lunch hour, every evening, and every weekend. He arranged his life to fit his dream, not the other way around. You can make time and space for your plans so that they will evolve naturally with much less effort.

➔ Start your day by setting intentions for what you'd like to have happen. And then be on the lookout for signs that support your intentions. Focus on who or what is connecting you to your future. Who might you see today who could help you with your plans? If you already know you have a tough day ahead, decide now how you're going to handle it.

↱ What's your soundtrack for the day? On the TV show *Grey's Anatomy,* whenever the medical students feel too stressed, over-whelmed, or depressed, they put on upbeat music and dance. They're shaking off any negative vibes and creating positive energy. What theme song plays in your head? How does it affect you throughout the day? Pick a song that will motivate you all day.

↱ Take your top three goals (some of which are probably not career related, by the way) and write them on sticky tabs. Place them everywhere—on your mirror, on your computer, and so on. As you go through the day, think about whether what you are doing is moving you toward one of those goals. If not, stop and think. Is it worth the time you're spending doing this non-goal-related activity? Only you know the answer. But if you find yourself continually doing things that take time away from your goals, it's time to use your analytic mindset to figure it out.

↱ Finally, can you think of a small object you could use to remind yourself of your goals or intentions? Professional writer Anne Lamott describes using a one-inch-square picture frame to remind herself to just write enough to fit in the frame when she becomes overwhelmed by a writing project. Remember Emily who was considering a career as a comic? A friend photographed her with her favorite comic at a venue recently and she keeps that picture in her notebook as inspiration. Brianna, who hopes to become an archaeologist, keeps on her desk a small arrowhead she found on a dig. Diego, who plans to become a heart surgeon, keeps a small heart-shaped tin *milagro* (a religious folk charm) on his desk. Think about something small that can represent your dream, and keep it where you'll be reminded on a regular basis.

2. MANAGING YOUR ENVIRONMENT

Now that you've set some goals or intentions, take a look around your living space. Have you set it up to make achieving your goals easier? Are your goals and intentions visible? If you have something you want to accomplish (write a paper, read a book, search the Web, play your guitar), can you just walk in and do it? Or do you have to clean up a bunch of junk first and remove last night's pizza crusts and beer cans? Your personal environment plays a big role in shaping your dreams. If you don't think your setting makes a difference, try studying in the middle of a fraternity party. Sit in the middle of the party with your chemistry book and see how much you learn.

When you're trying to set new goals and move forward in your career plans, it's important that your lifestyle support those plans. The college environment doesn't always support job searching—students are often working with last-minute deadlines, distractions, and time-wasting activities. With so many choices to make, procrastination can easily become your lifestyle.

Let's say your goal is to manage a golf resort, and one step toward that goal is to improve your golf game so you can get a job at a local country club where you'll likely develop a great network. You've even found a way to get credit for pursuing golf by taking a phys ed course on golfing. Take a look around—what in your room supports your goal? Do you have some clubs? Are they readily available? Do you have some golf magazines or books?

A professional musician friend leaves his instrument in his hallway and every time he walks past he plays a scale or a short song. He has found that short exercises throughout the day make his scheduled longer practice sessions go much better and he plays much more than he otherwise would. The same idea applies to the job search: are your job search materials easily accessible?

- Keep all your job search–related materials in one place—a notebook or file.

- Keep your résumé near your phone or maybe in your wallet in case you get a call on your cell phone.

- Keep the materials you need for an interview in one place so you don't forget them.

Here are some areas to assess and possibly change in your environment:

> ❯ **Time.** There's an adage that says we don't manage time; time moves on regardless of what we do. We manage ourselves. Do you have a system for managing your time? How's it working for you? If it's not helping you, or you're constantly late or missing events, it might be time to find a new system.

> ❯ **People.** Your roommate or friends may be great, but may not be your best support system unless they share your goals and values. It's not unusual for others who aren't working as hard as you on the job search to be jealous or resentful. So enjoy their friendship, but look elsewhere for support if necessary. All sorts of people can help you: professors, coaches, alumni, career center staff, advisers, family members, supervisors, older students in your major, even clubs devoted to your interest areas.

> ❯ **Health (Diet, Exercise, and Sleep).** You probably know what's going to be said here. Is there a way you can eat healthier and stay away from too much fast food? Are you staying fit and getting enough sleep so that your energy level stays high? Nothing will torpedo your goals faster than being too tired to take action or even think about your plans. College is hard and intense, and you need to find a way to restore your energy without relying on supercaffeinated drinks to keep yourself awake and energized.

> ❯ **Other Distractions.** Are there areas of your life that are distracting you, causing worry, or keeping you from focusing on your job search? Does your car need repairing, is your room a mess, are you in a troubled relationship, are you having financial problems such as overdue bills or maxed out credit cards? Worrying can deplete any energy you might have to tackle the job search. If you can't fix the problem on your own, figure out who can help you and seek the help. Colleges are filled with people who can assist you at no charge from financial aid planners to mental health counselors to academic advisers.

3. PSYCHOLOGY AT WORK:
PREMACK'S PRINCIPLE

Keeping yourself motivated is the key to the job search process. For that matter, if you hope to supervise other workers, it's important to start thinking about how you might motivate them. Consider Premack's principle. It states that a behavior is more likely to occur if it is *followed immediately by a more preferred behavior.* What this means is that you (or those who might be working for you) will accomplish more if you set up a reward system for each of your goals and objectives. Certainly one reward is how much better you'll feel when you can check another item off your to-do list. But sometimes special accomplishments require special rewards. This can be the fun part of planning if you turn it into a brainstorming session.

By finding reinforcements that are similar in nature to the task involved, you could apply Premack's principle to your current job search. Conducting research related to a career interest might be worth a coffee break. Completing your résumé and uploading it to ten carefully selected employers is probably worth an afternoon off pursuing your favorite hobby.

FINAL QUESTION

What could you do in the next twenty-four hours to move forward with your plans?

_____

_____

_____

_____

_____

CHAPTER 7

PAGING DR. FRANKENSTEIN

EXPERIMENTAL WANDERINGS WITH BIG PAYOFFS

> Science, my lad, is made up of mistakes, but they are mistakes which it is useful to make, because they lead little by little to the truth.
>
> —JULES VERNE, *JOURNEY TO THE CENTER OF THE EARTH*

Are you ready to wander? Ready to take action, have fun, and pick up job leads at the same time? One misguided notion about the job search is that it consists of an onerous set of tasks you have to take on in addition to all the work you're already doing. Make no mistake: the job search is challenging at times and it does require you to do certain tasks well, but there's no reason you can't have some fun along the way. And that's what experimental wanderings are all about—doing things that are sometimes fun and sometimes related to your goals and intentions, and always being ready to say yes to the butterfly.

Through your wanderings you will get to experiment with all sorts of environments and people and make wise choices based on what you learn. You may be surprised to read some of the suggested wanderings because another myth about the job search is that you have to be extra careful and pick the "perfect" experiences in order to succeed. For instance, if you want to work in banking, then you must do an internship in banking. Obviously, that's logical and a great idea. But what if that's not an option for you? What if you can't find a banking job? Where else could you wander that might add value to your potential banking career? From your Wandering Map, you know you can build skills and develop networks in a variety of locations, and experimental wandering will allow you to do that.

Experimental wanderings are designed to help you with four main goals: identifying the best prospects for finding jobs, finding hidden opportunities, developing your network, and positioning yourself as the best candidate. Whether you're on a probable path, pursuing several Possible Lives, or seeking the butterfly, the actions provided in this chapter will propel you quickly forward. Experimental wanderings will strengthen your vision of the future, possibly provide interesting résumé entries, make you stand out from your peers in the job search, and very likely help you encounter a butterfly or two.

The chart below demonstrates the key results of experimental wanderings.

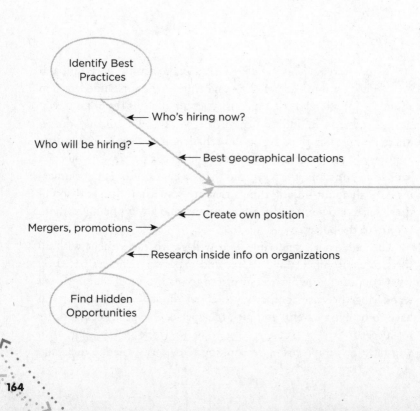

So how do you achieve these results? By wandering two ways: first, by using traditional research methods such as books and Web sites, not unlike what you've done when you've researched a paper for a history or English class, and second, by putting yourself in situations where you are likely to acquire needed skills and knowledge or meet people who can help you.

As you prepare to start experimental wanderings, consider what you hope to uncover:

- Is there a specific body of knowledge you're seeking?

- Are you hoping to find someone who can help connect you with your field of interest?

- Are you looking for inspiration or for a career that might interest you?

- Based on your goals or intentions, and your personality type, would you prefer to start with some Internet or book-based research, or would you like to wander into people and places?

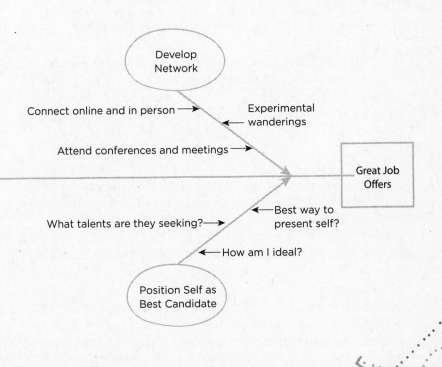

) Which approach would likely yield the most information efficiently?

) If you want to learn more about careers in publishing, for example, do you know someone in the field?

- Do you have enough information to approach them intelligently about the field with good questions?

- If you don't have a connection, then start with traditional research to see if you can find one.

The type of information you're seeking will help you determine whether to do your wandering in the library, at your computer, or experientially.

EXPERIMENTAL WANDERINGS AT YOUR DESK

The art of research is the ability to look at the details and see the passion.   **—BILL PULLMAN AS DARYL ZERO,** *THE ZERO EFFECT*

Let's start with the method you already know a fair amount about: research. Instead of researching an academic topic, though, your mission now is to assess what you know and what you don't know about the workplace, and then set out to become a pseudoexpert in your field of interest before you apply for the job or the graduate program.

Did you know that the number one complaint employers have about college students and recent graduates is their failure to do their research before the interview? Recruiters are offended by interviewees who don't know what the company produces or does, don't have a basic understanding of the position they're applying for, and ask questions that could be easily answered on their Web site or in their promotional material. You see, from their perspective, the point of the interview is to get to know *you*, not explain basic information about their company. The good news in this, of course, is that thanks to all the work you've done so far, you have an extensive and rich collection of information about yourself to share in an interview.

And the better news is that thanks to the Internet and the plethora of books on career-related topics, much of the company research has already been done for you. The downside of all this information, however, is that it's easy to be overwhelmed and lose track of your purpose, which is why this chapter is designed to help you access the information you need quickly and efficiently.

FIND THE REALITY BEHIND THE IMAGE

As entertainment, TV shows are great. As reality, they fall a little short. The characters go to work occasionally, never seem to work long hours, hang out in coffee bars or restaurants, and magically have nice apartments. The media is actually the worst place to get an idea of the working world. Remember, there's a reason they call television and movies entertainment. People would quickly turn off a show that presented a realistic picture of many workplaces. Only insomniacs would watch a lawyer show that placed a camera in front of an attorney researching and writing a brief at his desk for fourteen hours. So enjoy your TV and movies, but don't make career decisions based on them. Do your research to uncover the reality. Kathy, a biology major working in a *CSI* type setting, is quick to point out that they don't *have the attractive blue lighting, no one wears leather pants, and absolutely no one looks like Marg Helgenberger.*

Sometimes finding a good metaphor for what you're about to do can make the process more interesting. You could consider yourself an anthropologist uncovering a hidden civilization. If you'd prefer, you can call yourself a scientist conducting research, an investigative reporter on a search for the truth, a CSI investigator seeking clues to solve the mystery, or perhaps you could just be what you are: a student or recent graduate in search of an interesting career or job. Armed with a metaphor or not, you are going to wander experimentally and gather information, which is probably the most important thing you will do in this whole job-seeking process. Chaos theory stresses that greater knowledge leads to better predictions, so the information you gather will help you make better decisions about your future. And as a student or recent grad, you get an added bonus most other job seekers lack: your youth opens doors to opportunities and helpful mentors because most people enjoy helping or mentoring young people who are enthusiastic and interested in learning.

It's easy to get overwhelmed as you begin your wanderings, so whatever you are seeking, take a few minutes to write down some goals or intentions before you wander. For instance, if you're sitting at your computer to do some Internet research, set a time limit and say to yourself, "For the next hour I'm going to find anything I can about_____." You can insert the name of a particular company, job field, city, or whatever topic you're trying to find information on. For those of you who aren't sure where you're headed, no problem. Focus on something you'd like to do for just the next month or two. Setting a time limit and having a specific reason for searching the Internet will keep you from wandering off, so to speak, to find that really good game site or interesting blog you can't resist. Be sure to bookmark the best sites (if you're using your own computer), write them in your notebook, or e-mail them to yourself so you can refer to them later.

Good research will take away the fear of the unknown, eliminate the future "abyss," increase the likelihood of the butterfly effect, help you develop a network, and gain a personal understanding of the culture of the workplace you are aiming for.

The more information you can fill in about the opportunities in your field, the better you will be able to match yourself to it and the stronger your interview, cover letter, and résumé will be. The form on the next few pages will help you organize the knowledge you already possess and identify what you need to learn more about. If you quickly discover you can't fill in much of the form, try a Google search or one of these top five career-related megasites:

The Riley Guide: http://www.rileyguide.com/

Quintessential Careers: http://www.quintcareers.com/

Vault: http://www.vault.com/index.jsp

Careerjournal.com: http://online.wsj.com/careers

Monster: http://www.monster.com/

Usually the best resource for more in-depth databases (like Hoover's or Vault guides) is a college or university library. If you're still in school, use your library to locate databases, journal articles, books, e-books, and other resources. Check with your career center: they likely subscribe to many of the job search databases, which would be expensive for you to get on your own. Many university libraries (particularly business school libraries) have already organized a section of resources for job seekers that will make your search even easier. If you're not in school, talk to the library at the nearest college or university. Often local residents are granted special permission to use the library resources. Public libraries may also have access to job-hunting materials; ask the librarian for assistance with your research.

So armed with all the information you're finding on the Internet and in great books like the Vault guides, try completing this information sheet on your area of interest. If you're still in the process of figuring out what might appeal to you, see if you can complete any of the lines.

POSSIBLE OR PROBABLE LIFE FACT SHEET

Career field: _____

Most interesting job titles:

_____

_____

Typical entry-level position: _____

General culture of the setting:

_____

_____

Education/training needed:

_____

_____

Experience needed:

_____

_____

Skills needed:

_____

_____

Typical terms used in the field:

_____

_____

Geographic locations with most opportunities (and cost-of-living information):

_____

_____

Sample job description/duties:

_____

_____

_____

How to move up:

_____

_____

What's needed to get started:

_____

_____

Best resources to learn more about this field:

Books:

_____

_____

Companies:

_____

_____

Web sites:

_____

_____

Internships:

_____

_____

People to contact:

_____

_____

_____

_____

Key information about myself and specific language to use in interview, cover letter, or résumé:

_____

_____

_____

_____

_____

If you've exhausted the resources recommended on the megasites, consider scheduling a time to meet with a librarian. They are experts at uncovering resources, and most college and university librarians are assigned to specialty areas within the library. Find out who specializes in business, nonprofit, government, or whatever resources you're specifically seeking.

EXPERIMENTAL WANDERINGS BEYOND YOUR DESK

What do you first do when you learn to swim? You make mistakes, do you not? And what happens? You make other mistakes, and when you have made all the mistakes you possibly can without drowning—and some of them many times over—what do you find? That you can swim? Well, life is just the same as learning to swim! Do not be afraid of making mistakes, for there is no other way of learning how to live!

—**ALFRED ADLER,** *ALFRED ADLER: A PORTRAIT FROM LIFE* BY PHYLLIS BOTTOME

If you've gleaned as much information as possible from Web sites and books, it's time to start the other kind of experimental wandering into people and places. The tougher the job market or the more competitive the position, the more important it is that you have done both types of experimental wandering. For those of you who are bored in a library, this part may be much more fun than sitting in front of a computer or a book.

Statistics vary but some studies say as many as 75 percent of all jobs are obtained through networking, and recent studies have shown that your connection to your eventual workplace is likely someone who's a stranger to you right now. Parents, neighbors, professors, friends, and other typical connections can be helpful, but you may get even better results by reaching out to new people and new places. You're already familiar with the basics of networking through Web sites such as Facebook or MySpace, where you met people and developed new friends through common interests. Now you're going to apply that to your job search. Whether you network online or in person, your goal is to become comfortable meeting people and letting them know what you're seeking. So armed with lots of knowledge about your strengths, and thorough research about the job (or not, if you don't have a job in mind yet), it's time to try a new type of experimentation.

Experimental wanderings are some of the most fun you can have in the job search. Some of them will be obvious and directly career related, such as an internship in your chosen field. But others will be just about you having fun doing what you like to do and encountering a chance connection or lead that will move you closer to your dream. Consider the story of Hannah:

Just prior to leaving school for the holidays, Hannah's hand-bell choir performed a concert at a local church. At the end of the concert, the minister asked the choir to introduce themselves

to the congregation. Most people just said their names, but on a whim Hannah said, "I'm Hannah and I'm a Russian area studies major, and I just returned from a year in Moscow and would love to go back again." The audience smiled and clapped. Hannah thought nothing more about it until a woman stopped her as she was leaving the church and said, "My husband is an executive with a local company that is just starting to do business in Russia. Would you like to meet him?" Hannah, of course, said yes, and the woman gave her the executive's home phone number. Hannah called him that evening, and a few weeks later she was on a plane to Moscow, escorting several company executives on a two-week fact-finding trip. She translated for them, showed them around the city, explained how many services worked, and even sat in on confidential meetings. When she returned for spring semester, she interned with the company and received a job offer at graduation.

Let's take a moment to analyze what Hannah did right:

1. She was doing something she loved: playing in a handbell choir.

2. She seized the opportunity to let a group of people know what she was seeking.

3. *She didn't ask for a job.* This is an important point to remember because timing is everything. Obviously, she was ultimately seeking a job, but if she had said, "I need a job," the executive's wife might not have even approached her because she wouldn't have known if her husband had any jobs. Hannah simple phrased her desire more like an intention, "I'm looking for a way back to Russia," which opened the gate to the job path.

Hannah's situation worked out beautifully. But not all experimental wanderings do, as in the case of Andrew, who wanted to work in South America.

Through a chance encounter on an elevator, Andrew met a gentleman who had some connections in Argentina and told him about an opportunity in market research for a dental organization. Andrew applied for the job and was told to report in about a month. He took off for Buenos Aires, excited about the prospect of working in his dream country. He vacationed and traveled for a few weeks first and then reported to his new job. Unfortunately, his dream quickly disintegrated when on his third day at the job (which turned out to be in a dentist's office), he was handed a book of dental procedures and told to read it and be ready to work as a dental assistant in one week. He protested his lack of knowledge and skill in this area and shuddered at the thought of cleaning people's teeth, but no one cared. He realized that because they were paying him in cash and he technically didn't have the proper working papers, he had no power to do anything. In two days he would have to sign a contract that would keep him there for six months, so he quickly packed and took a flight back to America. Now, it would be easy to call this experiment a failure, and Andrew did feel frustrated and angry when he returned home, but within a few days he had decided he could turn his experience into something good. First, he had traveled all over Argentina, which he had always wanted to do, and second, he had strengthened his language skills. Moreover, he had a great story to tell a future employer. He even wrote a short essay for the career center at his college to help students prepare for an international job. He decided to pursue another of his Possible Lives: becoming a Spanish professor. He has enrolled in a master's program in Spanish (he used his Argentina story as his essay) and will remain to get a Ph.D. And now that he can laugh about the experience, he has a great educational story for his students.

What did Andrew do right ?

1. He engaged with someone who helped him find an opportunity in a country he had always wanted to see.

2. He took a chance and reached for his goal.

3. Once he discovered unforeseen problems, he made quick decisions and cut his losses.

4. He used his negative experience to catapult himself forward into a new and better experience.

Andrew's and Hannah's experiences confirm the value in approaching all your experimental wanderings with two questions: What can I learn? and What stories could I tell about this experience? By constantly considering what you're learning and the story you will tell, you mine the experience for its learning value regardless of whether it is positive or not.

Most students enjoy experimental wanderings (particularly when they discover how interesting and valuable they are), but if you're a little anxious about it, try using one of the metaphors discussed earlier and casting yourself in a role—it might help you detach yourself from your anxiety. Why not focus on being curious? Curiosity can take you a long way in the job search process and a little curiosity might be all you need to take a step forward. Remember the positive mindset in Chapter 3? What if you replaced worry with wonder? The key to finding experiments is asking questions such as How could I . . .? or What's great about . . .?" or

→ What would happen if

- I wandered into that program tonight at the college and asked the guest speaker how she or he first started?

- I started writing a blog about my interest in foreign policy?

- I took a semester off to test out my dream?

- I called a graduate who's a social worker to find out whether or not I really need to get that M.S.W. degree?

Or

→ I'm curious:

- Just what do I need to do to be able to ____?

- How could I make a better learning experience out of this ____?

- What are the salaries of ____?

- Would I really like working with_____?
- Where is the best place to work if I'm interested in_____?

The point of the experimental wanderings is to move you forward. There aren't any rules per se about these wanderings, because there's no way to predict what experience or research finding will be the key to your future. So the best thing you can do is take action. Doing something, anything, may move you a step closer to your dream. Here are some guidelines that should spur you on to start experimenting immediately.

TEN GUIDELINES FOR EXPERIMENTAL WANDERINGS

1. Wander anywhere.

2. Wander anytime.

3. Say yes.

4. Forget perfect. No experiment is a failure if you've learned something.

5. Assume there will be messiness, detours, blind alleys, and new adventures.

6. Be sure to actively engage:

   a. Express an opinion.

   b. Speak for someone who can't.

   c. Provide a solution.

   d. Focus on and state what you want.

   e. Ask how you can help.

   f. Ask good questions.

7. Find the story.

8. Be curious.

9. Be flexible.

10. Seek part of your dream if the whole dream isn't available.

It's hard to add one more commitment to an already over-committed schedule, so design your experiments to fit with your schedule. You're less likely to experiment if the cost seems too great for the benefit. Don't set yourself up for ten hours a week of volunteering if you don't have the time. Find a volunteer project that you can do in an afternoon. You'll get a taste of whether you like it and can add more time as you go along. The trick is to take some sort of action. You can audition for a Possible Life without committing to it. You define the level of commitment—one hour, one day, one semester, or one year. As you experiment, be sure to pay attention and look for the stories and possible career touchpoints: moments of contact with potential employers. Remember Hannah as you make your connections: don't ask for a job—talk about what you're looking for. Just treat everything as an experiment and see what happens.

TRADITIONAL EXPERIMENTAL WANDERINGS

There are several well-known traditional sources for experimental wandering that many students have found helpful. One reason they are successful is that they tend to be longer-term experiences that give you time to really gain new knowledge and develop your skills in a particular field. You can also list them on your résumé under the experience category (see Chapter 8), regardless of whether you were paid or not. Employers like seeing these experiences because they demonstrate commitment; they show that you successfully complete an experience and that you are hardworking and focused. The chart on the next page illustrates the top seven experiences you can acquire and their value to both you and the employer:

TRADITIONAL EXPERIMENTAL WANDERINGS	SOME OF THE VALUE TO YOU	SOME OF THE VALUE TO EMPLOYER OR GRAD SCHOOL
STUDY ABROAD	Intellectual challenge. New perspectives. Build language skills. See new places. Get to know a culture. Handle problems.	Comfortable in new environments. Language and culture skills. Active learner. Risk taker. Shows initiative.
STUDENT EMPLOYMENT (WORK STUDY OR OTHER)	Acquire workplace skills. Learn about college from a different perspective. May be given professional duties depending on position—seek these out. Acquire recommendations.	Demonstrates initiative and is a hard worker. Manages time well if grades are also good. May acquire specific skills related to job depending on position.
LEADERSHIP IN STUDENT ORGANIZATIONS	Practice motivating and leading others. Learn new skills and develop relationships. Be recognized on campus. Connections with administrators and faculty. Acquire recommendations.	Future management potential. Someone who can motivate others. Handles variety of management tasks including budgeting. Takes initiative and demonstrates team-playing ability.
INTERNSHIPS	Preprofessional experience valuable on résumé. Immersion in work environment. Learn whether you want to pursue as career. Acquire recommendations.	Experience in field demonstrates commitment. Shows initiative. Demonstrates skills directly related to job.
SUMMER JOBS	Money. Shows you work hard. May acquire skills related to future depending on job. Learn what you like and don't like about workplace.	Demonstrates initiative and hard work. Depending on position may have specific skills needed for workplace.
VOLUNTEERING/ SERVICE LEARNING	Good feeling knowing that you helped another. May acquire work-related skills. Provides understanding of nonprofit organizations.	Demonstrates character. May have acquired relevant knowledge to workplace. Generally valued by all employers.
TEMP WORK	Learn about a variety of workplaces; acquire valuable office skills; build customer service skills; can get promoted or lead to a full-time job. Many sources for recommendations.	Demonstrates flexibility; able to handle a variety of situations; quick learner; will fit in with new workers

SEEKING THE BUTTERFLY: FIFTY-PLUS LESS TRADITIONAL EXPERIMENTAL WANDERINGS

The goal of experimental wandering is to put yourself in a place where something might happen. *Everyone knows the phrase "six degrees of separation":* the notion that you are only five people away from anyone you want to meet. You never know who might know someone who could help you. So as you pursue these experimental wanderings, keep Hannah's lead in mind: whatever you're doing, introduce yourself, and state what you're seeking (avoid *job*—use *experience* or another word). Ask yourself: Who am I connected with already? Have I used my current connections to find opportunities? And if you're considering something new, ask yourself: What could I do? How could I help? What could I learn from this? What is the story?

Below is a list of over fifty experimental wanderings, in no particular order, many of which might not seem job-search related. Remember your overall goal is to collect information and learn, and these activities can help you by either contributing to your understanding or knowledge of a subject, or connecting you to people who can help you. As you read the list, highlight the ones you'd like to try first or jot them down in your notebook as intentions or goals. And add your own as well!

JOIN, INTERACT, AND MEET PEOPLE

→ Talk to everyone you know or meet about your plans for the future.

→ Join or create an organization and demonstrate your unique gifts and talents.

→ Take on tasks you enjoy and build your résumé.

→ Shadow someone: spend a day with a person doing what you want to do.

→ Do an externship: spend a week or two with an alumnus in your field of interest.

→ Put yourself in a place where you'll meet the people you want to meet. When asked why he robbed banks, Willie Sutton said,

"Because that's where the money is." If you want to work in_____, where are the people who are already working in that field? Find out where they hang out and go there. If you're over twenty-one, bars can be a great place to connect. There are several bars in Washington, D. C., that are known as hangouts for congressional aides and political types. Police usually have a favorite watering hole, as do newspaper reporters. Doctors and nurses might stop for a quick after-work drink in bars or restaurants near the hospital. Traveling business executives often stop for a drink in the bar of a five-star hotel. In Austin, Texas, where I live, there's a chili parlor frequented by lawyers, judges, legislators, and others who work in the capitol nearby.

➔ Join a team—whether it's sailing or the chess club, you will meet people.

➔ Sing in a choir or play in an orchestra.

➔ Pursue a hobby with others.

➔ Play tennis or other sports, even if you're awful at it. You'll have a good laugh and meet new people.

➔ Learn to play golf if you're going into business.

➔ Join one of the thousands of professional organizations, such as the American Marketing Association or the American Philosophical Association. You'll get a bargain student rate, newsletters and journals about the field, and access to private job listings.

➔ Set a goal to meet a new person in each class you're attending.

➔ Set an intention to find helpful people who can assist you on your search.

➔ Never miss an opportunity to make a new friend—people of all ages, in your classes, on your floor in the dorm, or in your apartment complex.

➔ Ask questions. A famous mystery writer used to go up to people at parties and ask them what they did for a living. When they told her, she would say, "Now why would someone want to murder a person in your profession?" Their responses gave her lots of inspiration for her books. What questions could you ask that might inspire you in your job search?

➔ Find hidden gems at your school.

- Many presentations, programs, workshops, and other opportunities are poorly attended or receive few applications. Show up. Ask questions. Participate. (Hint: Even if you've

graduated, most schools advertise their special programs and
lectures and allow the public to attend. Here's your chance to
connect with the speakers you didn't have time for when you
were in school.)

→ Select an office at your school that interests you. Ask if they
could use your help with a survey they don't have time to do,
writing brochures or information sheets, greeting visitors, or
whatever you're good at.

READ, LISTEN, AND RESPOND

→ Find textbooks related to your career field if you didn't major in
the subject. Usually your school library will have them, so you
can read them for free. Mine them for keywords, industry terms,
phrases you should know, and so on.

→ Read bulletin boards and kiosks. Look for interesting
opportunities.

→ Start your own blog about your interests or what you're learning
about your career plans (keep a positive mindset—no whining).
Several students have gotten job offers from their blogs.

- Encourage readers to respond with helpful information or
suggestions for you.

- Respond to other people's blogs.

→ Find podcasts with tip-of-the-day–type information about
management, marketing, or other things everyone in the
workplace needs to know.

→ Find podcasts that will help you learn or keep up your skills in a
foreign language.

→ Play music on your MP3 player that inspires you to move and
take action.

→ Read your professors' Web pages. Find out what research
activities they are involved in and offer to help. For free. At the
very least, you'll get a recommendation letter out of it. Maybe
even credit or some money.

→ Get books on CDs from the library on management or other
business ideas and download them to your MP3 player, or play
them in your car while commuting to school or work.

→ Surf the Internet. Google words related to your interests.

⇥ Read a magazine devoted to something you know nothing about. How could what you're reading apply to your interests? Remember, creative thinkers connect the unconnected.

⇥ Subscribe to a magazine in a field of interest. If you're interested in working in a spa, for example, and the nearest one is fifty miles away, reading *Spa* magazine (http://www.spamagazine.com/) each month might keep you informed about the field and identify sites for future employment.

⇥ Subscribe to (or read the Web site of) the newspaper from the location where you want to live. Become as knowledgeable as a native before you've even lived there.

⇥ Check out your school's alumni database. If they don't have one, talk to someone in alumni relations to get some names of alumni who might help you.

⇥ Join LinkedIn (http://www.linkedin.com/), the professional version of Facebook and start networking.

⇥ Join Meetup.com (http://www.meetup.com/) and find groups in your area interested in what you're interested in. No groups? Form one.

⇥ Look for opportunities for grants, scholarships, and funds. Start reading about them as soon as you can, because many have long application periods.

WATCH, ANALYZE, AND FIND THE CONNECTION

⇥ Watch a movie and analyze it for what you can learn about life and/or the workplace, even though you know not to expect a completely realistic portrayal.

- *Ocean's Eleven* for leadership and team development

- *Dead Poets Society* for what can go wrong in a first job and how it all could have been prevented

- *Wall Street* for a look at a trading floor and the pressured environment

- *Peaceful Warrior* for perspective and developing a wonderful mindset

- *Office Space* so you'll know the importance of a red stapler (just kidding)

❯❯ Take random photos across your campus and analyze the culture.

❯❯ Watch a football game and analyze it.

❯❯ Go to a cultural event (one that is not part of your culture) and discover what you appreciate about it.

❯❯ Read the advertisements in a magazine related to your interest area. Are there hidden jobs with any of those companies? For instance, if you're interested in sports and read *Sports Illustrated,* notice the advertisements. Would you be interested in working for a company that manufactures athletic gear or energy bars?

BE BOLD AND DARING

❯❯ Tell ghost stories late at night to your friends to practice your storytelling skills. (See Chapter 10 for the importance of building these skills.)

❯❯ Move: get a summer job in the city where your best opportunities are.

- Have you always wanted to live in _____? What about moving there now?

- Set an intention: "I want to find a way to live in Washington, D.C., this summer."

- Can you find others interested in spending a summer elsewhere as well? Maybe you can share an apartment? Check colleges for cheap summer dorm rentals.

- Take a "survival" job that puts you in your desired location. While waitressing or bartending in Washington, D.C., you can use your free time to learn all about the city, decide where you might want to live, and so on.

❯❯ Write a poem about the job search. Read it at a poetry slam.

❯❯ Ride a horse. If you can manage a thousand-pound animal, you can tackle a lot of things.

❯❯ Write a reality show based on your job search experience. Pitch it to a network.

❯❯ Go up to a famous guest speaker at your school, tell him or her what you want to do and seek their advice.

→ Get lost in a strange city and explore.

→ Write a screenplay, memoir, poem, or short story and submit it to a contest.

TAKE TIME FOR REFLECTION AND INSPIRATION

Inspiration is everywhere and some of these activities are designed simply to give you the downtime you need to process all the thoughts whirling in your head. Remember the value of reflective mindset in Chapter 3?

→ Go to an art gallery and ponder your favorite pieces, but also spend some time studying ones you don't like. What turns you off and why?

→ Get near water: a lake, swimming pool, or even a shower. Some creative thinkers say their best ideas come when they're near water.

→ Download some meditation or hypnosis podcasts—maybe even one on anxiety to help you get through college and the job search!

→ Throw the I Ching coins and ask about your future.

→ Go to bed an hour earlier and set an intention that while you're sleeping, a new career idea will come to you . . . and then let it go.

PUTTING IT ALL TOGETHER

So how does this all experimental wandering come together? Obviously, it's going to be different for each of you, but here's one story of how a student found a job by conducting experimental wanderings at his desk and beyond:

Brandon had been planning to go to law school since his junior year of high school. He started working as a residence hall adviser in his sophomore year of college just to help with college expenses. He discovered he enjoyed living with the first-year students and helping them with typical issues they faced, such as homesickness or getting along with their roommates. After reading about an opportunity posted on a campus kiosk, he found a summer job in Baltimore, a city he had always wanted to see, working as a resident adviser for high school students attending special summer programs at a college. He learned that he truly enjoyed this type of work and now was less enthusiastic about going straight to law school. His senior year he was asked to sit on a freshman orientation panel along with the dean of admissions to talk about college life. Even though he was applying to law schools, Brandon began thinking that he might want to work in a college or university setting for a few years first. He talked to the staff in the residence life program at his college about working in a college setting. Everyone gave him lots of information and advice about the field and recommended he start his job search in February.

To carry out his job search, he defined what he wanted: a position in a college or university setting working directly with students. He then identified the likely offices that might hire him: residence life, housing, financial aid, development, and admissions. If he was unsuccessful in his initial search, he figured he would expand his search to boarding schools and junior colleges. He isolated the areas in which he most wanted to work: New York, Pennsylvania, and New Jersey, knowing he could expand this as well if he needed to. To his delight, he learned that just those three states had over six hundred colleges and universities. He then created an online folder called College Jobs and bookmarked the human resources Web sites for each college in which he was particularly interested. He also created his résumé and a cover letter that he modified as needed. Every week he searched the sites and applied for positions for which he was qualified. Ultimately he uploaded twenty-two résumés and cover letters for positions at a variety of colleges.

Within a few weeks he began to get calls and e-mails from colleges, and started completing phone interviews. His research and knowledge of the field paid off, and he was then invited to several campuses until, ironically, the dean of admissions with whom he had served on the panel called to ask him if would be interested in applying for a job in the admissions office. And that's where he's working.

You could say Brandon got his job because of the butterfly effect—a random job he took to pay the bills and a coincidental appearance with a college administrator. But it was Brandon's work and his knowledge of the field that ultimately sealed the deal. The butterfly just got him started. And now he knows how to do the search if he wants to again in the future. He's now planning to start taking classes to get his master's degree in higher education with a specialty in counseling so he can go even further in the higher education field. Key steps for Brandon included:

1. Applying to law school while seeking a Plan B: a residential life position

2. Targeting his résumé to the settings for which he was applying

3. Creating a basic cover letter that he modified based on the position and school

4. Speaking with people already doing the job he wanted so he could be better informed

5. Targeting a large but manageable range of potential employers

6. Creating a system for checking on job openings that fit the field

7. Knowing the right season for applying for the job

8. Being flexible yet focused in his search—wanting a college setting but willing to work in a variety of areas

WISDOM BUILDERS

I. EXPAND THE SCOPE OF YOUR EXPERIMENTAL WANDERINGS

You may have settled on a particular field of employment, but particularly in tight job markets or situations where you face a lot of competition, it's a good idea to think of ways to expand your options. You can expand geographically by changing the location of your search, and/or you can expand within the career field by considering related job titles or occupations that are in the same general area as your prime target.

The simplest way to expand geographically is to start where you are and connect with family or friends who might know about opportunities in your field. Pay attention to what's going on right at your college or university if you're still a student. Is there an opportunity to learn the skills you need through working in an administrative office or department on campus? No jobs? Ask if you can volunteer a few hours a week or offer to work on a special project using your skills. If you're in school, branch out to see what's happening in the town or city where your school is located. By changing the location of your search, you might change the nature of the work. For instance, if you're in a social work field and living in a small town, you may find you'll provide more direct client service. If you're in a big city, you may work for a large agency where you won't have much client contact but will provide other services that ultimately benefit the client. If you're working at the national headquarters of a nonprofit organization, you might even be involved in lobbying for legislation or setting policies.

Alyssa is considering a career working with homeless individuals in some capacity. She has already volunteered at a local shelter and is looking to expand her job possibilities. She brainstormed about the different opportunities she might have depending on her geographic focus, and developed the chart on pages 188–89. She's filled in the opportunities for her vision; there are two blank rows for you to write in your vision and how it might grow if you choose a different level of involvement. Don't worry if you don't know all the answers to the questions: that's what research is for.

	HOMELESSNESS		
At college or university	Fund-raising; take sociology and economics classes.		
Hometown or school location	Volunteer or work at local shelters and services. Check with churches to see what programs they operate.		
County	Speak to the City Council about the needs of the homeless; find out what county services are provided—any job openings?		
Nearest large city	What services are available in the nearest large city? Larger service organizations might have more opportunities.		
State	What is going on at the state government level? What state agencies work with homelessness?		

	HOMELESSNESS		
Region	Are there any agencies that provide services across several states or in specific regions like the Northeast or Southwest?		
Country	What national organizations deal with issues related to homelessness? Where are they located? Are they specialized to areas like housing or alcohol or drug abuse?		
International	What relief organizations are helping with housing and homelessness around the world? What types of positions do they offer?		

Not only is Alyssa expanding her geographic opportunities, she's also noticing that the opportunities start to vary in scope. When she volunteered at the local agency, she dealt with all the issues of her clients. But if she goes with a state agency, she might find she can specialize in one area. She will want to consider her specific skills and strengths and seek a variety of positions within those larger agencies.

A second way to expand your career possibilities is to consider a variety of jobs within a particular field or to consider related fields. On the work sheet on the next page or in your notebook, try listing up to three industries or fields you might be interested in. Then list several places where you could work within those fields. Finally, indicate possible job titles or functions you would be interested in within those industries. The first one is filled out as an example. If you're having trouble identifying the locations or titles, keep researching!

EXPANDING YOUR CAREER POSSIBILITIES WORK SHEET

FIELD: Writing

POSSIBLE EMPLOYERS:

a. Publishing firms

b. Computer or high-tech companies

c. Professional trade organizations (newsletters and journals)

d. College alumni, admissions, and development offices

POSSIBLE JOB TITLES: Freelance writer, Web writer, technical writer, assistant editor, science writer, training and development specialist, editor, copywriter, proofreader, grant writer

Now you try it:

FIELD: _____

POSSIBLE EMPLOYERS:

a. _____

b. _____

c. _____

d. _____

POSSIBLE JOB TITLES: _____

_____

FIELD: _____

POSSIBLE EMPLOYERS:

a. _____

b. _____

c. _____

d. _____

POSSIBLE JOB TITLES: _____

_____

> FIELD: _____

> POSSIBLE EMPLOYERS:
> a. _____
> b. _____
> c. _____
> d. _____

> POSSIBLE JOB TITLES: _____
> _____

2. ANALYZE THE CULTURE OF THE WORKPLACE

Company cultures are like country cultures. Never try to change one. Try, instead, to work with what you've got.

—PETER DRUCKER

You're about to enter a foreign land. Most of the people are older than you, and they gather around a water cooler laughing and joking. The only person close to your age is an intern. They dress more formally than you. They're pleasant to one another, but your attempts at making light conversation aren't working. They seem to use certain words or acronyms over and over and you don't know what they mean. You were given a name tag on your first day, but you forgot to wear it and now you realize you stand out. Despite some joking or friendly banter, there's a serious atmosphere to the setting. Sometimes you even sense fear, but you're not sure why. The rules seem odd and not all of them are written. Welcome to the workplace.

A culture is defined as a set of shared meanings, values, and assumptions, and in general, it is the responsibility of the individual to adapt to the culture. Just because some rules are unwritten doesn't mean you don't have to know them. It's important for you to quickly size up the culture so you can determine whether you are a good fit or not, and good research can help you uncover the information you need.

Cross-cultural understanding is imperative in today's workplace. An HR executive at a California-based Marriott Hotel once stated that their employees speak over one hundred foreign languages, including the special dialects within each language category. Can you image the challenges of communicating with that workforce and how important it is to be aware of your culture and what you bring to the workplace?

It's not unusual for students to experience a certain culture shock at their first professional job. You might be used to sleeping in, having long breaks over the holidays and in the summer, being surrounded by people your own age and being immersed in other common characteristics of college life. The first step in analyzing a culture is understanding your own. Take a few minutes to describe your culture. Where are you from and what implications does that have for where you want to live? Noticing your own cultural perspective will make you more cognizant of what you consider "normal." Can you think of a time when you felt you didn't fit in somewhere? Why? Did cultural differences have anything to do with your feelings?

Some books and Web sites (such as the Vault guides) interview employees to give you the inside scoop on an organization. You definitely want to get past any bias you might have from watching *The Office* or reading *Dilbert* cartoons. You can also gain a perspective through reading the organization's Web site and corporate or annual reports to see what they say about themselves.

- How do they present themselves in writing?
- Are their publications creative, conservative, visionary, or traditional?
- Do they state their organizational values or mission?
- Is the leader clearly identified and does she or he dominate the publications?

While all of that information is helpful, the best way to ascertain the culture is when you visit the organization for an interview and see for yourself. People tend to view things through their own perspective, and Web sites that rate organizations (just like the Web sites which rate professors) are often biased with either extremely positive or extremely negative perceptions. Take a look at the environment where you're considering working. You won't be able to assess everything on a single visit, but you might be able to assess culture through some visual cues:

- Buildings
  - Is it in a freestanding building or a suite within a larger building?
  - What is the architectural style? Modern, stylish, conservative, nondescript?
  - Location of the office: rural, urban, suburban?
  - How safe is the location?
- Ambience of office
  - How do they greet strangers?
  - Is the reception area formal, informal, elegant?
  - What kind of furniture/decor? How attractive is the environment?
  - Is the general noise level quiet or loud? Is music piped in? Or do a lot of workers have headphones on?
  - How neat are the offices?
  - Does there appear to be a policy for the appearance of the offices?
  - Do people wear name tags?
- What are the characteristics of the workers you can observe?
  - What is their age range?
  - Are they friendly, neutral, or tense?
  - How diverse is the workforce? Will you be one among many, or will you stand out for some reason?
  - How much are they interacting?
  - How do they dress? Is there a dress code? Do they wear uniforms?
  - Are most workers in cubicles or offices?

FINAL QUESTIONS

What experimental wanderings are you going to try in the next twenty-four hours? What is your goal in doing this?

_____

_____

_____

Is there a secret experimental wandering you would love to do, but are concerned that you might not do well in it? If you knew you couldn't fail, what would you do?

_____

_____

_____

CHAPTER 8

MY JOB AS A KRACKEL BAR

CREATING IRRESISTIBLE RÉSUMÉS THAT WILL GET YOU THE INTERVIEW

Ken, Barry was looking at your résumé and he agreed with me that eating with chopsticks is not really a special skill.

—*BEE MOVIE* (2007)

A popular theory holds that there are four stages to learning:

1. Unconscious incompetence (where you don't know what you don't know)

2. Conscious incompetence (you now know what you don't know and are completely overwhelmed)

3. Conscious competence (you know it but you have to concentrate to do it)

4. Unconscious competence (you know it so well you can do it without thinking)

You probably went through these stages when you first learned to drive a car: remember how easy it looked when you watched your parents drive? And then you got behind the wheel for the first time, and suddenly it seemed as if you had a million things to remember at once? You started driving, but you had to focus intensely on everything. After a while, though, you could drive without thinking about it all, and even talk on a cell phone at the same time.

So why do I bring this up in a chapter about résumés? Because writing a good résumé is one of the hardest tasks you'll undertake in the job search process, and despite the thousands of books and Web sites dedicated to résumé writing, most college students do not produce a good résumé, at least not the first time out. Most employers can eliminate over 75 percent of their candidates by a brief glance at their résumés. And that's a tragedy because a well-written résumé can beautifully encapsulate your experiences and serve as the bridge between you and the interview.

Résumés are a form of creative writing and have their own special rules and methods of construction that are different from virtually any other form of writing. So when it comes to résumés you're probably in that first stage of learning, unconscious incompetence. You are used to writing five-page papers and maybe even used to starting a paper the night before it's due, so you see this rather bland, innocent-looking one-page document and figure you can do it in an hour or so.

You've probably even seen those books that claim you can "write your résumé in an hour" or "overnight." So you set aside an hour and sit down to write your résumé. Then you glance at your watch and forty-five minutes have flown by and you're still trying to structure the education section. Poof—you've moved into stage two: conscious incompetence.

You suddenly realize that there are all these strange rules about formatting and language structure, and you're not sure what information to include, much less how to organize it. If you have acquired a lot of experience, how do you cut it back to one page (that is the rule, isn't it)? Or if you don't have much experience, how do you make a whole page out of it? Use a size 28 font and list everything from tenth grade on? After an hour of this, like most people in the conscious incompetence stage, you walk away. Frustrated. Because it's one thing to have the motivation of a fifteen-year-old who wants to drive—that will pull you through any tough stage of conscious incompetence— but you probably don't have the same sense of urgency about writing a résumé, at least not today. Maybe tomorrow. And then you procrastinate until you discover a great job opportunity, it's 11:00 p.m., and the deadline to upload your résumé is midnight.

It doesn't help that so much of the résumé advice out there is conflicting and creates confusion or, dare I say, résumé chaos? For every employer who says "Job objectives are unnecessary" you'll find another who says "I won't read a résumé that doesn't have a job objective." For every résumé guide that says "The résumé must be one page only" another says "Two-page résumés are fine." I've always told my students to spell everything correctly because spelling errors stop the job search. But I've heard employers say, "Oh, I overlook the occasional spelling error on a résumé if the candidate is really qualified." See what I mean? Chaos. Well, once again, you can relax. Here's what you need to remember: résumés are evaluated based on opinions, not hard and fast rules. So ultimately every piece of résumé advice comes down to one person's opinion. Let's just say that some opinions are more consistent and helpful than others. In this chapter, you're going to get an opinion based on years of experience and reviewing thousands of résumés: good, bad, and ugly. The opinions expressed will fall well within the bell curve of traditional advice and are endorsed by a majority of employers. If you follow the guidelines presented here, you will produce a résumé that will serve you well in the job search process and place you ahead of a majority of other applicants.

Before we move into the details of résumé writing, here's one recommendation: don't try to do it all alone. You will need more than this book to write a great résumé. You should take your résumé to your career center or to someone who is familiar with current résumé styles for suggestions and feedback. Use this book and others to help write your draft, but *always* find other people to assist you. This chapter will give you the key information you need to write your résumé, but it can't cover résumé writing with the thoroughness of a complete book on the subject. The goal is to make sure you articulate your wanderings in the best possible way, so this chapter will give you key guidelines to make your résumé stand out. Soliciting other opinions is always helpful. Just remember that ultimately it's your résumé, so when you get conflicting information, go with what you think is right.

With that in mind, though, you still need to write your résumé yourself. Do not pay a service to write it for you and do not copy a résumé verbatim from a book or Web site. You might think you're saving time and energy by paying someone else to write your résumé, but the work you'll do answering their questionnaires and filling in your experiences will take almost as long as writing it yourself, and the résumé won't really be yours. And if you copy some great lines from the sample résumé on your career center's Web site, you can bet twenty other students did as well, and the employer will catch the similarities in a minute. Even résumés that have been created by special computer résumé-writing programs need editing, if only because a lot of the programs use the same formatting and recommend boilerplate phrases that students like and use, resulting in a formulaic résumé. Employers can spot a formulaic résumé a mile away. In fact, boilerplate formatted résumés that resemble every other résumé get rejected just as quickly as résumés with obvious errors. So use one of those computer programs if you'd like to start your résumé, but edit and adapt your résumé from there on, incorporating your unique background and taking advantage of all the help available.

You now know that it's going to take more time than you think, so plan for that and give yourself time to rewrite and rework it. Your final résumé will be worth every extra second you put into it. In tight job markets, employers are looking for easy reasons to reject candidates and the résumé is one of the quickest and easiest ways to do that. While the résumé won't get you the job, it will get you the interview that will get you the job, so your goal is to create a document that is interesting and compelling enough to convince an employer you're worth meeting. If you've already written a résumé, get it out and review it as you go through this chapter. And if you haven't, well, it's time to start with that blank piece of paper again. Although this time I recommend you use a blank word processing screen instead of paper.

Before you get started, think back to Chapter 3 and get ready to apply many of the mindsets you developed as you work on the résumé, including analytic, strategic, creative systems, and perhaps most important, the positive mindset and right mind. It's easy to get bogged down in the résumé-writing process, so keep your focus positive and remember how much you have to offer an employer. You may be tempted to read some of the rules and decide that you're not going to follow them simply because you don't want to. Try not to do that. You break the rules and guidelines at your own risk. In some very specific and special situations (such as in highly creative fields) the rules can be broken without consequence, but in general it's better to follow them. So when you read that your résumé should be one page, don't think "I'm going to write a three-page résumé to impress employers with how much I've done." Instead, think "I'm going to impress employers by conveying the most relevant information on one page." When you start to think "I'm going to print my résumé on a brightly colored piece of paper so it will stand out," think instead "I'm going to print my résumé on standard résumé paper—the content of my résumé will make it stand out."

While you're digging up old résumés and your mindset list, get out your Wandering Map as well. Review it for any forgotten strengths or experiences you want to work into your résumé. Is it time to update it and add more experiences? Have you discovered some new themes or threads, or done any experimental wanderings since you wrote your map? Be sure to add the new information to your map and note where it connects with other themes and experiences in your life.

The last section of this chapter breaks down résumé writing into five distinct sections you can complete all at once or one at a time, depending on your schedule. You will be creating a basic résumé that will serve as your template, which you can adjust as needed to fit specific opportunities that come along. First, however, you're going to learn three secrets that will keep your résumé at the top of the stack.

THREE SECRETS ABOUT AN IRRESISTIBLE RÉSUMÉ

OK, so I'm exaggerating a little. These aren't necessarily secrets; you'll read similar advice elsewhere. But they are far and away the three key aspects of résumé writing most ignored by college students and new résumé writers, so they might as well be secrets. Consider these vital elements as mantras to be repeated over and over while you write, critique, and edit your résumé:

1. To whom am I writing and why will they care?

2. Can I picture what I've written and can my claims be substantiated?

3. Is every word spelled correctly and is my résumé professional and attractive?

Let's look at each of these vital elements in detail.

VITAL ELEMENT 1: TO WHOM AM I WRITING AND WHY WILL THEY CARE?

> Well, I suspect there's more to come from Dave Scott. But, in the meantime, "Brought back original crust from the moon" should weigh pretty impressively on your résumé, you know?
> —**DR. LEE SILVER,** FROM *THE EARTH TO THE MOON*
> (1998 MINISERIES)

A classic adage in writing is to know your audience and write to them. If you're writing a book on dogs, you need to know if your primary audience will be veterinarians or first graders. You wouldn't write to a professor in the same style and language as you would to your best friend, and because a résumé is intended for a potential employer or graduate school admissions panel, you need to put yourself in their mindset and focus on what they are seeking. As you write each section of your résumé, ask yourself "Why am I telling my audience this?" and "What is my reader most interested in?" Constantly consider how you can add value to an employer: "What should this employer know about me?"

Asking these questions will help keep your résumé relevant, giving you a major advantage over other job seekers. The job to which you're applying becomes your thesis statement, so to speak, and your résumé should support that central point. One way to do this is by using language common to the field (keywords). For example, if you are applying for a human resources job and you have tutored students, you might want to say "trained" students, because the word *training* is commonly used in human resources. Your keywords should be relevant to the field, particularly if your résumé is likely to be scanned. Using keywords is one of the best ways to demonstrate how your experience and education match the requirements of the position. You can find keywords in books about the field you're interested in. The text for an introduction to an advertising course, for example, will likely contain all the keywords you need for an advertising job.

Have you ever tried to open one of those annoying plastic packages that are vacuum sealed around an electronic device or a pack of batteries? You have to really want what's inside the package to go to the effort of opening it. Focus on that image when you're writing your résumé. Are you making it easy for employers to find the information they're seeking? Or do they have to read through all sorts of text before they can find what they're looking for? Most recruiters will scan your résumé in less than fifteen seconds, and if they don't see what they want right away, they'll probably quit looking.

Part of knowing your audience is anticipating what they will like or dislike. You don't want to set yourself up to be rejected by presenting your politics, religion, unusual hobbies, or other aspects of your personality if they are not relevant to the employer. Your participation in a particular church's activities would be relevant in an application to a faith-based social service program; your hobby of playing "World of Warcraft" probably would not. On the other hand, if you're applying to work for a gaming company they're going to be much more interested in your knowledge and experience with online gaming than the church you attend. If you're applying to work with a Republican senator, you might want to list your work with the college Democrats as "managed a campus political organization." You can use your interview to explain the details if necessary. In the same vein of relevance, résumés are designed to reflect what you've done since entering college, so after your sophomore year, do not include high school information unless you are applying to work in a high school.

VITAL ELEMENT 2: CAN I PICTURE WHAT I'VE WRITTEN AND CAN MY CLAIMS BE SUBSTANTIATED?

> You know, for someone who's got "Watcher" on his résumé, you might want to cast an eye to the front door every now and again. —SPIKE IN *BUFFY THE VAMPIRE SLAYER* (1997)

To put it bluntly, there are a lot of bad résumé-writing guides out there. Maybe it's because the writers are trying to make their guides unique, but some of their advice is just plain lousy and out-of-date. One of the worst examples of bad advice on many Web sites and in books is the promotion of fluffy language. Fluffy language, for lack of a better term, is sometimes called marketingspeak. It relies on phrases that sound important and meaningful at first glance, but really don't say anything or tell the reader what you have done. Some examples include:

- → Hard worker with great communication skills
- → Team player who regularly upgrades collateral to ensure successful responses
- → Experience with fast-paced environment and multitasking requirements

Your résumé should substantiate your strengths; it should show what problems you solved, what skills you possess, what experiences you have had, and how you were valued in the workplace—but not through buzzwords and trite phrases. Use numbers, percentages, dollar amounts, and other specifics to support your statements, particularly if they are impressive. Don't just say "sold merchandise." Say "increased weekly store sales by 20 percent in first month of employment" (if it's true, of course). Instead of "raised funds for charity," say "raised over $2,000 for the American Cancer Society." Some impressive examples would include managed a $5,000 budget, supervised ten people, advised over fifty students. On the other hand, these figures are not as significant: worked eight-hour days, supervised one person, managed a $200 budget. It would be better to say, "supervised staff and managed a budget," and let it go at that.

Working eight hours a day is expected, so leave it off unless you also took classes on those same days, making your typical day longer than twelve hours.

So just what is fluff? When I review résumés, I use two rules to uncover it: (1) can I picture it?, and (2) if I use the opposite words, does it sound dumb?

Here's an example that answers the "can I picture it?" question: Ashley spent a summer working at Hershey Park, a family theme park in Hershey, Pennsylvania, known, of course, for its chocolate. Her title was something like guest services specialist, and she described her experience as "assisted guests and promoted a fun environment for parents and children." I had trouble picturing it. How does one promote "a fun environment"? It sounded like fluff. So I asked her. It turns out she spent the summer dressed in a Krackel bar costume and basically roamed the park, helping children find lost parents, signing autographs (!), giving people directions, and playing little games with the children. It's possible she even saved the life of a guest by using CPR, but her favorite part of the job was watching the children's faces light up when they would see her. "I had no idea anyone would want to run up and hug a candy bar!" she said. So we changed her job title to Krackel bar and rewrote her résumé entry to include:

- ➔ Greeted more than twenty thousand families, including posing for photographs, signing autographs, and playing with the children, ensuring a pleasant visit and encouraging return visits

- ➔ Located lost parents, and solved numerous problems from answering mundane questions to providing CPR and quickly obtaining emergency medical assistance for guests

- ➔ Consistently maintained pleasant demeanor despite heat and fatigue, and received award for highest number of positive comments from guest satisfaction surveys

Now I can picture her job. And so could the employers—she received numerous requests for interviews with the on-campus recruiters because they all wanted to meet the Krackel bar!

The second question I use to determine whether claims can be substantiated is what I call the rule of opposites, that is, does it sound dumb if I use the opposite words? Some career guides recommend that you use phrases designed to impress employers, such as "team player," "hard-worker," or "strong communicator," because that's what employers are seeking. And it's true, employers are seeking those strengths, and in Chapter 10 you'll learn to use those phrases in a much more powerful way. But on a résumé they just sound boastful and empty. After all (and here comes the rule of opposites), who's going to put on their résumé "loner who can't work with others," "lazy worker," and "poor writing and speaking skills." That's how you know you're writing fluff. Fluff shows up a lot in job objectives as well: "seeking a challenging position in a growing organization with potential for promotion." This would be as opposed to "seeking a position where I can do nothing in an organization that's likely to go out of business and fire me."

Rather than tell an employer your strengths, show them. We can assume that Ashley is a patient, hardworking, and naturally friendly person who is a good problem solver because of the way she described her position. She never had to *tell* us; she *showed* us. Verbs and nouns are much more powerful than adjectives.

Use action words to start your phrases and follow with a description that can be pictured. Avoid weak phrases such as "was responsible for," "duties included," "did some work with," and "handled assorted jobs." Those phrases are passive and don't illuminate your skills. Instead of writing "was responsible for managing the front desk," write "managed the front desk, including answering phones, greeting visitors, and assisting staff with a variety of projects." Depending on the space you have available, you could expand that entry to describe the projects if your work was meaningful and of interest to the employer. If all you did was staple reports, it's probably not worth mentioning, even if you're applying for a job that requires stapling reports. Go back to your Wandering Map for more powerful themes and ideas to put on your résumé.

VITAL ELEMENT 3: IS EVERY WORD SPELLED CORRECTLY AND IS THE RÉSUMÉ PROFESSIONAL AND ATTRACTIVE?

> So, under experience, you've listed here on your hat-shaped résumé that you can skin a buck, run a trout line and that all your rowdy friends. . . ." —*SQUIDBILLIES* (2005)

In his excellent book *Does Your Marketing Sell?* British writer Ian Moore says, "Think fast—your audience is whizzing by." In general, your résumé will only receive a few seconds glance, so the information needs to be easily accessible and readable and spelled correctly. Keep your entries short and to the point. Lead with verbs and nouns and don't use the word *I*. Think of it as translating your experiences and education into sound bites for the six o'clock news. Write what is most important. If you've buried your most important experience somewhere in the middle, it will likely be missed. Keep in mind that image of the plastic packaging that's hard to break through. Make sure the important information pops off your résumé. Here are five tips to ensure your résumé complies with Vital Element 3:

→ **Format and print the résumé in an attractive, consistent, and professional manner.** Your creativity should show in your phrasing and writing, not through a funky-colored résumé or a strange font. Creativity expert Edward DeBono describes the shift beyond creativity as crossing over the line from creativity to "crazytivity." As in the quote from *Squidbillies* above, if you have a hat-shaped résumé, you've probably crossed that line. Printing your résumé on green paper with images of money on it probably won't thrill a bank. But always consider the job you're seeking. One student who applied for a job as the Oscar Mayer Wienermobile driver put her mustard-colored résumé inside a pickle relish jar. It worked. That was a unique marketing trick and she was applying for a unique marketing job. Remember Vital Element 1: Know your audience.

→ **In general, keep your résumé to one page, particularly if you're going into business.** If you have a lot of experience and *it is all relevant*, you can have a two-page résumé. But make sure the most important information is on the first page. Employers disagree on this topic and many are amenable to two-page résumés from new graduates (particularly in the nonprofit and education fields), but tread carefully: one page is usually best for a recent graduate entering the business world.

↪ **Always proofread and proofread again.** Spell-checker is wonderful but it doesn't catch everything: homonyms can slip by, as can a faulty word. I've seen résumés where students "mange" projects as opposed to manage them, work with "perspective" members rather than prospective members, or who claim to "writ" well, rather than write well. One poor student applied for a job in "pubic service," and neither she nor the spell-checker noticed the missing *l* until a savvy roommate laughed herself silly and wished her luck finding that job. Correct spelling can't be stressed enough. Employers are looking for reasons to eliminate résumés from the stack and spelling is an easy way to do this.

↪ **Use bullet points for emphasis,** but if you start to have more than five bullet points in one entry they will lose their emphasis. You may need to write a few short phrases and then use bullet points to highlight key accomplishments. As you write your phrases, you may be tempted to abbreviate common words like *assistant* to *ass't.* Don't abbreviate unless the abbreviations are well known. You can use the standard two-letter abbreviations for states, for example, or for well-known companies like IBM or ESPN, but don't use abbreviations for words like administrative assistant.

↪ **Use reverse chronological order** (your most recent experience comes first), and if you start by naming the employer, the location, and then your title, you should use that order in every entry.

STEP-BY-STEP GUIDE TO WRITING YOUR RÉSUMÉ

This guide will help you write a general résumé that will serve as your template for the targeted résumé you will develop as you move along in your search. *The general résumé you create may be several pages long and will contain virtually everything you've done since high school because you won't actually be sending it to anyone.* Instead, you will draw from it to create your targeted résumé by selecting the most relevant information that will appeal to a specific employer or career field. If you don't have a specific field or employer in mind, you can use your general résumé to create a one-page condensed all-purpose résumé that will highlight your best experiences and accomplishments. As you move through the steps, remember three things: it will take longer to write than you think (sorry), conscious incompetence will creep in and you'll want to quit, but most important, *writing your résumé can be one of the biggest self-esteem and confidence-building activities you can do.* So make this experience as enjoyable as possible: reward yourself, work on it in a fun setting, break the task into small pieces by taking it a step at a time, seek help from your career center or whatever works best for you. Here we go . . .

STEP 1: COLLECT THE INFORMATION YOU NEED

Start by gathering the information you collected about yourself and your plans in Chapters 6 and 7. If you've already written a résumé, print it out. As previously stated, this chapter won't give you everything you might need, so check out résumé Web sites, particularly the information posted on your career center's Web site. When you see a résumé you like, print it out and use it as a model. Just remember: do not copy the wording verbatim. You must write the entries yourself, because most of your fellow students are copying them as well, and your résumé will read like everyone else's. Big mistake. Employers don't like lazy résumé writers and they can spot them a mile away.

STEP 2: WRITE OUT YOUR EXPERIENCES

Take out your notebook or tablet or open a file on a word processor and at the top of each page write one experience or activity you plan to include in your résumé. Use as many pages as you have experiences or activities. If you had a title or several titles, write them down. Take a few minutes to jot down everything you can recall about that position no matter how silly. Think about what made you unique or stand out;

think about promotions, the skills or knowledge you learned, the mindsets you used, commendations from supervisors, what you did during a typical day, and so on. Was there a special event or activity that occurred while you were there? What problems did you solve? What responsibilities did you have? What types of people did you work with? Your list doesn't have to be in any particular order and you don't have to write it the way it will ultimately appear on your résumé. Just do a quick-writing exercise and complete it as quickly as possible.

As we consider résumé entries, we're going to follow Justin, a senior international studies major at Longstreet College in Washington, D.C. Here's an example of one of his pages describing his work as an administrative assistant and legal assistant for a law firm one summer:

ORGANIZATION: SRLQ Law Firm, Washington, D.C.

TITLE: Administrative Assistant/Legal Assistant

DATES: Summer 2008

BASIC DESCRIPTION OF WORKPLACE: SRLQ law firm consists of five attorneys practicing mostly corporate law, including occasional trial work.

WHAT I DID:

- Kept the office running smoothly so that the attorneys could do their work
- Opened the office at 9:00 in the morning and closed it at 5:00
- Answered phones—clients, other lawyers, judges, professionals from banks, expert witnesses
- Welcomed visitors politely and offered coffee, etc.
- Maintained visitor and call log for legal records and billing purposes
- Created and mailed bills—organized better billing system using Excel
- Had to cope with changing needs, last-minute deadlines, emergencies, etc., on a regular basis: flexible mindset
- Dressed professionally every day—first impression for law firm
- Learned to write basic legal documents
- Prioritized workload because all attorneys wanted their stuff first. Used strategic mindset and team mindset.
- Delivered documents to clients or to courthouse—needed to be punctual— five minutes too late and a deadline might be missed—pressure
- Assisted one attorney with a sales presentation at a bank by creating a PowerPoint presentation
- Trained replacement when I left
- Dealt regularly with sensitive and confidential information
- Did a lot of stuff at once because some days I was the only assistant for all the attorneys—had to manage time and multitask. Flexible mindset
- Converted documents to PDF format and e-mailed them
- Learned legal guidelines for maintaining and/or shredding files
- Used my Spanish skills to assist with case involving a Mexican restaurant

---

Depending on the job he's applying for, Justin has a basic list of his experiences to pick and choose from. For instance, if he were to apply for a job requiring a high level of security or integrity (such as the CIA or FBI), he might select the entries that focus on his work with confidential information and dealing with pressure and deadlines. If he's applying for a management position, he might focus on the independent projects he worked on, training his replacement, and his Excel and multitasking skills.

Now it's your turn. Go ahead and fill out as many sheets as you can with your experiences. Doing these sheets now will save you tons of time when you're writing your targeted résumés. Don't forget to do a sheet for all your school activities or groups, volunteer experiences, or even classes that required work above and beyond traditional note taking and test taking. Some sheets may only have two or three entries, and that's OK. The point is to get as much down on the paper now so you don't forget it later when you're quickly writing your targeted résumé to meet a deadline. Write quickly, write casually, and don't censor yourself.

STEP 3: WRITE THE HEADING SECTION OF YOUR RÉSUMÉ

This step is rather simple, although mistakes can be made. You should include your name, address (current and/or home address), a phone number where you can be reached, and your e-mail address. You can bold your name, but don't make it more than one font size larger than the text in your résumé (that is, if your résumé is in Times New Roman 12, your name shouldn't be larger than 14). Do not use creative fonts for your name; stick with the same or a similar font you use in your résumé. Some preformatted résumés use different styles for the heading with special fonts, underlining, and so on. As long as it looks professional, you can use the style you prefer.

Here's one way Justin could write his heading:

Justin Matthews
123 Maple Street
Smalltown, MD 55555
e-mail: jmmd
Cell phone: 301-555-5555

Remember the discussion about being sensitive to new cultures in Chapter 7? Your phone and e-mail habits can label you as stuck in the student culture if you're not careful. Be sure your e-mail address is professional sounding. Create a new e-mail account for your job search and keep "lilsuzieq@" or "buysthebeer@" for your friends. If you give employers your phone number, they might actually call you, so make sure you answer your phone professionally and create a professional voice mail. Turn your phone off (or scrupulously read the caller ID before answering) at parties or other events where you might not present your best self.

STEP 4: WRITE THE JOB OBJECTIVE AND/OR STRENGTHS SECTION

Employers are mixed in their reactions to this aspect—some insist on a job objective; others don't care. But they all agree that a bad job objective (fluffy, poorly written, or not appropriate for their organization) will greatly hurt your chances, so tread lightly here. Remember you will likely be creating several résumés, so you can use a different job objective on each one.

Do you have a specific job or career field in mind and are you sending it to organizations that hire for that position? Then go ahead and state it:

> **⇢** Technical writer

> **⇢** Research analyst

> **⇢** Market researcher

If you have some ideas, but aren't completely sure, try considering the following:

> **⇢** What activities would you like to perform (writing, editing, teaching, managing, and so on)?

> **⇢** In what setting would you like to work (outdoors, education, insurance, banking, nonprofit, and so on)?

> **⇢** What kinds of people, data, or things (children, the elderly,

money, stocks, computers, statistics, laboratory equipment, electronic equipment, and so on) interest you?

↦ How does the position mesh with future career plans?

Pull it all together, as in

↦ Management training position in retailing leading to a career as a buyer

↦ Secondary-level history teacher and soccer coach in private-school setting

↦ Marketing or grant-writing position for nonprofit organization

Instead of a job objective, you might find it more effective to have a strengths section. A strengths section can help pull together a varied background and focus the employer's attention on your most important accomplishments. This section should list your top three or four strengths in a bulleted format. Remember to tailor your strengths to fit what the employer is seeking and show concrete accomplishments, not fluffy boasting. Here is an example:

↦ Extensive experience with PC and Mac operating systems; software knowledge includes Microsoft XP, SPSSX statistical software, and Adobe Creative Suite

↦ Bilingual Spanish/English

↦ More than three years' experience in customer service occupations

Notice the lack of fluff—no "hard-worker who will bring a team spirit to your workplace." The skills should be tangible and relevant to the employer.

Justin is considering three Possible Lives after graduation: working in a law firm for a few years and then going to law school; working in a bank; starting in a customer service capacity; and/or working in the sports/recreation field—he's not sure exactly where or how. Because the three industries he's selected are different, Justin will need to create three résumés, targeting each to the specific industry. As you read through the next stages of creating the résumé, note how the different sections of Justin's résumé change depending on his focus.

STEP 5: WRITE THE EDUCATION SECTION

Most résumés of college students and recent graduates should list the education section before the experience section, because that is the primary feature they are selling to an employer. In addition to listing your school, graduation date, and major(s), you can add other information as appropriate. Consider if any of the following education-related elements are relevant to your future employment. You can expand or contract the information based again on relevance to the employer.

- Special courses beyond your major

- Skills, knowledge, or training you acquired in classes

- Projects you worked on

- Presentations you gave

- Research you conducted: What type of research? What instruments or methods did you use? Was it published? Did you assist a professor with research that will be published?

- Papers you wrote

- Honors you received

- Study-abroad experiences

Justin studied abroad in Mexico. He thinks his experiences aren't particularly relevant to the recreation/sports field, so he's going to keep his entry short, as in:

Study abroad, Guadalajara, Mexico (August 2007–June 2008). Immersion program.

On the other hand, for the banking and legal positions, his knowledge of Spanish and his ability to work in a different cultural environment might be more relevant, so he will expand his entry as follows:

Study abroad, Guadalajara, Mexico (August 2007–June 2008). Immersion program. Intensive study of Mexican culture, history, language, and international politics. Resided with Mexican family. Courses taught entirely in Spanish. Taught English to children of Mexican family.

If you have completed an internship, you can list that in the experience section. If you have not started the internship yet, but plan to do one soon and would like to include it in your résumé because it is relevant, you can put it in the education section and call it "anticipated internship," indicating the anticipated dates when you will complete it and what your duties will be.

STEP 6: WRITE THE EXPERIENCE SECTION(S)

The experience section is usually the most time-consuming part of the résumé, but it won't be for you because you have already listed the important aspects of your experiences back in Step 2. Start creating your experience section by reviewing those lists you created. Wherever possible, focus on the *outcome* of your actions, not just what you did.

As you look over your experiences, you need to make a key decision—in general, which is more appealing, your job titles or the places where you've acquired your experience? If you have job titles like manager, vice president, legal assistant, and so forth, then you will probably want to lead with your titles. On the other hand, if your titles are clerk, intern, or waitress, you will probably want to lead with the names of the organizations.

Now that you've made that decision you can start listing in reverse chronological order each of the experiences you described on your pages. For the moment, you only need to include the names of the organizations and their locations, your title, and the dates you worked for them.

Justin has a total of six significant experiences between his summer jobs, internship, and college activities. As he looked over the list, he determined that the places he worked were more impressive than the titles he held, so he decided to list his experiences with the organization first. This listing (with all entries described, of course) would be fine for a generic résumé with no particular focus.

Longstreet College Sports Office, Washington, DC	(Fall 2009–present)
Office Assistant	
Longstreet College Campus Activities Board, Washington, DC	(2007–present)
President	(2009–present)
Treasurer	(2008–9)
Member	(2007)
SRLQ Law Firm, Washington, DC	(Summer 2009)
Legal/Office Assistant	
The Woodlands Inn, Barclay, MD	(Summer 2008)
Lifeguard	
Commissioner Bill Smith's Office, Annapolis, MD	(Summer 2008)
Coordinator/Intern	
Underwater Canoes, Cambridge, MD	(Summer 2007)
Customer Service Representative	

As you look at your list, are there any patterns to your experiences that would interest the employer? For instance, are you seeking a nonprofit job and have several jobs or experiences where you worked for particular causes or with a particular population? Perhaps you are seeking a position that requires creativity, and several of your experiences had elements of creativity to them. If you have two or more experiences that can be combined in a manner relevant to an employer, consider doing that and labeling them concretely. Cut and paste your list to sort it according to the categories. Now, instead of a generic experience section that would simply list all your experiences in reverse chronological order, you might choose to have a Nonprofit/Community Service section if that applies to the position you're seeking. Or a Creative/Communications section, and so on.

By dividing your experiences into these specially labeled categories, you are making them pop from the page so the recruiter will see them. Some students use Relevant Experience as their lead experience category, but it begs the obvious question: relevant to what or to whom? It's better to identify why you're placing certain experiences above others with a term that specifically describes it. You can then create a second experience section to include the other experiences that didn't fit under your initial category. If these experiences fit a category as well, use that word. If not, you can call it Additional Experience.

Here's Justin's first attempt at organizing his law résumé:

LAW/OFFICE MANAGEMENT EXPERIENCE	
Longstreet College Sports Office, Washington, DC	(Fall 2009–present)
Office Assistant	
SRLQ Law Firm, Washington, DC	(Summer 2009)
Legal/Office Assistant	
Commissioner Bill Smith's Office, Baltimore, MD	(Summer 2008)
Coordinator/Intern	
Underwater Canoes, Cambridge, MD	(Summer 2007)
Customer Service Representative	
LEADERSHIP EXPERIENCE	
Longstreet College Campus Activities Board, Washington, DC.	(2007–present)
President	(2009–present)
Treasurer	(2008–9)
Member	(2007)
The Woodlands Inn, Barclay, MD	(Summer 2008)
Lifeguard	

For his résumé for sports/recreation employers, Justin might lead with Sports/Recreation Experience and include his sports office, lifeguard, and canoe sales experience, and then list his other work under Additional Experiences. For his banking résumé, Justin might lead with Customer Service/Office Experience and include his law firm, commissioner's office, canoe shop, and lifeguard experiences. In each case, he will likely change the bulleted point phrases under each job listing to indicate the most relevant parts of the experience.

Are there experiences you listed on your pages that don't fit, or don't seem as relevant? Consider leaving them off. You don't have to list every job and every experience you've ever had on a résumé.

Now that you have decided which experiences fit best in the

categories you've selected, look over the list of duties you compiled for each experience. Which aspects of your experiences best fit this field? Which skills most apply to your potential work setting? Can you phrase them to fit the language of the field to which you're applying? Rank them from most significant to least significant, based on your job objective. Use action verbs followed by specific explanations of what you did. Remember to show, not tell. In general, you should leave out the insignificant or less important tasks.

Justin is going to include his law firm experience in all three of his résumés. For the law firm job, he plans to select his most valuable and responsible roles to highlight perhaps as follows:

- Researched cases, and created and filed documents for five attorneys
- Designed efficient billing system resulting in 20 percent greater collection of fees
- Organized office tasks to ensure all deadlines met and files properly maintained

For the customer service banking job, Justin might list the following entries under the law firm position:

- Provided daily customer service to clients, consultants, vendors, and staff
- Maintained financial records, created invoices, and reconciled accounts
- Interpreted and translated for Spanish-speaking clientele

For the sports/recreation field, Justin might choose to focus on organizational and management skills, such as:

- Explained legal documents and reviewed basic laws to clients
- Created PowerPoint marketing presentation for law firm
- Worked in a fast-paced environment, completing numerous tasks under pressure, never missing a deadline for over fifty cases

As you can see from the example above, one job or experience can lead to a variety of other careers—you just need to think about the way your experience fits the position you're seeking. You'll notice that the word *I* does not appear on Justin's entries. He leads with an action verb and then the subject, trying to make his descriptions as clear as possible and free of fluff. Below is a list of common action words that might help you develop your experience entries.

Action Words

Achieved	Created	Initiated
Adapted	Critiqued	Inspected
Administered	Delegated	Instructed
Advertised	Demonstrated	Interpreted
Analyzed	Designed	Launched
Approved	Developed	Led
Arranged	Directed	Lectured
Attained	Drafted	Maintained
Authorized	Earned	Managed
Balanced	Effected	Marketed
Budgeted	Eliminated	Mastered
Calculated	Enabled	Motivated
Chaired	Established	Negotiated
Collected	Evaluated	Operated
Communicated	Executed	Ordered
Compiled	Expanded	Organized
Completed	Expedited	Originated
Computed	Facilitated	Oversaw
Conceptualized	Generated	Participated
Condensed	Guided	Performed
Conducted	Identified	Pinpointed
Conferred	Illustrated	Planned
Consulted	Implemented	Prepared
Controlled	Improved	Processed
Coordinated	Increased	Produced
Corresponded	Influenced	Programmed

Promoted	Reviewed	Transferred
Proposed	Revitalized	Transformed
Provided	Revived	Translated
Publicized	Scheduled	Treated
Published	Strategized	Tutored
Purchased	Strengthened	Unified
Recommended	Summarized	United
Recorded	Supervised	Upgraded
Recruited	Surveyed	Used
Reduced	Systematized	Utilized
Reinforced	Tabulated	Won
Reorganized	Taught	Worked
Repaired	Trained	Wrote
Represented	Transcribed	

STEP 7: THE INTERESTS SECTION

This is a completely optional section of your résumé and another area where you will get mixed responses from employers. Some say they like it because it shows your personality and can provide a common ground for conversation. Others say they aren't interested. So let two factors help you make your decision: space and relevance. If you have extra space to fill on your résumé, an interests section is one way to do that. (Just make sure you don't have a larger interests section than experience section! It might look as if you aren't interested in working.) Also, if your interests are relevant to your career field, by all means include them. Just be sure they don't conflict with your field (for example, someone whose hobbies are sewing and reading applying for a high-pressure sales job) or are risky activities that might indicate an insurance liability for an employer (motorcycle racing, skydiving, and so on).

That's it! You're done. No need to put "References available on request" at the bottom of your résumé unless, again, you have lots of extra room. Instead, create a separate word file that has "References of *Your Name*" and list your references' names, job titles, addresses, phone numbers, and e-mail addresses. If you want, you can include one line for each reference indicating how you know the person if it's not obvious from title or place of employment.

So before we end this chapter, let's go back and visit Justin one more time. The more Justin considered his after-graduation options, the more he found himself leaning toward a career related to sports and recreation, even though he had no idea what he could do. He started researching careers related to sports and found that many of them required advanced degrees or special athletic skills. But then he found a Web site called CoolWorks.com, which had a job listing for an office assistant at a tourist resort in Alaska. It was a short-term opportunity offered from May until September, and it involved working in the office of a resort that offered hiking, biking, kayaking, and all the other activities he loved. The salary wasn't exciting, but housing was included, and the company was ranked one of the best employers in the nation, so he figured if he did well on that job, they might promote him or help him find other opportunities. Not only that, he'd get to live in Alaska for five months, which sounded like a great adventure.

The title was "office staff" at the resort and required strong organizational skills, basic bookkeeping/accounting skills, and strong knowledge of MS Word, Excel, and Access computer programs. He would be greeting customers and selling various adventure packages and tours. The advertisement also indicated that because the job involved arranging backpacking, rafting, and hiking itineraries for customers, outdoors experience was a plus. So armed with the job description in hand, he began adjusting his résumé to fit the position.

You may recall that Justin had originally planned to keep his study-abroad experience brief on his résumé for the sports/recreation area, but then he realized that while he was studying abroad he had spent his spare time hiking, biking, and doing all the activities listed in the job description. So suddenly a completely different aspect of his study in Mexico became important. He also decided that based on the job description, it would be better to lead with his office management skills rather than his recreational skills, since the advertisement led with office skills.

On the next page, you'll see Justin's final résumé for his possible career at a resort in Alaska. It would have been just as easy for Justin to create a résumé for a law firm or a bank, and he can still do that when he returns from Alaska in October.

Now it's your turn . . .

What could you do in the next twenty-four hours to make your résumé stronger?

_____

_____

_____

_____

If you knew you couldn't fail, where might you target your résumé? Is there a dream place where you'd like to work, or a field you'd like to try even though you might not succeed? It seldom hurts to write a résumé and see what happens.

_____

_____

_____

_____

Justin Matthews

123 Maple Street, Smalltown, MD 55555 ~ (301) 555-5555 ~ e-mail: jmmd@internet.com

OBJECTIVE: Office Assistant Position for Vacation Resort

EDUCATION
Longstreet College, Washington, DC   May 2010
B.A., International Studies   GPA 3.25

Study Abroad, Guadalajara, Mexico   **August 2007–8**
Immersion program. Intensive study of Mexican history and culture. Utilized time off to explore outdoor recreation, including kayaking, backpacking, climbing, and scuba diving. Resided with Mexican family: strengthened Spanish-speaking skills by interpreting and translating for family.

ADMINISTRATIVE/OFFICE MANAGEMENT EXPERIENCE

SRLQ Law Firm   **Washington, DC**
Legal/Office Assistant   Summer 2009
- Provided daily customer service to clients, consultants, vendors, and staff.
- Explained legal services and costs to clients, including service packages and discounts.
- Maintained financial records, created invoices, and reconciled accounts on Excel.
- Coordinated over 40 legal cases simultaneously with 100% accuracy in meeting court deadlines.

Commissioner William Smith's Office   **Baltimore, MD**
Coordinator/Intern   Summer 2008
- Supervised office, handled calls and correspondence (including e-mails) with constituencies.
- Resolved complaints and found solutions for constituents' financial and legal problems.
- Maintained a positive demeanor, increasing constituent satisfaction rating by 20%.
- Designed and updated constituent database regularly to ensure accuracy.

SPORTS/RECREATION EXPERIENCE

Longstreet College Sports Office   **Washington, DC**
Office Assistant   Fall 2009–Present
- Recorded student statistics for official records and answered incoming office calls.
- Called students, supervisors, and officials to remind them of their scheduled working times.
- Supervised sports games and maintained order within the gymnasium and sport fields.

Longstreet College Campus Activities Board   **Washington, DC**
President (2009–Present) Treasurer (2008–9) Member (2007)   2007–Present
- Coordinated and promoted sports-related events, including whitewater rafting and caving activities.
- Negotiated contracts with agencies providing outdoor expedition activities.
- Served as liaison with faculty and administration and organized executive board meetings.

The Woodlands Inn   **Barclay, MD**
Lifeguard   Summer 2008
- Maintained cleanliness and order around pool. Monitored water daily and adjusted chemicals as needed.
- Ensured safety of patrons by maintaining constant vigilance and providing rescue services.

Underwater Canoes   **Cambridge, MD**
Customer Service and Sales Representative   Summer 2007
- Rented and sold canoes, boats, and kayaking equipment and accessories.
- Instructed clients in the operation and safe use of equipment, resulting in no injuries during season.

CHAPTER 9

CHANNELING JANE AUSTEN

WRITING THAT WILL GET YOU HIRED

> You don't write because you want to say something,
> you write because you have something to say.
> —**F. SCOTT FITZGERALD,** *THE CRACK-UP*

Ernest Hemingway wrote a short story using just 6 words. Actress/writer Portia Nelson wrote her autobiography in less than 150 words. Think you can write a good cover letter in four paragraphs?

During your job search you will encounter several opportunities to write. Everything you send out during this process has the power to cast you in a positive or negative light. You will be evaluated on many things, and well-written correspondence can be a decisive factor in your employment. It is your chance to make a good impression, demonstrate your writing skills, and convey your enthusiasm for the position or company. If you fail to represent yourself well in writing (even when it's "just an e-mail"), you have given the employer a reason to choose someone else. Because cover letters, just like résumés, are so important to the job search, you will see hundreds of books and Web sites on the subject. And once again you're going to find all sorts of conflicting advice: cover letters should be just two or three sentences to introduce your résumé, cover letters should be at least three paragraphs but never more than one page, cover letters are completely unnecessary, and so on. In this chapter, we're going to cover the basics of good business writing and provide you with several illustrations to use as starting points for creating your own brilliant letters. And just as was recommended in Chapter 8, you will want to seek examples of good cover letters and other business writing from Web sites and books, and you will want to enlist someone to critique your letters.

No matter what career field you're considering, good writing will not only help you get the job, it will also help you keep the job and get faster promotions. That's a rather bold statement: I can hear some of you saying "Wait a minute. I'm going to be a_____. I'm not being hired for my writing ability." And you may be right. But do you think you might have to send an e-mail at some point to your supervisor? Is there a chance you will need to craft a letter to sell a product or your services? Do you dream of becoming an entrepreneur and developing your own business? No matter what field you're in, you will write; and because so few people take the time or energy to hone the craft, good writers easily stand out from the competition. And good writing will serve you throughout your career.

Want one more reason for developing strong writing skills? *Money.* Good writing skills are consistently one of the most sought-after skills by employers. The employee who can write a great memo, send the perfectly composed e-mail, write grants that result in funding, or write the perfect proposal will stand out for promotion every time. In fact, even now you're about to be "paid" for your ability to write a good cover letter and other business correspondence by landing a job, internship, or a volunteer opportunity that will lead to something better in the future.

For years you've been writing to please your teachers or professors with the hoped-for result of an A. Some of you have perfected this skill; others would prefer to avoid it and have mastered the art of finding courses that require tests rather than papers. If you haven't enjoyed academic writing, the good news is that the type of writing you'll be doing for the job search differs from the writing that professors have expected. Business writing is generally more direct and easier to write. If you're a strong academic writer, you will find that you can adapt your style quickly. The basic rules of good writing apply everywhere, but business writing (the term we're going to use for the kind of writing you'll be doing to land a job) is a new skill even for experienced A writers.

It's a myth that writing is some kind of natural gift bestowed upon only certain people. Sure, not all of us can write like Jane Austen or Maya Angelou, but good basic writing skills can be developed and learned by anyone. So if you're still in school and you've been avoiding those writing-intensive courses, consider taking one. If that's too intense, take a creative writing course that allows you to write about your interests, or a workshop on journaling or blogging, because practice and feedback from your professor or facilitator will be invaluable to your goal of becoming a better writer. Some colleges even offer business writing courses that would be a great place for you to practice your technique. If you're out of school, there are still lots of options for improving your writing skills, from getting a book on business writing to taking a Web-based writing class. Even your local bookstore might host writing groups where you could practice your writing and have it critiqued by fellow writers. And by the way, because good writing is good writing, you don't always have to take a business writing workshop or course if that doesn't sound appealing. Learning to write science fiction, creative nonfiction, mysteries, poems, or other forms of writing will also develop your business writing skills.

One of the common challenges for students accustomed to writing five-hundred-word essays or twenty-page research papers is the myth that the longer a piece of writing is, the better it is. Good writing isn't about length. It's about covering the subject and then stopping. An apocryphal story about Ernest Hemingway places him in a bar where he bet someone that he could write the shortest short story ever written. Supposedly he won the bet by writing a six-word story on a napkin:

"For Sale. Baby shoes. Never worn."

Now, that's not exactly a mood lifter and arguably Mr. Hemingway would have benefited from some of that positive mindset in Chapter 3, but in six words he beautifully encapsulated character, plot, and story. You can picture it, can't you, and fill in the details yourself?

Right now many of you are well versed in academic writing. And that's good because academic and business writing have many characteristics in common. Good academic and business writers strive for clarity, know their purpose for writing, know their audience and write accordingly, organize their writing in a logical manner, and use the amount of space needed to adequately cover their points. Both types of writing have three key elements: format, style, and content. The table below illustrates some of the differences and similarities between academic and business writing:

KEY CONSIDERATIONS	ACADEMIC WRITING	BUSINESS WRITING
Audience	Faculty: well educated and knowledgeable about subject	General: education varies; sometimes unknown
Subject	Topic appealing to academic world, such as humanities, history, and so on	Topic appropriate to workplace needs: job finding, promotion, informative memos, and so on
Expected Length	Usually lengthy: three-plus pages	Minimal: one to two pages
Tone/Style	Academic, formal, learned. Focus is on research/theories	Attention getting, professional, businesslike, straightforward, sales oriented
Vocabulary	Academic, formal, technical, specialized	Short words/short sentences. Can be technical or specialized, but must be clear and to the point
Use of References	Bibliography, sources, careful citations	Simple references—no formal bibliography, less formal citation
Purpose	To inform, advance, and demonstrate knowledge, demonstrate research and writing skills	To inform and inspire the reader to take action, to sell a product or an idea

In this chapter we're going to focus on the cover letter, the key piece of job-hunting correspondence. We will briefly discuss other correspondence in the job search process, but the writing knowledge you acquire when crafting a cover letter can be easily transferred to other documents. You are going to use a system for developing your cover letter that will help you avoid writer's block and keep your letter interesting and focused. You will also learn to avoid the five fatal errors that can ruin your chances of getting a job: a lack of focus in your writing, poor sentence structure and/or bad grammar, misspelled words or typographical errors, an inappropriate style (too casual or academic), and a failure to focus on the reader's interests and needs.

PREPARING TO WRITE

Your cover letter and other correspondence (including e-mails) related to the job search are a part of your marketing campaign. A good marketing campaign sells the product. Have you ever stood in the grocery staring at the myriad toothpastes available, unable to make a decision because there are just too many? Do I want the whitening or the fluoride or the one with the little speckles or the one that says it has breath freshener? Well, while no one is comparing you to a tube of toothpaste, you *are* selling yourself to an employer who likely has many candidates to choose from, and is sometimes just as confused and overwhelmed as you are in the toothpaste aisle. So it's your responsibility to make sure they consider you first.

A good marketing campaign is designed to connect you to your future employer by establishing a relationship that will lead to a personal interview and a job offer. Other aspects of your marketing campaign include your résumé, your interview technique, and any portfolio of work you've compiled related to your chosen profession. A well-executed marketing campaign can place you miles ahead of the other individuals seeking the same position. With your marketing campaign, you control what is said. You can tell the employer only what you want them to know about you by selecting the most important and relevant aspects of your background.

As you prepare to write your letter, you can expect to spend about one-third of your time *planning* your writing, one-third *writing*, and one-third *rewriting and editing*. You will need space and time to write these documents, so find a place where you can focus and won't be disturbed. You need to clear all the clutter from your mind—this is not the time to make that to-do list or help your room-mate find his or her lost shirt. Try sitting still and breathing for a few minutes before you begin. For inspiration, try checking your career center's Web site first and read a few of the sample cover letters to get the general gist of what you'll be writing. *Just don't copy the sentences verbatim.* Don't worry; the letter you write will be equally good or, more likely, even better.

In the next section of this chapter you will learn a series of guidelines to help you develop the best possible letter. Stay within the guidelines as appropriate, but remember that your letter is the best place to demonstrate your less tangible strengths, such as teamwork or detail orientation. Develop your own style and let your personality shine through, always keeping in mind the line between creativity and crazytivity discussed in Chapter 8. And just as recommended with your résumé, bring your letter to your career center or writing center for review. If you don't have access to a career center, let several friends read it and critique it for you.

Before we move to the letter-writing process, the issue of marketing or selling brings up a common concern among students and recent graduates: How do you sell yourself when you're not even sure you want the customer to buy you? That is, how do you write a compelling letter when you don't know if this is *the* job—the one you really want? Back to chaos theory: focus on what you know, what you don't know, and what you need to learn. Right now you probably don't know enough to know whether it is *the* job. And you probably won't until you do the interview. The great psychologist Alfred Adler had a wonderful phrase for people who weren't sure about something. He would say "act as if" you're sure—in other words, sort of a fake-it-till-you-make-it theory. Because you won't know if this is *the* job without more information, the best way to get that information is to "act as if" it is and move forward. If at any point in the process you discover it's not for you (whether it's the moment you upload your résumé and cover letter to their Web site or ten years after you've been working for the organization), you can always change plans. Right now your goal is to get the interview. During the first interview you will be better able to determine if you might be a good match and during a longer second interview at the site you'll have a much better idea. So let's get started.

> The aim of marketing is to know and understand the customer so well the product or service fits him and sells itself.
> —PETER DRUCKER

When conducting interviews for a pharmaceutical sales position, one recruiter hands the students a pen and says, "Sell me that pen." It is an anxiety-provoking moment for the students, but it is a good test of how quick they are on their feet and whether they have any feel for the selling game. After the interview, the recruiter shares with students the three basic ways to sell a product: tout its features, tout its benefits, or put the pen down and ask questions to help you understand your customer so that you can sell more effectively by tailoring your sales pitch to his or her needs. In a résumé you are generally limited to the first two aspects of selling: your features and your benefits, although you can focus those features and benefits to fit what the employer is seeking. In your letter you have the opportunity to develop the third and most powerful element of selling: establishing or developing a relationship with the reader. Let's examine those three methods of selling and how they apply to your marketing campaign.

- **Features** are the basic characteristics that define you. They tend to be hard facts or data easily observed or quantified. Features appeal to logic because they provide tangible evidence of accomplishment. Your features might include your major, your GPA, your job or volunteer experiences, and so on.

- **Benefits** are less tangible and are more likely to be your "soft" skills, the special talents and features you bring to a job, such as hard working or team player. You already discovered many of your benefits when you did the Wandering Map and identified your strongest mindsets. Benefits appeal to emotion and logic, particularly if you can back up your statements of talent with examples.

While both of these selling points are necessary, in order to use them effectively the third aspect of sales must come into play: What is your potential employer seeking and how can you build rapport and demonstrate that you fulfill that need?

⮑ **Asking appropriate questions** might seem more applicable to an interview than a cover letter, but as you write your letter, answering certain unasked questions will help you frame your correspondence in a way that will state your qualifications, demonstrate your knowledge of the company and the position, and address any potential concerns. Extend your research, if necessary, to find answers to the following questions about the cover letter you're preparing to write:

- To whom am I writing? Do I have a specific name and address?

- What action am I hoping this person will take?

- How do my features and benefits fit and support the position, the organization, and/or the career field?

- What features and benefits should I include/exclude from the letter?

- How knowledgeable is this person likely to be about my features? For instance, will she or he already know a lot about my major, or will I need to include a line or two explaining the connection between my major and the position or industry?

- Why do I want to work for this employer and how can I convey my knowledge and understanding of the position or the field?

- How am I connected geographically to this opportunity?

- What else does this person need to know about me?

Writing your letters with these three key sales elements in mind will help you build rapport with the reader and establish your credibility. As in your résumé, you want to develop brief short stories that convey a lot of information in one or two sentences. The reader will know that you have done your research because you will be showing (rather than telling) the reader through your stories and examples.

Perfectionism is the voice of the oppressor.   —ANNE LAMOTT

Following the five-step method presented below will help you avoid the form letter look that is generally rejected by employers and reviewers, and it also has an added benefit: it is designed to eliminate, or greatly reduce, writer's block. Most students sit down to write their cover letters, and fully aware of the importance of the task, immediately freeze. You stare at the blank piece of paper waiting for the inspiration to start your letter. The five-step process will guide you through your letter in a manner that will destroy the usual causes of writer's block: the lack of a great opening line, not knowing what information to include, the fear that you will be rejected, and the need to be perfect. You can write the opening line later; in fact, it will likely come to you without effort once you're in the middle of writing your letter.

Certain characteristics are common to all good letters, and for this reason a sample letter is presented. You may not agree with the example. In fact, you may think it's terrible and that you wouldn't write like that. Actually, that's the point. Writers have to write in their style, not someone else's, and as long as you're following the basic guidelines, you'll produce a document that represents you in the best possible light.

FIVE-STEP PROCESS FOR CRAFTING LETTERS

I. ESTABLISH YOUR AUDIENCE AND YOUR REASON FOR WRITING.

If you already answered the questions on page 230, you won't need to spend as much time in this step. Consider how formal or informal your writing style needs to be. Are you writing to someone you've never met? Then your style will be more formal. To an alumnus you met recently? Then you can be less formal, while still remaining professional. The important component in this step is recognizing what your audience is expecting from you and getting their attention from the first line on. You want to persuade the employer to want to speak with you. If you're writing a cover letter, you will likely establish your reason for writing in the opening line, which is designed to hook the reader and motivate him or her to keep reading.

For now, though, *don't write anything.* The goal in this stage is to know your audience well so that you keep their point of view in mind as you follow the next four steps.

2. SWOT MAP IT

Got another blank piece of paper handy? In this step you're going to brainstorm your ideas for your cover letter by combining two techniques: a SWOT analysis briefly mentioned in Chapter 3 under strategic mindsets and the mapping skills you've developed throughout the system. This technique can be used to write a specific letter for a specific job, or to draft a generic cover letter you can modify later when you see a position that appeals to you. There's only one rule: you must start with one mindset—that of the employer. Remember, it's not "What do I want to say?" It's "What does the employer need to know or want to hear?" Just like your other maps, creating a SWOT Map is fairly easy:

⇢ Are you directing your letter to a specific job opening? Then start by placing the job title in the center of the page and draw a circle or rectangle around it. If you're writing a generic letter, put the general field or type of job you're seeking in the center.

⇢ Draw four rectangles or circles around the center and label them with the following words: *Strengths, Weaknesses, Opportunities,* and *Threats.* As you focus on each of these areas, start drawing lines from their boxes with examples that demonstrate your connection to the position and/or the ways you can overcome a discrepancy between you and their ideal candidate:

 • *Strengths* refers to your features and benefits as they apply to the position you're seeking. Why are you the best candidate? What do you want the employer to know about you in particular? What three skills or talents do you want to be sure to mention?

 • *Opportunities* refers to the learning opportunities and other benefits you see about this job. Is this a place where you'd really like to work? What is appealing about it? Is there an opportunity for you to use and build your skills and/or provide a service? Does the organization focus on a longtime interest of yours? Are there opportunities for growth and challenge?

 • *Weaknesses* refers to what you might be lacking from the point of view of the organization. For instance, the

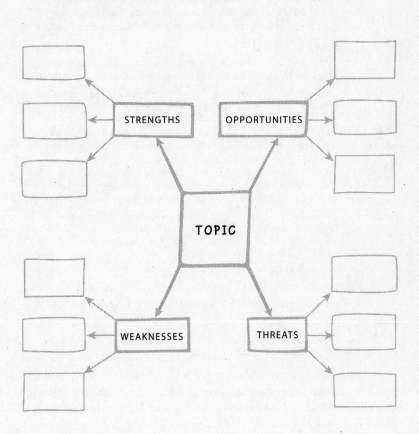

advertisement might say they're seeking an advertising major. And there you sit with your American studies major. What arguments do you plan to use to overcome their resistance? What could you say about your American studies major that would interest an advertising firm? Keep the employer's point of view in mind.

- *Threats* is kind of a scary word. While no one is threatening you, the truth is there are outside factors that could influence your situation. Who might be your competition for the position? In the example above, a threat might be those pesky advertising majors who tend to apply for advertising jobs. Another threat might be the economy: How hard is it to get a position in this field or company? Another threat could be your geographic location: Are you living in Utah and applying for a job in Atlanta? How do you explain that to an employer? If they assume their ideal candidates already live in Atlanta, how do you overcome their reluctance to consider you? (Hint: Do you have relatives or other connections to the area? Are you going to be in Atlanta and available for an interview at no cost to the employer? Mention that.)

Let's follow Kayla, a recent college graduate who is currently working at a coffee shop in Oregon, through this SWOT-mapping process. She's going to apply for a position in a different geographic area that is not related to her major.

Kayla graduated from college with a music major and an English minor. She has always been interested in environmental issues and found an interesting job posting for a field associate with an environmental organization in California. According to the job posting, she would need to be knowledgeable about environmental issues, including global warming, clean water and air, energy policies, and so on. In addition to surveying the general public about attitudes toward environmental concerns and acquiring signatures for petitions, the field associate would work with local media to promote environmental causes and increase awareness of issues. The position requires that the individual be outgoing, have an understanding of local and statewide politics, be familiar with sales or customer service and/or fund-raising, and have a bachelor's degree, preferably in environmental science. Preferred experience includes grant writing and managing staff. Applicants are asked to submit their cover letters and résumés directly to the agency via e-mail. To preserve the environment, no paper-based applications will be accepted.

Kayla knows she could do this job, but she's concerned that employers won't look past her major when they see her résumé. She knows she needs to immediately overcome some reservations an employer might have. Her SWOT map is on pages 236–37.

3. CREATE SAMPLE SENTENCES AND POSSIBLE PARAGRAPHS

Now that you've outlined the pluses and minuses of your candidacy for the position, you're ready to start developing your ideas into sentences. Do not try to write the full letter yet. Use your SWOT Map information to identify the key points (strengths, experiences, education) you want to emphasize, and try writing some sentences or phrases around them. Create a list of the sentences you might use in no particular order. What do you most want the reader to know? Or more important, what does the employer need to know about you? Can you articulate that information in a sentence or paragraph? Refer to your original source (the position announcement or whatever) as necessary. Keep the tone of your sentences positive and natural. You want your letter to be specific and persuasive. Presenting challenging or novel thoughts will motivate the reader to meet you, but always be careful to avoid crazytivity.

Here are some suggestions for writing your sentences:

⇢ Use an active voice and focus on action verbs.

- Write "As chairperson, I organized . . .," not "The event was organized by . . ."

⇢ Connect your experiences to the position you're seeking, establishing mutual interests or similarities between your background and the position or industry:

- "During my three years as a night desk clerk for Hilton Hotels, I learned the importance of good customer relations. I believe my knowledge prepares me for your sales division because . . ."

- "Your job description indicates you are seeking someone with leadership potential. As captain of the soccer team, I developed a strong team spirit by . . ."

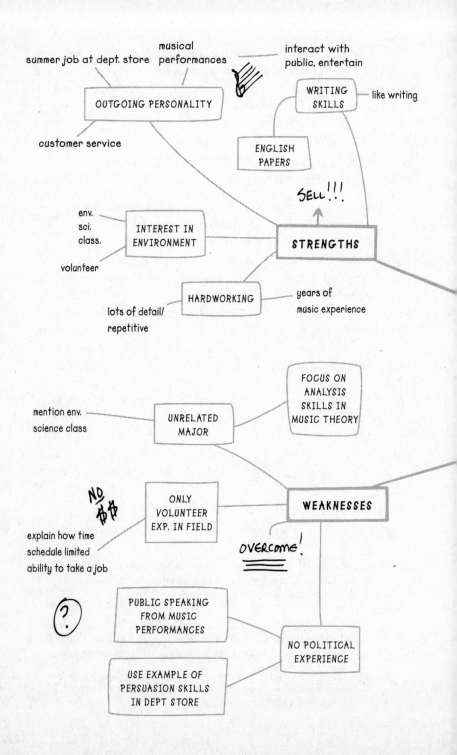

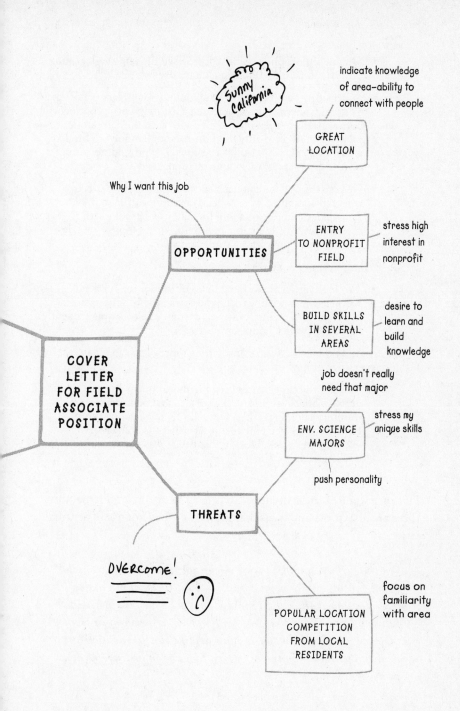

- "In my philosophy course work, I used the same logical and analytic thinking a good consultant uses when . . ."

- "I led a Boy Scout troop throughout my four years of college. To fund troop activities, I created a list of twenty prominent corporations in the area and met with each of their public relations staff. Not only did I raise enough money to fund a week-long camping trip for the boys, I acquired interesting observations about the public relations field . . ."

- "My history major emphasized the importance of precise research combined with concise communication of knowledge and information. I would use these skills to research your product line to develop the best possible sales presentations for you."

‣ Back up what you say with evidence.

- "Your advertisement stated that you're looking for a hard worker who is willing to 'go the extra mile.'" This past year, in addition to maintaining a B+ average as a full-time student, I worked twenty hours . . ."

‣ Expand on your résumé by providing more depth about an experience or new information.

- "One of the experiences I list on my résumé is as a server at Pizza Shack. While on the surface that position seems uninteresting, in reality I learned valuable lessons about business management when I served as the manager two evenings per week. During that time I was particularly challenged by . . ."

Here are some of the sentences Kayla is working on (and remember, these are just drafts and ideas that she may or may not use in her final letter):

On the surface, a music major might not seem particularly relevant for an environmental position. But through my major I have developed an analytic mindset that helps me take apart and fully understand an issue, an ability to easily perform in front of people, and a focus on minute details, not to mention the dedication and commitment needed to learn an instrument at a professional level.

I managed a busy schedule of classes, performances, and practices, but still found time to volunteer for a cause I consider imperative in today's society: the environment.

I was required to take a science course and specifically chose environmental science due to my interest in acquiring more understanding of the issue. We studied not only the science of global warming and the management of natural resources, but also the political forces which have an impact on those issues.

I am originally from the region of California where your office is located. I am quite familiar with the environmental policies of the politicians in the area as well as the way the citizens have voted on environmental issues in recent elections.

Now it's your turn. See if you can craft some sentences that might ultimately fit into your cover letter.

4. WRITE A FAST DRAFT

I wanted to write "very fast," but the voice of my ninth grade English teacher still haunts me: "You mean as opposed to 'unvery'?" Fast writing is a common and successful exercise for a first draft because it clears away the cobwebs and heightens your focus. See if you can write the letter in less than ten minutes.

Sit down at your computer or grab your pen and notebook and just write and write and write. Try using the sentences you've already developed or write new ones. Don't try to make it perfect: it's not supposed to be. It's a draft. Let it be as bad as any draft can be. If you can't think of an opening line, skip it. Write the middle of the letter first if that works best for you. Write the closing line first. You'll clean it up later. The goal now is to get everything down on the paper. Ready? Set? *GO!*

See Kayla's first draft on page 240. You'll note that it's too long, contains some misspelled words, and isn't all that well organized or styled. But she has captured a lot of the information she will use in her final letter, and that's the point of a first draft.

Dear_____:

I read your job announcement for a Field Associate position in Santa Barbara, California and I would like to apply. I read your website and I was particularly impressed with the work you've done to save national forests and strengthening the clean water act. I am originally from Santa Barbara and I believe that my background in environemtnal issues and my knowledge of the politics of the region could be valuable in your fund-rasing and advocacy efforts.

I am a hard worker and understand the importance of dedication to an important cause. As a musician, I had to be very dedicated to my craft, and devoted numerous hours to practicing and perfecting my skills. In addition to managing a busy sechule of classes, performances and practices, but still found time to volunteer for a cause I consider imperative in today's society: the environment. I also worked in a department store where I developed my skills of persuasion. I received an award for outstanding sales person because I increased sales in my department (juniorwear) by 20% in one month.

The first thing you will likely notice on my resume is that I'm a music major. On the surface, a music major might not seem particularly relevant for an environmental position. But through my major I have developed an analytic mindset which helps me take apart and fully understand an issue, an ability to easily perform in front of people, and focus on minute details, not to mention the dedication and commitment needed to learn an instrument at a professional level.

I was required to take a science course and specifically chose Environmental Science due to my interest in acquiring more understanding of the issue. We studied not only the science of global warming and the management of natural resources, but also the political forces which have an impact on those issues.

As I mentioned, I am originally from the region of California where your office is located. I am quite familiar with the environmental policies of the politicians in the area as well as the way the citizens have voted on environmental issues in recent elections. I hope you will consider my resume and experience. I look forward to hearing from you regarding this important opportunity.

5. EDIT AND PROOFREAD IT RUTHLESSLY

Congratulations! You've finished the hardest part: getting that first draft down on the paper. Now it's all about refining it: seeing what works and changing what doesn't. Someone once said that all good writing is rewriting, and one of the best ways to start rewriting is to read your letter out loud. The minute you stumble over a phrase or something doesn't flow smoothly, chances are you need to make a change. Most people find their first draft starts falling apart after about the fifth word (!). Not to worry. You're going to turn your draft into a better draft and then to the best final copy you can write. Notice you haven't seen the word *perfect*. There is no perfect letter—like résumés, reviews of letters are based on opinions, not hard facts. One person's "perfect" is another person's "OK." Edit and organize your letter now, using some of the suggestions below. Once you've worked it up to the better draft stage, get other people's opinions. Ask your friends to read your letter (or try reading it aloud to your friends). If you're still in college, ask someone at the career center to review it with you.

> Cover letters are generally three to five paragraphs, but you can break this rule if you have a good reason, and have carefully considered your audience.

> - In the first paragraph connect yourself with the reader by explaining what you're applying for, how you heard about the job opening, and some sort of indication as to how/why you are qualified for the position or they should consider you for it.

> - The middle paragraphs allow you to expand on your résumé and bring up the "soft" skills that you couldn't explicitly state in your résumé such as teamwork or your personality. Use the sentences you developed in the third stage, keeping brevity in mind and distilling your letter to the most important information of interest to the reader. Remember, your reader has little time to devote to your document (unlike a professor or teaching assistant who actively reads your papers), so get to the point.

> The final paragraph closes your letter with an indication of what action will be taken. You will need to know your field to determine the best close. In general, the more sales, marketing, or business oriented the position, the more appropriate it is to end with the action you will be taking.

- With government, nonprofit, or educational fields you can often get away with a less assertive close. In education, for example, it's common to write something like, "I look forward to hearing from you . . ."

- In the business arena the previous ending would be less acceptable. There you would close with a more assertive, "I will contact your office in one week to discuss the opportunities in greater detail." (And by the way, take that action. If you say you're going to contact them, do it.)

- If you're going through your on-campus recruiting program, an appropriate close would likely be, "I look forward to having the opportunity to interview with you when you visit . . ."

⇒ Vary the openings of your sentences. Make sure each sentence doesn't begin with *I* or another common opening.

⇒ Remove any fluffy language. Just like résumé guides, many cover letter guides recommend fluffy phrases. You have way too much substance at this point to waste your time writing phrases like

- "I am looking for a position in a growth-oriented company that will utilize my many skills."

- "I am a team player who enjoys hard work. Don't hesitate to contact me."

- "I am seeking a position in a well-known company such as yours."

- "It is for this reason that I am hopeful you will consider me for this position."

- "I believe I would be a strong asset because I have exceptional communication skills."

⇒ Don't brag, deprecate yourself, complain, or appeal to sympathy.

- "You'd be lucky to have me working for you."

- "Don't miss this opportunity to interview me."

- "Although I don't have any experience in your field . . ."

- "I know that this letter is late, but . . ."

⇒ "I didn't major in business, but . . ."

⇒ This probably goes without saying, but don't exaggerate or lie. If you're caught, you could lose your job and your reputation.

FORMATTING YOUR LETTER

So your content is strong and you've created the best possible document to market yourself to employers. Let's make sure you don't ruin those beautifully turned phrases with poor formatting. Here's what you need to know about formatting a business letter, whether you're sending a paper copy or uploading an electronic version.

1. If you're printing the letter, always use good quality white, gray, or cream-colored 8½ by 11 bond paper. Use the same paper to print your résumé. Do not print the final letter or résumé on the typical paper found in most copies.

2. When possible, address the recipient by name, and use the appropriate courtesy title: Mr., Ms., Dr., and so on. Do not use "Dear Sir or Madam" or, worse yet, "Dear Sir" or "Gentlemen." Even if the job announcement doesn't show a name, a little detective work on the Internet can often uncover it Lacking that, use "To Whom It May Concern" as an absolute last resort.

3. Proofread. Repeat. Let someone else read it. Proofread again.

4. Copy traditional business letter guidelines (headings, locations of dates, spacing, and so on) from the sample letter in this book and/or on your career center's Web site.

You'll find Kayla's final cover letter, which she sent via e-mail, on the next page. Remember, this is just a sample letter and not intended to be the only style of letter acceptable to employers. You should visit your career center's Web page (even if you've graduated) to see if they recommend a different style or have other suggestions you might find helpful.

August 10, 2009

Ms. Susan Smith
Employment Manager
Environmental Agency
10500 East Main Street
Santa Barbara, CA 93102
s.smith@email.net

Dear Ms. Smith:

I was pleased to discover the field associate position listed on your Web site recently. As a former resident of the Santa Barbara area with a deep concern for the environment, I am particularly impressed with the work your agency has done to save state forests and strengthen the Clean Water Act. I would like to be part of the team that assists you in your efforts, and I believe I have the fund-raising and advocacy skills you are seeking.

I worked in sales throughout my college years while pursuing a challenging and time-intensive major (music), but I always found time to demonstrate my concern for the environment. I received an A in the two-semester environmental science class I took in college and volunteered for numerous environmental projects, doing everything from highway cleanup to canvassing and fund-raising to protesting at the state capital when it appeared that much-needed environmental legislation might not pass.

I suspect you do not often receive applications from music majors, but it is my music background that actually honed many of the skills I would use at Environmental Agency. I developed my strong analytic skills through music theory classes, my dogged determination and attention to detail through endless practicing and rehearsing, and my communication skills through performances and presentations.

As requested, I have attached a copy of my résumé. I will be in the Santa Barbara area the week of September 7–14 and would like to arrange a meeting if that would be convenient for you. I will contact your agency within the next week to confirm that you received this e-mail. Thank you for your consideration and I look forward to hearing from you.

Sincerely,
Kayla Jones

100 Pine Street
Portland, OR 97212
kaylajones@email.com
Cell: 503-555-5555

Résumé attached as MS Word document

WISDOM BUILDERS

I. COVER LETTER HAIKU

One fun way to prepare to write your cover letter is to write it as a haiku, an ancient Japanese form of poetry consisting of exactly seventeen syllables. That sounds a little odd for a cover letter, but the structure of haiku requires you to be succinct and make every word count. In haiku, the first line has five syllables, the second has seven syllables, and the third five syllables. Here are some samples:

Nursing Position

Lifelong dream to heal
Tough, smart, caring hard-worker
How can I serve you?

Social Worker in Youth Program

Adolescents rock.
I enjoy challenge and growth.
Hire me to change them.

Event Planner

Details. Beauty. Class.
Organized. Experienced.
Work wonders. Call me.

Investment Banker

Money. More Money.
Never stop working for you.
Bottom-line results.

If you had to distill your cover letter to these essentials words, what would you include?

2. CONSTRUCT A GOOD HOOK FOR YOUR COVER LETTER

You will want to open your letter with a good hook. A good hook keeps you reading; a bad hook doesn't. Did you ever think about using your favorite authors as inspiration for your writing? Now, don't get all stressed and think you have to be John Grisham or James Baldwin to come up with that perfect opening line. You just need to create an opening sentence that is interesting to the reader and conveys necessary information. Try to avoid the obvious "I am a senior at . . ." And don't cross over the line into crazytivity with a silly or weird opening like quoting a famous author ("It was the best of times, the worst of times . . .") or writing "You don't know it yet, but you have just discovered your best employee."

If you received the reader's name from a mutual friend or contact, mention it. Mention where you heard or read about the job opening.

- "Your advertisement in the *New York Times* captured my attention for two reasons . . ."
- "My sociology professor, Dr. Sara Jenkins, suggested I contact you regarding . . ."
- "While preparing an economic analysis for the United Way program in San Francisco, I . . ."
- "The *Washington Post* recently reported that Apple is opening a new facility in . . ."

One source of inspiration could be your favorite author. Think about your favorite writers and stories and how their opening lines hooked you. Here are the opening lines of some of my favorite books and writers It may just be that their opening lines kept me reading and taught me something about writing.

It is a truth universally acknowledged, that a single man in possession of a good fortune must be in want of a wife.
—**JANE AUSTEN,** *PRIDE AND PREJUDICE*

My wound is geography. It is also my anchorage, my port of call.
—**PAT CONROY,** *THE PRINCE OF TIDES*

In my younger and more vulnerable years my father gave me some advice that I've been turning over in my mind ever since. "Whenever you feel like criticizing anyone," he told me, "just remember that all the people in this world haven't had the advantages that you've had."

—**F. SCOTT FITZGERALD,** *THE GREAT GATSBY*

I am doomed to remember a boy with a wrecked voice—not because of his voice, or because he was the smallest person I ever knew, or even because he was the instrument of my mother's death, but because he is the reason I believe in God; I am a Christian because of Owen Meany.

—**JOHN IRVING,** *A PRAYER FOR OWEN MEANY*

The very first thing I tell my new students on the first day of a workshop is that good writing is about telling the truth. We are a species that needs and wants to understand who we are. Sheep lice do not seem to share this longing, which is one reason they write so very little. —**ANNE LAMOTT,** *BIRD BY BIRD*

If you really want to hear about it, the first thing you'll probably want to know is where I was born, and what my lousy childhood was like, and how my parents were occupied and all before they had me, and all that David Copperfield kind of crap, but I don't feel like going into it, if you want to know the truth.

—**J. D. SALINGER,** *THE CATCHER IN THE RYE*

3. FOUR HOT TIPS FOR CREATING THE BEST RESPONSE TO A JOB POSTING

I. READ THE AD CAREFULLY, UNDERLINING KEYWORDS, SKILLS, OR POINTS

Immediately Google the organization to learn as much as you can before you respond. A ten-minute Internet search should give you the information you need to write your letter. Note how the position is described, not just its title. Assume that the duties mentioned first are the most important and focus your letter accordingly, linking your strengths to them.

2. NOTE THE QUALIFICATIONS FOR THE POSITION

Create a SWOT Map to analyze your relationship to the position. If your qualifications don't match exactly, explain why you might still be qualified for the position. Be positive and don't lead with "Although I'm not a business major, . . ." but rather with "Through my____major I acquired many of the skills you are seeking, including . . ."

3. FOLLOW THE INSTRUCTIONS FOR CONTACTING THE ORGANIZATION CAREFULLY

If the advertisement requests three letters of recommendation, send three letters. If it says "no phone calls," don't call. Failure to follow directions could cost you the interview. Spell all names correctly, including the name of the organization.

4. INCLUDE ALL REQUESTED INFORMATION

Sometimes employers will ask for more than your résumé. They may want a writing sample, letters of reference, or more specific information, such as your salary requirements. Always include all requested items, including a salary requirement. The salary requirement is always a challenge: shoot too high and they won't interview you; shoot too low and you might not earn what you deserve. Because it is likely that this is your first or second professional job, and you don't have a long track record of professional compensation, simply state that fact in your letter, and if you want, indicate the general range of salary for the field. You will need to research this (try the Occupational Outlook Handbook at http://www.bls.gov/OCO/). For example: "Salary is not my prime consideration for this position and I am willing to consider a reasonable offer. My understanding is that salaries in this field tend to range from____to____, which seems to be an appropriate compensation range."

4. RESOURCES TO DEVELOP YOUR WRITING SKILLS

Here are some of my favorite books on writing. While they are not specifically related to the job search, their ideas and exercises will help you improve your writing for all purposes. They will also help you deal with writer's block and learn to think like a writer.

The Artist's Way by Julia Cameron

The Right to Write by Julia Cameron

On Writing: A Memoir of the Craft by Stephen King

Bird by Bird by Anne Lamont

Write Mind by Eric Maisel

Writing from the Inside Out by Dennis Palumbo

One Continuous Mistake by Gail Sher

The Elements of Style by William Strunk Jr. and E. B. White

A FINAL QUESTION

What could you do in the next twenty-four hours to begin crafting your best possible cover letter?

_____

_____

_____

CHAPTER 10

WANDERING INTO THE WORKPLACE

INTERVIEWING AND IMPRESSING

Once upon a time there was a liberal arts student named Emily. She was a French major and wanted to interview for a marketing position with IBM. IBM came to campus, and she signed up for the interview. The recruiter expressed some surprise when he looked at his schedule: he had a day full of business and economics majors and then this one French major. When Emily arrived for her interview, the recruiter tackled his concern head-on. "You're a French major," he said, "What can you do for IBM?" Emily calmly looked at him and said, "You know, when I came to college I wanted to take a Spanish class, but they were full. My adviser suggested I take French instead. It's four years later: I've majored in French, I studied abroad in France, I lived with a French family who spoke no English, I worked for a French corporation, and I speak French fluently. I know and understand a language, a culture, and a country. I've already started researching your product line and customers, and I'm excited about learning how to best reach your market."

Take a look at the story above. If Emily had said: "Well I think a French major is valuable for many reasons" or "I've developed a lot of skills with my French major" or even "Well, aside from my French major . . . ," would her response have been as compelling?

What makes Emily's response so memorable and powerful is

the story—the "frame" she created that *demonstrated* her knowledge, confidence, and quite frankly, her sales ability. She didn't avoid the question. She answered it head-on, weaving a thread between what she had already done with her French major (answering **THE QUESTION** the recruiter was really asking) and then pulling the thread directly into the new position she was seeking. (I don't know if she lived happily ever after, but she got the job and within a year was promoted to a marketing management position.)

This chapter is about weaving threads into stories: connecting those threads you discovered in your Wandering Map to your future employment by managing the interviews, meetings, and other encounters you will have with people who can help you move forward in your job search. Like Emily, you will now confront **THE QUESTION** on a regular basis. It will be worded in a variety of ways (have you seen those monstrously long lists of "typical questions" asked at job interviews? Just Google "typical interview questions" and be prepared to be overwhelmed instantly), but the bottom line for most employers is "Will this person fit in our environment? Does he or she already possess the skills or have the potential to learn quickly so that he or she will be an asset to our organization and not a liability?" Through storytelling you will be able to demonstrate convincingly to an employer just how well you are prepared for the workplace.

Before we get into shaping your stories to impress future employers, let's take a look at the interview itself. Like most job seekers, you probably haven't given much thought to the employer's perspective. You've been focusing on answering questions correctly, assembling the right interview outfit and reading up on etiquette and table manners (you have done all that, right?!?), but you haven't stopped to consider what the employer is thinking. And, as you saw in the previous chapter, one of the keys to marketing yourself is to make a connection, to get out of your mindset and into your audience's. So, just what is that employer thinking?

THE INTERVIEWER AND THE INTERVIEW

What is a date, really, but a job interview that lasts all night? The only difference between a date and a job interview is that in not many job interviews is there a chance you'll end up naked at the end of it. **—JERRY SEINFELD,** *THE SEINFIELD CHRONICLES*

Let's start by examining your interviewer, with the caveat that there's no one type of interviewer out there. Some organizations have professional human resources staff who devote most of their time to interviewing candidates for positions. They travel all over the United States to find the best talent for their organization and they pretty much have interviewing down to a science. They know exactly what questions they're going to ask, what replies you will likely give, and they have honed their ability to separate the sheep from the goats, so to speak. You will often encounter this type of interviewer in a typical college recruiting program or at large corporations.

It's just as likely, however, that you'll get Bob, the guy who actually works in the field and has just been told by his manager to "go interview some college kids" for an upcoming opening. Bob is usually well meaning and sincere, and is probably very good at selling widgets or whatever he does, but he's no expert in interviewing and his questions may be odd or seemingly haphazard. Some might even be illegal, technically, because Bob hasn't been given any formal training in interviewing. Bob will ask weird questions, such as "Where's a good place to get a drink around here?" (Yes, that question has been asked at interviews.)

And of course, there are all shades of interviewers in between with varying skills in interviewing and assessing candidates. Regardless of their training or experience, interviewers have one thing in common: they want to hire the best person for the job. They want individuals who demonstrate skills such as problem solving, communicate well verbally and in writing, have an understanding of the industry, common sense, and a strong work ethic. Ultimately, they are seeking fit: that indefinable and vague quality that says others will enjoy working with you and you'll enjoy and be productive in the work setting. Their worst nightmare is that they hire the wrong person and then are stuck with a bad employee whom they have to fire and start all over again. And no one wants to do that. In some organizations, professional recruiters are reviewed annually for their hiring record, not unlike a football coach who is judged on the ratio of wins to losses. So they are under pressure, just like you. (And here you thought that you were the nervous one during the interview!) The last thing they want are surprises, particularly bad surprises. They don't want to hire a person who can't do the job, has a bad attitude, or leaves the company within a year. Hence, all those odd questions designed to trip you up or weed you out. But no matter what type of interviewer you get, or what type of questions you're asked, your smart and well-chosen stories will tell them what they need to know and in a way they will remember. You will present them with responses that will break through their fears or concerns about your suitability as a candidate.

Let's add one more element of pressure to the interview: a typical one-day college interview schedule will likely involve about twelve interviews. Odds are, the recruiter will select two people, at best, to move to the next stage of the interview process. And that doesn't include all the other schools the recruiter may visit. (And outside of a college recruiting program, the sky's the limit. There's virtually no way to know for sure how many people are being interviewed.) In general, though, you can assume that at least five (and potentially a lot more) individuals have made it to a final interview stage for each available position, no matter what position you're seeking. So your interviewer is listening to your responses at a deeper level than you might expect and you are being directly compared to the other people the recruiter is seeing. If you need an image, think of those long lines at the *American Idol* auditions versus the number who actually make it to the Hollywood tryouts. Fortunately, your odds of getting the job are better than most *American Idol* candidates, but it doesn't hurt to remember you're not the only candidate.

The same numbers game applies to the short encounters you might have with employers at a job fair as well. They may greet hundreds of candidates at a fair, but it's likely that only about ten or so résumés will be placed in that special pile designated for follow-up. And the decisions are based on a two-minute conversation with you in a noisy and crowded room teeming with people in suits.

Are you grasping the importance of preparing for your encounters with people who have the potential to hire you? Particularly when the economy is slow or the unemployment rate is high, employers can afford to be very selective in their hiring choices. And unfortunately, you seldom get a do-over in the interview-encounter process. Just like résumés that receive a few seconds' glance, your quick encounter with a potential employer is going to determine your fate.

Hey, what happened to that positive mindset in Chapter 3? Where's the rainbow in the midst of this rain? It's you. You're going to be the person who moves forward in the process, because you will be better prepared for your interview or chance encounter with the daunting amount of wisdom you've acquired about yourself, the job search process, and the position you're seeking. You will have stories and responses crafted that will leave a lasting and positive impression on the interviewer. There's a little-known fact about career books: only about 10 percent of the people who buy them actually read them the whole way through, so if you're reading this paragraph, you've already surpassed 90 percent of your competition. You already have more knowledge and are better prepared for the process. And now that you know how steep the competition can be, just like those *American Idol* contestants you will practice, practice, and practice to get better.

INTERVIEW SHAPES AND SIZES

When you think about an interview, what image comes to mind? If you're like most people, it's a vision of you and one other person in a small room asking and answering questions. Perhaps you get an immediate visceral sensation of anxiety. Or maybe you see yourself skillfully answering whatever question is asked. You might hear someone asking you that annoying typical opening line that's almost as bad as **THE QUESTION**: "Tell me about yourself." Or maybe you've read about stress questions such as "I've seen lots of good people today. Why should I hire you?" Or case interview questions where you have to answer strange queries, such as "How many gas stations are in Los Angeles?" Or requests for behavioral responses, such as "Tell me about a time when you solved a problem under pressure."

As mentioned earlier, it's easy to search the Internet and find list after list of possible interview questions. And that's actually a good idea. Gather up the questions and practice answering them, because you will likely get one or two of them. The problem is no list can cover every single scenario. There are simply too many questions and too many types of interviews and interviewers. Chaos theory has returned. Employers often have a personal favorite question they like to ask each candidate, and that question varies widely. Some like asking slightly off-topic questions, such as "What are you reading aside from your textbooks?" Others like to know what you already know about their company or position. The situation is too complex to be reduced to a few simple answers. That's why you have to be prepared to answer anything that is thrown at you, whether it's predictable ("Tell me about yourself") or out in left field ("Why are manhole covers round?"). But don't worry; you'll learn how to approach these situations with confidence. You are already skilled at taking the complex (your life) and making it manageable (identifiable threads and themes). Interviewing is no different. Strong interviewing skills rely on your knowledge of yourself (features and benefits), the position, field, and/or organization you're seeking, and your ability to quickly establish a relationship.

Interviews come in basically two sizes: short and long. The shorter interview is a screening interview and constitutes your *first conversation* with the potential employer. These interactions can last anywhere from two minutes to thirty minutes and take place at a job fair, in an office, on the phone, or even via e-mail. Sometimes they are called screening interviews and they rely on relatively quick answers to basic questions. Notice the emphasis on first conversation—even when you're simply answering a phone call to set up the interview, you're being interviewed. It is the first impression (aside from the résumé/cover letter if that's been part of the process) that the employer will have of you. In addition to the stories you'll be creating shortly, it's helpful to have a short speech about your plans prepared, what some career specialists refer to as an elevator speech or a sound bite.

The long interview usually takes place at the workplace, but again, it could occur over lunch in a restaurant, or at a neutral site like a hotel meeting room. A long interview is any conversation that lasts more than thirty minutes. Long interviews are more comprehensive, with questions that will dig deeper into your background and knowledge. A longer interview may last all day and include meetings with several managers and executives.

As for the style of the interview, much depends on the interviewer and the industry. Certain industries, such as investment banking and consulting, are known for case interviews where you (and perhaps a group of fellow interviewees) are presented with problems to solve in an allotted period of time. You are not only being judged on your ability to formulate an answer (and by the way, there may be no one correct answer), but also your thinking skills, and if it's a group setting, your teamwork skills and leadership potential. It's not unusual to experience some of each of these interviewing styles with one organization due to the personality of your interviewer. Some of the basic interview styles include the following:

- Directive interviews that rely on a series of preselected questions and proceed rather matter-of-factly

- Nondirective or free-flowing interviews that are more like a conversation or exchange (but be careful here—sometimes that approach is taken to make you relax and let down your guard)

- Panel interviews where a group of current employees will ask you a variety of questions

- Behavioral interviews that encourage you to provide examples of your skills and use your past as an indicator of the likelihood of future success

- Case interviews that present special problem-solving situations that may or may not be related to the actual job

> Last time I gave an interview, they told me to relax and say what I felt. Ten minutes after broadcast, I got transferred to an outpost so far off the star maps you couldn't find it with a hunting dog and a Ouija board.
>
> —**COMMANDER JEFFREY SINCLAIR** IN *BABYLON 5* (1994)

So are you grasping the complexity and chaos of the interview process—how challenging it is to predict what questions you'll be asked or the type of interview you're going to have and how it will be conducted? While it's a good idea to develop some basic responses to common questions, your time will be much better spent focusing on two key preparation strategies: storytelling and SWOT analysis.

WHY IS STORYTELLING IN A CAREER BOOK?

How important do you think it is to be:

Remembered

Trusted

Persuasive

Authentic

Considered a leader

in the job search process?

And how would you like a remarkable tool for making sense of the chaos of an interview? Well, once again, you're only a few blank pieces of paper away.

With all the information you've been developing from your Wandering Map, your collection of mindsets, your experimental wanderings, and the various exercises you've completed so far, I suspect you are starting to see how some of your findings could be crafted into stories that would resonate with a prospective employer. Even though you may not know how or where you're going to use these stories, taking the time to develop them now will help you clarify your experiences and view them in a new way.

Great storytelling is one of the most powerful skills you can master for the job search and interviewing process. And the good news is that you have been telling stories all your life. Whether you were entertaining your friends with a saga about that white-water rafting trip where you almost drowned or explaining to your parents the mysterious dent on the bumper of their car, you were developing plots, creating characters and dialogue, and forming compelling themes about your bravery or innocence.

Stories abound in college—and not just in English class. Courses in anthropology, history, psychology, sociology, Latin-American studies, and so on, all use stories to convey meaning and information. And outside the classroom, stories surround the legacy of the sports program, the rumors about that odd professor, ghosts haunting buildings where something bad happened one time, and other folkloric tales of your institution.

When you tell a story, you convey a piece of yourself, a snapshot of your life that allows the listener to know more about you and builds trust. In the same way that you needed to "show" rather than "tell" your skills in a cover letter or résumé, stories help you show the interviewer the veracity and sincerity of your statements. People distrust self-serving statements such as "I'm a good leader," but if you follow that statement with a description of how you raised funds and created a management team to develop an evening program on global sustainability involving guest speakers and catered food, the employer will know that there is substance behind the style.

Telling great stories in an interview can mean the difference between a job offer and a rejection letter. My first employer after college told me that the key reason she hired me (the only liberal arts major in a management-training program full of retail-merchandising and textile majors) was the story I used to explain how I knew the store from my childhood and how I had an understanding of who shops there and why. Your ability to describe your skills, your character, and your experiences in a manner that compels the interviewer to listen will be the beginning of an amazing career. And when you're on the job, your ability to tell the right story at the right time will impress colleagues and supervisors, settle disputes calmly, and give you the reputation of someone who is intelligent, thoughtful, insightful, and valuable. You can even build powerful long-term relationships through the impact of your storytelling.

Can you recall a story you learned from a family member, a professor, or maybe even someone at a job you held that has been memorable for you? What did it teach you? What did you learn?

One of my favorite stories is from the time I served on a housing board for a college that was in the process of moving the fraternity houses from one concentrated area (the quad) to smaller houses along the periphery of the campus. At an open meeting scheduled for the fraternity members to voice their opinions of this change, the volume level steadily increased as the members talked over one another, all arguing the same basic theme: that the social life of the campus would be ruined because they would not be able to hold their parties in the quad. The quad parties had been the source of many wild weekends and happy memories for both students and alumni. Where and how would students party?

Several members of the housing board tried to reason with the students; some even began raising their voices as well. The associate dean who chaired the committee sat silently throughout. Finally, as the last of the members argued his point again, the dean quietly said, "How many cat skeletons do you see in trees?" Everyone froze, not sure they had heard the statement correctly. The dean repeated himself, "How many cat skeletons do you see in trees?" The room was silent as participants looked at one another trying to make sense of what he had said. All eyes refocused on the dean. "The reason you don't see cat skeletons in trees is because they figure out a way to get down. Now you fellows are much smarter than cats. I suspect that even though this location option is removed, you will find a new way to hold your parties. I have total faith in your ability." And with that, the fraternity members sat mute, and even smiled a little at the dean's faith in them (knowing, of course, that he was right).

That meeting happened more than ten years ago, but the story remains fresh in my mind. That associate dean is now the president of another college. His brilliant observations and stories have endeared him to many colleagues and students throughout his career. And I tell the cat skeleton story again and again when the situation warrants. It never fails to amuse and calm people down.

OK, so you get that telling stories is a good thing. Maybe you've even read on the Web somewhere that you should tell a story in an interview about your greatest strength. But here's the catch: while it may be known that storytelling is a great interview technique, most students and recent grads tell monstrously *awful* stories.

They ramble on for ten minutes, causing the interviewer to forget the original question. Sometimes they've only prepared one story and tell it repeatedly regardless of the question. They tell stories that don't answer the question. Or they tell stories that are too brief, assuming that "I am great at solving problems; I did it all the time in my classes" is a story. They even shock employers with the topics they select for their stories (such as one demonstrating their ability to get things done by describing the night they drank too much yet managed to stumble back to the dorm at 3:00 a.m. and write a paper for a 9:00 a.m. class). Telling a weak story or telling a story badly pretty much guarantees your job hunt will continue. You must tell the right story at the right time and in the right way.

Storytelling is an art. And fortunately, it's an art you can acquire. In fact, you're going to acquire it by using the information from your Wandering Map and many of the mindsets from Chapter 3, such as creativity, flexibility, analysis, synthesis, and reflection. But it takes time. Mystery writer Raymond Chandler once said that "a good story cannot be devised. It has to be distilled." You have to let it sit a little and refine. You have to practice it repeatedly. And the last thing you want to do is try to create a story the night before an interview.

CREATING COMPELLING
INTERVIEW STORIES

Get out the blank paper again—it's time to control the chaos and create several powerful stories that will serve you in the job search and beyond. Like Emily's story at the opening of this chapter, a good story helps you build a frame around your experiences. You get to control everything—the plot, the characters, the action, and the outcome. A properly selected and developed story will be persuasive, help you establish rapport with the interviewer, and focus your vision. Use your systems (Big Picture) thinking to go above the situation and look down upon it as you consider the story in its entirety. Replay the story in your mind as you ponder it. And remember, your story needs to be believable. A phony story will betray you.

To start constructing your stories, identify three strengths or points you want to make in your interview, for instance, your attention to detail or your ability to handle difficult situations. Then begin thinking of two instances that illustrate each point. Take each instance and see if you can create a short short story—just a few sentences—to illustrate your points so you'll have at least six stories when we're done. As you build your stories, remember you only need to tell two or three in an interview. You won't answer every question with a story. Stories are powerful when they are carefully interspersed with more traditional responses to questions. If you can create two story ideas for the three key points you want to make in your interview

Wandering off:

WHEN STORYTELLING GOES AWRY

As powerful a skill as storytelling is, there are some common mistakes you can make that will undermine the value of your story. Watch out for:

- Stories that are superficial, trivial, too long, or too personal. Ask yourself if the story is interesting and worth the time it will take to tell. Make sure you're not giving the interview TMI (too much information).

- Stories that make you sound arrogant or superior. "I couldn't believe they asked me to answer the phones. I expected something more challenging than that."

- Boring linear stories: "This happened and then this happened and then this happened." Are you bored already?

- Stories that evoke negative emotions like fear, guilt, or sadness. Keep your stories uplifting. Remember the positive mindset in Chapter 3? For the most part, you want your stories to fit that style.

- Stories that are irrelevant or don't answer the question.

(six stories in all), you will likely be prepared for almost any question anyone can throw at you.

Now that you have generated a few ideas for stories, let's examine storytelling in greater detail. There are three equally important steps to creating great stories: finding inspiration and ideas, constructing your stories, and telling your stories.

STEP 1: FINDING INSPIRATION AND STORY IDEAS

Where do you find stories? In general, *you* will be the best source for your stories. Events that have happened to you or your family, challenging times you've worked through, moments in which you achieved new knowledge or understanding, or something you observed that left an imprint are all possible fodder for a great story. Be a good listener and pay attention to your surroundings. What stories are unfolding before you?

You don't always have to invent your own stories: you can use anecdotes or small stories you read or hear about, as long as they are relevant to your situation. Every book you read and every movie you see contains a story, metaphors, or moments of understanding. Your family has probably told some of the same stories several times. What do they show about the people in them? You may need to travel into your past to create stories for your future. But don't try too hard to come up with them: forcing yourself to think of a story can lead to some of the worst ideas and weakest stories. *Relax: Put your mind on storytelling and the stories will come to you.*

Some possible sources for your stories include:

➔ The Wandering Map you completed in Chapter 2: what stories can you tell from those experiences, both successful and unsuccessful?

➔ The mindsets you analyzed in Chapter 3: When did you use them and what was the successful outcome?

➔ Significant events that caused you to take action.

➔ Problems or challenges you've faced.

➔ Your unique way of successfully handling a situation.

➔ A time you felt proud of yourself or someone else.

Are you bursting with ideas? Suddenly recalling that time when . . .? Then get your blank paper or notebook and jot down your ideas as quickly as possible: this is not the time to censor yourself or judge what comes into your head. Just write out brief narratives or ideas that might be worth turning into a story. Here's a sample from Jim, whose Wandering Map was described in Chapter 2:

Sample Idea: *The time I volunteered at a center for victims of the Katrina flood The site didn't have enough food for all the evacuees and no one took charge. I found a phone book called the Governor's Office and called it. I told them about the problem and within hours food arrived for the people.*

> *I think I could tell this story as an example of my problem-solving skills, or my ability to take charge, or my initiative even when something isn't necessarily my responsibility.*

Now it's your turn to write your story ideas on your paper or in your notebook. You can use the following questions as a starting point if they're helpful:

IDEA 1: _____

WHAT'S THE BASIC OUTLINE OF THIS STORY?
_____
_____

WHY WOULD I TELL THIS STORY IN AN INTERVIEW?
_____
_____

IS THIS STORY RELEVANT AND/OR WHAT SKILLS AND STRENGTHS DOES IT HIGHLIGHT?
_____
_____

Write as many ideas as you can to find stories that illustrate different skills or experiences. Remember, you don't need ten stories that all show your leadership skills. One or two stories per key strength will work.

STEP 2: CONSTRUCTING YOUR STORIES

You now have anywhere from one to six ideas that might develop into useful stories. How do you craft them so that they're interesting to the listener and send the intended message? Focus on your audience: the interviewers who are trying to decide if you're the right person for the job. Why would they care about your story? How can you make them care?

Remember Emily's story at the opening of the chapter? She opened her story with the fact that she began studying French. The middle of her story emphasized all the ways in which she built up her knowledge of France and the French language. She ended it by linking her experience and knowledge with the position she was seeking. Your stories will also consist of three parts: a beginning, a middle, and an end. You should carefully consider each part, keeping in mind that you want to provide enough detail to make the story interesting without bogging it down with unnecessary detail. We didn't learn about every class Emily took or every experience she had in France. We only learned the key elements of her experience. Include only characters who are integral to the story. Emily mentioned that she lived with a French family but she didn't go into any detail about the family. She also stayed on her point and did not go off on any tangents.

Here are five questions to ask yourself as you develop your story. We'll use Jim's experience with the Katrina flood as an example.

I. HOW DOES YOUR STORY BEGIN?

Jim: *I was watching the TV coverage of the Katrina flood in New Orleans and they said volunteers were needed at a local shelter.*

2. WHAT ACTION DID YOU TAKE?

Jim: *I went to the shelter's medical area and asked how I could help.*

3. WHAT HAPPENED THEN?

Jim: *The buses arrived and the chaos grew tenfold. The noise level was unbelievable. Then a serious problem quickly arose: we didn't have enough food to last beyond the night. And these people were hungry—some had not had food for a day.*

4. WHAT DID YOU DO?

Jim: *Everyone was panicking about the food situation but no one knew what to do. And it just hit me: the governor of Texas was on TV talking about how Texas would help its good friends from Louisiana, so I figured why not call his office? I found a phone book and called the number. I had to go through a bunch of people, but ultimately I reached his assistant, who promised to speak to him.*

5. WHAT WAS THE RESOLUTION OR OUTCOME?

Jim: *Within a few hours, the governor had released the food supplies from the local schools for immediate use. What a rush. I was still in a state of shock—this nobody college kid getting on the phone to the governor's office? What was I thinking? And yet it worked, and people were so happy and appreciative.*

Obviously, Jim's story isn't quite ready for prime time, and he will want to rework it so that he can tell it quickly in an interview. He'll need to identify the skills he developed and what he learned in the situation. He'll want to relate it to the job he's seeking: How would that experience or the skills he gained from it serve him in this potential job? But he has the makings of an excellent story that will fit a variety of situations.

So now it's your turn. Try taking one of the ideas you developed earlier and begin to expand it into a story. Your story might not be as dramatic as Jim's, but don't censor yourself. It's your story and you can make it work for you. You can keep it fairly short—remember, you only have a minute or two to tell it. As you write your story consider

- ◆ What are the key points of my story?
- ◆ How do I want to open my story?
- ◆ What details should I include?
- ◆ How do I want to end my story?

  - What was my reward? Did I learn, did I grow, did I receive something tangible like an award?

  - What skills or knowledge did I acquire and how will I now use the lessons or skills I learned?

  - What is the meaning or moral of my story? How is it relevant to the job I'm seeking? Have I made that relevance clear?

Start writing—and have fun! You are an interesting person and you have lots of stories in you. You'll be surprised at what shows up on the paper if you just give yourself some time to reflect and allow the ideas to flow.

STEP 3: TELLING YOUR STORIES

Have you ever heard someone ruin a good joke just by telling it badly? The best story in the world can be ruined by weak storytelling, so this is an important skill to master. Now that you've crafted your stories, it's time to practice telling them. In general, the first time you tell the story it will likely be awkward. You may forget parts and have to go backward, or you might include too many details or get sidetracked. Not to worry. Practice will improve all of these problems and you can learn to tell your stories with authenticity and passion. Don't try to memorize your story: it will sound stilted and flat. And if it's too well rehearsed it may lose the personal touch and sound insincere. Just remember the key events or points you want to make and let the story flow from them.

So how do you practice? Over and over. Try telling your story to a friend and ask for feedback. Tell it when you're driving your car or taking a shower. Tell it once and then let it sit for a few days. Tell it again to the same friend and ask for more feedback. Usually when you tell a story a second time to the same audience, you cut down the unnecessary components without even realizing it.

Try watching some of your favorite comedians: they are often the best storytellers, and their stories tend to be short because they want to keep the audience laughing. Notice the rhythm and inflection in their voices as they tell their stories. Notice how smoothly their stories flow, grabbing your attention as you wait to hear the ending. What words or sections of the story do they emphasize? How do they make the last line (usually the punch line) work? Can you change the tempo or rhythm of your voice to suit your story? (Be careful not to go overboard, because that might sound theatrical—like the old *Saturday Night Live* sketch with the character Master Thespian, who preened dramatically and spoke with false accentuation and flair.) Keep your delivery simple but smooth. And always make sure you have identified your reason for telling the story and that the story fits the situation.

CREATING STORIES AND OTHER RESPONSES TO TYPICAL INTERVIEW QUESTIONS

While there is no definitive list of interview questions, it is likely that you will encounter at least half of these as you go through the interview process:

1. Tell me about yourself.

2. How would your friends describe you?

3. Why are you pursuing this position?

4. Describe the accomplishment of which you are most proud.

5. Why do you want to work for_____?

6. What makes you different from other candidates?

7. Why should we hire you?

8. What strengths/weaknesses do you bring to this position?

9. How did you select your college and/or your major?

10. What would you like to be doing five or ten years from now?

11. Your background doesn't really fit. Why do you think you can do the job?

12. What would you like me to know that's not on your résumé?

13. What books, magazines, or newspapers do you read regularly?

14. What do you enjoy doing in your spare time?

15. Have you ever failed at anything?

As you read through this list, are any of the questions particularly hard to answer? Those are the ones you should tackle first. Which of the questions most lend themselves to a story for you? For some people, the question about what friends would say about them might be answered with a short response, such as "My friends always say I'm the creative one because I have so many ideas." But for you, that question might be the start of a story about the time you were challenged by your friends' behavior and how you handled the resulting awkward situation.

PREPARING FOR THE INTERVIEW USING A SWOT ANALYSIS

You already know the value of the SWOT analysis from Chapter 9, where you used a SWOT map to develop your cover letter. Now you're going to work with a simple SWOT diagram to help you quickly identify how prepared you are for an interview.

Here is a basic SWOT design with some questions to get you started on your analysis:

INTERNAL AND PERSONAL FACTORS	EXTERNAL AND PROFESSIONAL FACTORS
STRENGTHS	**OPPORTUNITIES**
What talents, experiences, education, or other factors do you have that would appeal to the interviewer?	What do you already know about this field, company, and/or job?
What three key points do you want to make at the interview?	What positions are available?
	What skills are they seeking?
WEAKNESSES	**THREATS**
What factors might concern an interviewer?	Who is your competition?
What skills do you need to build?	Who else wants the same job or wants to get into the same school?
What knowledge or experience might you lack?	What is their preparation?
	What might give them the edge?

As before, you have four areas to work with: your personal strengths and weaknesses, and the external opportunities and threats. When you've completed your SWOT analysis, go back and focus on two factors related to the interview: (1) how you're going to accentuate your strengths, and (2) how you're going to minimize any weaknesses or threats. The positive factors you want to stress are your strengths (S) and the opportunities (O) available with the company. As you analyze these, you'll want to think about connections between the two. How do your strengths fit with what the company is seeking? How can you make an interviewer see the connections?

Minimizing the weaknesses takes some more planning. If you complete a SWOT analysis early enough before the interview (that is, not the night before!) you might have time to diminish some of your weaknesses (W) or outsmart the competition (T). For instance, suppose you're interviewing for a position that sounds really interesting, but the description indicates that one of the skills the company is seeking is experience with Excel worksheets, and you've never used Excel, so your lack of Excel experience is in your W box. What could you do between now and the interview to become familiar with Excel? Could you get a book on the basics of Excel? Perhaps you could try creating a simple Excel worksheet. Within a few hours, you could become familiar with the typical components of Excel worksheets, the typical tasks you could use it for, and even some basic entry guidelines and formulas.

Then when you're in the interview and the interviewer asks you about your skills with Excel, you have a choice. You can simply say, yes, I've worked a little with Excel and I'm sure I could learn it quickly. Or you could use the marketing technique of asking questions and telling a story, as in, "Can you tell me how Excel is used most often in your company?" Once the interviewer answers, you can then say, "You know, I didn't have any experience with Excel, but when I discovered that it was part of the job I decided to quickly learn it. I took an online tutorial and I set up several spreadsheets to experiment with. While I'm not an expert, I've been using it for a few weeks now and I've already learned how to. . . ." You can finish the story as it fits your experience.

Opposite is a blank SWOT diagram which you can fill in (or simply draw on a piece of paper). Take an interview you have scheduled or expect to have in the future and try doing a preliminary SWOT analysis. If you can't fill everything in, then you know what you still need to research or learn about the field. If you can fill it all in, then you have the beginning of a plan for impressing your future employer at the interview.

POSITION I'M INTERVIEWING FOR:

MY STRENGTHS	THE OPPORTUNITIES
MY WEAKNESSES	THE THREATS

WISDOM BUILDER

· ⟶

CORPORATE STORYTELLING: WHY YOUR EMPLOYER WILL CARE ABOUT YOUR APPRECIATION FOR STORYTELLING

Storytelling is used daily in corporations, government and nonprofit agencies, and even in entrepreneurial small businesses. Because storytelling has such a strong ability to influence, control, and even manipulate behavior, it can be an indispensable tool for an organization. The most obvious use of storytelling is in advertising, marketing, and public relations, which help organizations build their reputation and convey their carefully constructed image and identity to the public. Storytelling can convey a large message in a small package: an illustration of a loving mother holding her smiling infant with an image of a jar of baby food superimposed on a lower corner of the illustration tells a complete story without saying a word. Millions of dollars are spent developing brands, logos, and other marketing pieces with the idea of conveying a story to the customer or client.

CEO's and other leaders use storytelling to convey the organization's mission or meaning to employees, board members, customers, clients, and stockholders. The stories they tell will capture the imagination of the audience, using both reason and emotion, and present themselves as credible and reliable and competent, perhaps even visionary.

Storytelling can help workers better understand the value of their work, bring them closer together, and build community. It can be used to help convey the beliefs or customs of an organization, and even to control or influence employee behavior. The new employee who is told the story of a former employee who expressed her dislike of her job in an elevator, not knowing the president of the company was standing behind her, quickly learns to be quiet in an elevator or in any setting where she doesn't know who might be listening. The supervisor could have simply said, "Watch what you say about the company," but

The Classics at Work:

ARISTOTLE MEETS *WALL STREET* AND ENRON

Think your classes on Greek myth or narrative structure are a little obscure? Think again. Greek dramatic structure is alive and well in fiction and in real life. The movie *Wall Street* follows traditional Greek narrative style as it presents a fictionalized version of money-obsessed 1980s investors, corporate raiders, and stockbrokers like Ivan Boesky, Donald Trump, and T. Boone Pickens. The lead character of *Wall Street,* Bud Fox (played by Charlie Sheen), follows the path of the flawed hero of Aristotle's tragedies. He falls at the end but not without learning valuable lessons and changing his life forever.

Fast forward twenty years to a real-life Greek tragedy played out in the news by executives of the Enron Corporation in Houston, Texas. The documentary *Enron: The Smartest Guys in the Room* proves that in the twenty-first century C.E., just like in the fourth century B.C.E., human beings fall prey to the same errors or mistakes, bringing about their own downfall. The next time you see a scandal in the news or watch an individual's fall due to misjudgment, error, or character flaw, remember Aristotle. His teachings can help keep you, and your employer, from making a similar mistake. Storytelling is invaluable on many levels in the workplace.

the story carries an emotional impact and gravitas that compel the listener to absorb it. Other stories can help workers know how the company prefers to solve problems, how willing they are to hear alternative points of view, or even whether the employee needs to be at work exactly at eight o'clock or whether it's OK to wander in at nine. Stories have power, and a smart new employee (you perhaps?) listens closely to the stories the workers and the managers tell and carefully reads the stories in the company's public relations material—a gold mine of knowledge and information exists in those stories.

FINAL QUESTION

What could you do in the next twenty-four hours to be better
prepared for your interviews than your competition?

_____

_____

_____

CHAPTER 11

WANDERING AFTER GRADUATION

YOU MEAN THE CHAOS CONTINUES?

In the last week I've uprooted myself from my home of fifteen years, moved all the way across the country away from everything I care about, and plunged myself into a frightening new career. In the first few nerve-wracking moments, I walk in here and find my producer lobbying to get herself transferred to another show.

Abe Lincoln had a brighter future when he picked up his tickets at the box office.

—KELSEY GRAMMER AS "FRASIER CRANE" IN *FRASIER*

Lisa, a medieval studies major, came into her appointment with a worried look on her face. "It's September," she said "and I still don't have a job. This is really frustrating. I totally blew the last interview I had, which would have been the perfect job if I had gotten it, and I have another interview this afternoon, but it's just for a part-time job, so I don't even know why I'm bothering. The worst part is all my friends have moved on and they're starting these really great careers." She pulled out her résumé and cover letter and asked me to look them over (again) to see if they could be fixed. "I really have to get a job," she said as she slumped back in her seat.

If you're like most recent graduates, a new form of culture shock has occurred. Some of you are experiencing the jolt of entering the workplace, with all its changes from the academic culture you've been in for at least sixteen years. You suddenly don't have your summers off, and the people you work with are all older than you (after being surrounded by a sea of faces your own age in school). You're trying to negotiate the strange new world with different expectations, less feedback (no more grades for better or worse), and an unclear future (at least when you were in tenth grade you knew you'd be in eleventh grade the next year).

Or you could be experiencing a different kind of shock: that sudden wide-open gap of time with nothing to do. Some of you have understanding parents who will let you cruise a little while you get your bearings, but others are starting to feel the pressure.

I'll bet the conversation and the anxiety have switched from **THE QUESTION** to **THE JOB:** that relentless pressure you're feeling inside or from your parents, society, and elsewhere to now "do something," and it had better be the "right" something. You know that you want to do something that has meaning in your life; you certainly don't want to be doing your own version of *Office Space* and wearing too much flair. But time is running out because graduation is here, or already passed, and you still haven't made a move. It can all feel pretty paralyzing. Maybe it's time I told you my story.

I graduated with a major in sociology at a time when the economy was verging on a recession and there were no jobs out there. At least that's what the newspapers said. I was determined to have a job by graduation, so I took the first job I could get: as a management trainee in retail merchandising for a large department store.

About a month later I was transferred to the human resources office at one of the stores. I didn't really like the job much, but the one thing I did like was working with the manager of the department store's restaurant. He liked to hire people with disabilities because he had a sister with a disability and he knew how much she had struggled in the job market (this was before the Americans with Disabities Act was passed). Because part of my job was to interview candidates for positions in the store, he taught me how to ask people about their strengths and focus on what they could do, not on their disabilities. I gradually learned that the only part of the day I truly enjoyed was when I was interviewing the candidates for his restaurant.

With that nugget of understanding, I quit my job to become a caseworker for a nonprofit agency serving individuals who were blind. I also took a huge pay cut. My first day on the job was disappointing. I remember telling my parents (yes, I had moved back home to save money) that it was going to be like working with my grandmother every day because the clients were so old. Within a week or two, though, I found it was actually fun and I enjoyed the freedom of driving from client to client on backcountry roads, helping them with everything from reading their mail to sharing cups of tea while they talked about their family issues. (If you've ever seen the movie Doc Hollywood, *it was like the scene where Michael J. Fox is reading letters about the Pakistani to one of his patients.)*

But after a year or so, I realized that with a master's degree, I could double my salary and move out of my parent's home. So I went to grad school where a whole new thread of an idea developed—working with children with disabilities—and then I went on and on through more jobs and degrees to the point where another butterfly emerged and an anthropology class taken during my sophomore year in college resulted in my finding an agent for this book in 2008.

Did I know exactly what I wanted to do? No. I had way too many Possible Lives that looked interesting. Was I stressed? You bet. I thought it was bad not to have one specific job objective. And my rocky path sure didn't seem as smooth and easy as my friends' careers. I had switched from worrying about **THE QUESTION** to worrying about **THE JOB**. When would I finally find **THE JOB**? How would I know which job was the right one to go after?

No one explained to me how the system works. I thought, as many of you do, that I had to have a fixed goal—I had to have a plan. No one had clued me in about the butterfly and how often it would change my life. No one taught me it was OK to wander and experiment, even though that's what I was doing. After all, I didn't have a specific goal or plan, but I did have intentions. Sometimes the intention was just to *have* a job, but even then I kept one mindset in place at all times: *learning*. What could I learn from whatever I was doing? And how might I use that knowledge in a job I'd enjoy even more than the one I was currently in?

But for a minute let's get back to Lisa, the semidesperate and discouraged recent graduate. In just a few sentences, Lisa summed up many of the thoughts, fears, and quite frankly, misconceptions that most recent graduates have about their future. Let's examine her statements and see if we can make her (and you) feel better:

"It's September, and I still don't have a job."

This statement comes from an arbitrary definition of time and where one should be or ought to be at that time. As Gail Sheehy noted in her book *Passages,* twentysomethings often feel as if everything they do (or don't do) is going to have a major impact on their lives. Clearly, Lisa has decided in her mind that not having a job by September is a failure somehow. On its face, her statement is true: it is September, she doesn't have a job, and she would like to have one. But she's putting a heavy emotional weight on her shoulders by telling herself what she *should* have. She would feel much better if she could treat it as a very simple statement of where she is now ("it's September and I'd like to find a job") and focus on the future, not the discouragement she's feeling. Feeling discouraged won't make things better, and here's a little tip from cognitive-behavioral psychology: feelings aren't always accurate. Just because you feel something doesn't make it true. But Lisa is thinking a whole lot more than just "I should have a job." She's also thinking that there's something wrong, that she's done something wrong, that she might never find a decent job, and so on. Here's where positive thinking and the problem-solving mindset need to kick in: refuse to buy the problem and instead focus on the solution.

"I totally blew the last interview. . . ."

Lisa and I discussed this, and yes, it did sound as if her last interview wasn't exactly superb. She explained that it had come up so quickly she didn't have much time to prepare and she simply didn't answer the questions well. So we took a few minutes to focus on what went right: Did she answer any questions well? It turned out she did. Did she dress appropriately for it? Yes, she did. And most important, did she learn something from the experience? You bet. Just because you didn't do well in one instance doesn't mean you won't do well the next time. Learn. Keep learning.

". . . which would have been the perfect job"

OK, let's clear up that fantasy right now. There is no one "perfect job." In fact, you'll be pleased to know there are numerous "perfect jobs." I've had several of them myself. You will too. You are turning yourself into a fortune teller when you tell yourself you missed the perfect job. How do you know? Besides, that type of thinking will take you nowhere but back to the land of regrets and "shoulda woulda coulda." You know by now what I think about regrets. Remember how you're no longer allowed to say "I should have majored in_____"? New rule: you're not allowed to say "That would have been the perfect job." You are where you are, so focus on the next opportunity. Author Merle Shain once wrote a book called *Some Men Are More Perfect Than Others.* I like to use that same theory in the job world: there are no perfect jobs, but some jobs are more perfect than others. Don't worry, a perfect job awaits. And there will be another perfect job after that. Because you will make it perfect with your strengths, talents, and gifts. You will craft it into the "perfect" job.

"It's just for a part-time job, so I don't even know why I'm bothering."

Why do we dismiss opportunities based on superficial characteristics or how they might look to others? Why is a part-time job automatically less valuable than a full-time job? Because here's what Lisa was missing: the part-time job involved doing exactly what she wanted to do—writing, directing, and producing video shorts for a local news station. It was a chance to get her foot in the door of the very field she was interested in (her ultimate goal was a position at CNN), but she was less than enthusiastic because it wasn't full time. Sure, full-time jobs pay better, they generally come with benefits, and they sound better when describing them to friends, but Lisa was missing the point—and the true value—of this part-time opportunity. She was upset because she would have to keep her waitress job awhile longer. That's short-term thinking. When you're pursuing a Possible Life, you have to focus on what you can accomplish now and where it might take you, not the problems. Remember the quote about driving at night? Lisa can only see a few hundred feet ahead at this point, but there's every chance this job will lead to a full-time one in her field once she gets the experience. And if it doesn't, and turns out to be a dead-end job, she'll figure that out soon enough and move on to the next plan. But when she moves on, she'll have more skills (and maybe some good references) to take with her.

"All my friends have moved on and they're starting these really great careers."

This is comparisonitis and it is a deadly disease. Here's the deal with comparing yourself to others: you're always going to look good or bad depending on whom you choose to compare yourself with. You have to be *you,* with all your gifts and talents and, yes, issues. The minute you compare yourself to others, you've lost your focus. Your career path is about you and where you want to go, not what your friends are doing. Besides, how does Lisa know that they're all happy in those "really great careers"? I've received many calls from people in "dream jobs" desperate to find a way out. Never assume how others are doing regardless of what they say.

MOVING FORWARD

There are lots of rules out there about the job search. And some of them are good to follow. It's hard to argue with the linear types who major in engineering, set those goals, and move right into that engineering career. But when you let yourself become discouraged or depressed by all the rules that don't fit you, then they're no longer helping you.

One potential criticism of a system that encourages wandering is that somehow the people who follow it aren't competitive with the more linear, focused people who have a specific goal and shoot right toward it. The system, goes the criticism, is too vague. Well, you can't be who you aren't. If you don't have a specific goal, you have to start where you are. But then you also have to be doubly prepared with the best résumé and cover letter possible and the best interview skills so that you can match (and quite often surpass) the more linear-focused candidates. And be willing to act as if you want the job you're interviewing for until you find a clearer direction.

A metaphor I like to use to demonstrate the power of Wise Wanderers like you is "the Chicago Way" from the movie *The Untouchables*. In *The Untouchables*, Sean Connery plays Jim Malone, a streetwise cop in Chicago. He's advising Kevin Costner, who plays FBI agent Elliot Ness, on the way to bring down Al Capone's gang. He says: "You wanna know how you do it? Here's how: They pull a knife; you pull a gun. He sends one of yours to the hospital; you send one of his to the morgue! That's the Chicago way, and that's how you get Capone. Now do you want to do that? Are you ready to do that?"

Now no one is suggesting you follow that advice literally. Knives and guns will not help you at the job interview, and there is *nothing* funny about campus violence. What Connery/ Malone is saying is that you have to know what your competition is thinking, you have to be better prepared than your competition, and you have to be willing to put in extra effort. So how should you, as a now certified Wise Wanderer, use "the Chicago Way" metaphor?

- ❯ While other job seekers just think about what they might want to do, you *use the Wise Wandering System* (and do the exercises again if necessary) to analyze your career plans and *create career scenarios*.

- ❯ While other job seekers try to fit into a linear path, you have taken advantage of *chaos theory* to get the most out of *synchronistic moments and the butterfly effect*.

- ❯ While other job seekers write résumés, you *have written a targeted résumé* that demonstrates the power and value of your education, mindsets, and experimental wanderings.

- ❯ While other job seekers prepare for an interview by reading a few things on the Internet, you have completed a *SWOT analysis* before each interview.

- ❯ While other job seekers tell their strengths to employers, you *have prepared powerful stories* to show your strengths.

⇢ While other job seekers might read the company Web site to do research, you *became a corporate anthropologist*, unearthing new information and insight.

⇢ While others just attended class (or not!), you have mined your classes and your major for the value of what you were learning and make sure you let the employer know about it.

You deserve to be the first person considered for whatever job you seek. But you'll only get what you deserve if you take the steps necessary to develop the skills and knowledge needed to tackle the job market.

Here are ten suggestions for moving forward with your life, whether you are still seeking that first real job or have found it and are ready to do something else:

1. Make Chaos Theory Your Friend

You've noticed that this book is not one of those "find a job in twenty-four hours" guides or a compendium of innumerable resources or suggestions for places to work. There's a reason for that: chaos theory. It's too complex. There is no way one book can reach everyone's needs, particularly when it comes to providing resources for every possible career field. And with everything changing so quickly, any Web sites or references I might recommend could easily be gone by the time you read this. I chose to teach you to fish rather than handing you the fish, with the confidence that you're smart enough not to starve while you find that first fish. There are literally hundreds of books and thousands of Web sites that can connect you to the most current information about paths you want to follow. And being a Wise Wanderer, you're an expert at researching and experimenting already.

The mindsets and skills you have developed through the metaphor of chaos theory will help you navigate any choppy waters you encounter in the future. You might be interested to know that chaos theory is increasingly appearing in articles about management due to the constant change and complexity in the world. New trends emerge constantly and companies have to be chaos based to handle the changes. Constantly assess what you know, what you don't know, and what you need to find out. Consider possible outcomes and create scenarios that will help you predict the future (but don't try to see too far ahead!). Build up your personal and professional resilience so that you can handle job or even career changes with aplomb.

2. Your Attitude (Mindset) Is Everything

Don't sabotage your own potential for success by focusing on what's not working or how bad things are. The parent of a recent graduate once called me, frustrated because her daughter couldn't find a job in Denver. She insisted (and wanted me to agree) that there were *no* jobs at all in Denver. I hadn't seen that on the news—and believe me, if there were *no* jobs in Denver, it would make the news. Unfortunately, this mother was actually enabling and reinforcing her daughter's negative attitude and fueling her feeling of being stuck. Remember that even when there's a 6 percent unemployment rate, there's a 94 percent employment rate among those who want to be employed. And anyway, those are just general statistics that may or may not apply to the field or geographic location you're in.

You have to look at what is under your control and work with that. You might say "I'd like to find a job in the nonprofit sector, but there's nothing open." Is that really true? Is there absolutely nothing, no way, no how that you could do to move toward the nonprofit field? There are no agencies in your town? There are no volunteer opportunities? Really? A finalist on the TV show *Last Comic Standing* talked about how he worked at a radio station doing a show for two years for free until he had perfected the skills (and the courage) he needed to start doing stand-up comedy. *For free.* (He bartended to make money.) And when he was onstage as a finalist for *Last Comic Standing*, I suspect he didn't have one second of regret for those two years.

3. Keep Your Focus on Lessening the Gap Between Where You Are and Where You Want to Be

Keep conducting experimental wanderings that take you closer to your desired outcome. Experimental wanderings will help you particularly if you ask yourself one simple question on a daily basis: What can I learn today?

You never stop being a student. As you know, when you ask what you can learn, you focus on the knowledge and experience you're acquiring in order to make better decisions and find what you truly love to do. By always being a learner you develop an innate curiosity that helps you become an expert in whatever subject you desire.

I used to joke with my students that most people spend their first job looking for their second job. The reality is a little more complex. Your first job after graduation is a start whether you know it or not. Even if it's a McJob and certainly not the job of your dreams, it still represents a step toward the next better job, and then the next. Don't ever assume you have reached your final destination, whether you're at your first job at twenty-two or your latest job at sixty-two. There's always more to come when you see yourself as a learner.

4. Try to Enjoy the Process of the Job Search

You've seen all those trite quotes about enjoying the journey as you get to your destination. That's all fine and dandy when you're confident you'll reach the destination. It's one thing to enjoy the journey of a study-abroad experience knowing that you will return home and go back to school at some point. But how do you enjoy the journey when you don't know your destination? Or when your destination seems unattainable in the current economy? It's easy to fall into negative thinking patterns such as "the job search is too hard" or "it takes too much time." It might help to hear what alumni have said about the job search after it's over (these statements are from actual alumni surveys I've conducted):

- ➔ "Writing my résumé was a real ego booster—I've actually done stuff!"
- ➔ "I learned what's important to me."
- ➔ "The process was actually a lot more creative than I thought it would be."
- ➔ "Looking for a job helped me clarify my goals. I could see what I've done so far and it helped me figure out what I need to do."
- ➔ "The alumni contacts I made were friendly and helpful, and gave me lots of ideas."
- ➔ "I thought I had found a really neat job, but after I researched it, I learned I would hate that job."
- ➔ "I discovered that interviewing is just a skill that can be learned."
- ➔ "I developed a lot of confidence in myself."

> ❧ "I had a horrible interview, but I survived and I learned I would never want to work for that company. I also realized that I was partly at fault, so I worked on my responses to typical questions and never had a bad interview again."

> ❧ "The job search really helped me develop ambition."

If you're feeling isolated and alone in your search, see if you can connect with friends who are going through it as well or seek out a local job support group. Knowing that others are going through what you're going through and helping other people with the process will make you less anxious and more confident. Just make sure whatever group you connect with has a lot of positive energy and focuses on the solutions rather than the problems.

5. Keep Your Focus on Your Gifts, Strengths, and Threads in Your Wandering Map

Or as Glinda, the Good Witch in *The Wizard of Oz,* said, "You had the power all along, Dorothy." I couldn't have said it better.

6. Make Sure Your Résumé, Cover Letter, and Interviewing Skills Are Perfected and Ready to Go at a Moment's Notice

You know how those butterflies are—they flit in and out pretty quickly and if you're not ready for them, you might miss out on a great opportunity. Always keep "the Chicago Way" in mind.

7. Show Up and Pay Attention

Are you keeping your goals or intentions in your mind as you go about your day? In the movie *The Peaceful Warrior,* Nick Nolte, who plays a character called Socrates, tells his college student protégé to "take out the trash." By that he means the student needs to eliminate all the clutter in his mind that is keeping him from truly focusing on what is important. And if getting a job, or getting a better job, is truly important to you, you, too, will need to take out the trash. Jobs and opportunities are out there waiting for you. You just have to show up and pay attention.

8. Keep Wandering and Conducting Small Experiments

It's like following the instructions on the back of the shampoo bottle: lather, rinse, repeat. The experiments don't end when you leave school; in fact, they've just begun and it's through them that you'll discover your dream.

After graduating, Jessica decided she wanted to work in publishing, preferably in an international location. She was hoping to return to London, where she had studied a few years earlier, but she was encountering the usual problem of working abroad: obtaining a work permit. She found an organization called BUNAC, which would make short-term work visas available, though the Web site stressed that most jobs were not professional or all that glamorous.

Jessica decided that it was more important to live in England than work in publishing, so she got the visa and left for London. With the help of the CIEE/BUNAC agency, she found a roommate and a job waitressing at a pub. Not much glamour about it at all, but she was in England, which made it all worthwhile. Customers in the pub noticed her accent and would ask why she was working there. Jessica had her story ready. "Well, I love England and hope to stay here. But my real passion is publishing, and I'm hoping to find a job in that field even if I have to return to America. Thanks for asking."

She didn't ask anyone for a job; she didn't say anything beyond what she hoped to do. Sure enough, within a few weeks someone she spoke to offered to connect her with a local publishing house. She got a job as an "Americanizer," someone who translates British English into American English. She translated several cookbooks, and the company liked her work so much they extended her visa.

Jessica ultimately married a British citizen, and while still keeping her American citizenship in case she decides to return, she is now a top editor at a children's book publisher in London.

9. Take Advantage of Your Career Services Office

If you're still a student, use the services now, and if you've already graduated, find out what services are still available to you. The biggest job-finding mistake most students make is not using the services when they're easily accessible and free. You paid the tuition for them, so why not take advantage? Once you're out in the real world, you can end up paying hundreds of dollars for a private career counselor or coach. Why not get the most from the free services at your school? But don't just wander in and ask if they can help you "find a job." Of course they can help you find a job. Be clear with them about what you want. Help them help you by setting some clear goals you would like to accomplish during your meetings with them. A better client makes a better career counselor and results in a better session.

> All his life, Ray Kinsella was searching for his dreams.
> Then one day his dreams came looking for him.
> —TAGLINE FROM THE POSTER FOR *FIELD OF DREAMS*

10. If There's Something You Really Want to Do, Do It

Do you have a dream? Is it still just rattling around in your mind? Even if you can't do it as a full-time job, find time in your life for it. Try taking some small action to move toward it. When I wanted to become a published writer, I read tons of books on writing and publishing. Their advice could pretty much be summed up in one word: *write*. That's really the only way to be a writer. Don't wait for the job or the publisher or the agent. Just write. And as you write, you will develop your plan for moving forward with your writing, whether it's to a job in the publishing field or a job in the law or psychology, or places unknown. You already own, or will soon own, everything you need to achieve your dreams. You have access to more wisdom than you currently use. Plan to act on your dreams and respond to the opportunities that come your way.

FINAL THOUGHTS

As you start to map out your path, keep in mind that there is no "right" or "wrong" way to pursue a career or handle your college days. When alumni are asked to give advice to current students, their advice is inevitably contradictory: for every graduate who says "I wish I had buckled down and gotten better grades" there's one who says "I wish I had partied more and had more fun." For every graduate who says "I wish I had taken a major in____; that would have been more practical" there's an alumnus who says "I wish I had taken more risks and taken classes that seemed hard or weird at the time." So to say there's a right way just isn't, well, right. There's only *your* way and that's what you're going to spend the next fifty-plus years designing.

> *So let me finish the story of Lisa. We didn't focus on her résumé at our appointment that day. We focused on the value of the part-time job she was interviewing for and how she would answer the interview questions. We quickly mined her background for stories and examples she could provide of times when she had performed similar duties as outlined in the job description. She recalled when she had filmed her sister's wedding and edited it down to a three-minute video she put on YouTube, which had been viewed by thousands of people and received numerous positive comments. She prepared and practiced telling another story about writing an article for her college newspaper and how well she was able to meet deadlines and handle last-minute assignments, another job requirement. She went off to her interview, and called me several hours later to say she had gotten the job. Imagine that: she went from unemployed and discouraged to employed and ecstatic in a span of about four hours. Within six months, the position was increased to full time and she stayed for another year before moving to a different market as the producer of a local Sunday morning news program. One of her segments is being considered for an award. She's not at CNN yet, but she's on her way. Unless, of course, a butterfly takes her somewhere else.*

So you're going to do what wise wanderers do best. You're going to take risks, try new things, and experiment with what interests you, regardless of its "usefulness." You're not going to give up or admit defeat. You're going to wander *wisely* into all sorts of interesting stuff, from the class where you learned all about the hero myth to the class where you studied Gauguin, to the internship you had with the FBI, to the summer job in a commercial real estate office, to the month you spent in Peru building housing units. You're going to look at the seeming chaos of your life and you're going to make it meaningful.

And you know what: instead of looking for just a job, you may find that *your life comes looking for you*. I hope if you take nothing else away from this book, it will be the notion that you keep learning, experimenting, and wandering (wisely, of course) through the rest of your life. There's a wonderful line in a poem by the Sufi poet Rumi that reads: "If someone asks you what there is to do, light the candle in their hand." Consider your candle lit.

You may not know the destination of your journey, but you're on it, so enjoy it. And if you're so inclined, I would love to hear your stories of butterfly moments and other tales of the job search. If you'd like to share stories about your wanderings please visit my Web site at: www.youmajoredinwhat.com.

And please bear with me while I ask you one last time:

What could you do in the next twenty-four hours to move forward with your experimental wanderings or chase the butterfly?

_____

_____

_____

_____

If you knew you couldn't fail, what would you do?

_____

_____

_____

_____

Visit me at www.youmajoredinwhat.com.

APPENDIX

DREAMS DEFERRED, DELAYED, OR DENIED: THE RELUCTANT WANDERER

Things aren't as happy as they used to be down here at the unemployment office.

Joblessness is no longer just for Philosophy majors—useful people are starting to feel the pinch.

THE SIMPSONS, EPISODE 5.10 (1989)

It happens.

- ❯ You fail the science class you need to get into a good medical school.

- ❯ You get turned down by the graduate program you thought would be a sure thing.

- ❯ You've always wanted to be a journalist and newspapers aren't hiring.

- ❯ CNN posts the latest unemployment figures and they're worse than ever.

- ❯ A family member is ill and you have to stop your education for a while.

You're disappointed. Angry. Frustrated. Scared. But you're not alone.

Speak with most people who've been in the workforce for a while and they will tell you about the time when they were laid off, times when "no one" was hiring, or when they had to change their plans due to a family situation. The date of *The Simpsons* episode in the opening quote (1989) tells you that periods of recession and job loss are nothing new—they will always come and go.

Even a strong economy doesn't always provide protection if a career field is declining. Sometimes an industry becomes too popular and more people want jobs than there are openings. And so-called recession-proof fields like nursing can have built-in limits if you can't get into nursing school or if health care funding changes. Millions of jobs were lost in the recession that began in 2007, and many are not expected to return.

Good thing you're a Wise Wanderer.

The Wise Wanderings system is ideal for those who want to succeed in a tough job market. As you know, chaos theory reigns supreme in the Wise Wanderings system, and chaos is particularly apparent when the proverbial wrench is thrown in your plans. Career development is a lifelong process—it is not an endpoint—and the nonlinear nature of Wise Wanderings will help you cope with whatever situation you're facing.

When something you've been planning for disappears, you aren't expected to get right back on your feet and do something else. You need time to adjust to the shock and develop a new plan. But that is what you'll do next: develop a new plan. Because, as you know from the butterfly effect, these very "setbacks" often lead people to better choices and new situations. Learning from your setbacks now will serve you well in the future. If nothing else, you'll have new stories to tell future employers about how you made the most of a challenging situation.

The two keys to mastering any setback and moving forward are thinking and action. If you can control your thoughts you can control your actions, and that's what a setback period is all about: controlling what you can control and ultimately conquering it. If you're reading this, we'll assume you've already read the previous chapters, and have developed the tools you need to succeed in the job search including

- → identifying your best mindsets;
- → creating a Wandering Map;
- → developing your personal action plan;

➔ creating targeted resumes and cover letters;

➔ mastering your storytelling skills for the interview; and

➔ experimenting with new opportunities.

All of these processes will put you in the best position to succeed regardless of any current setbacks. But even if you haven't done all the processes, keep reading and you'll be guided back to them as needed.

Let's check back with Jim, the job-seeker you met in Chapter 2, on page 37. Jim created a Wandering Map and identified some key strengths and themes in his background. Later, in Chapter 10, on page 265, we watched him create a great story for his interviews. Given his interesting background and many talents, you would think his progression into the employment world would be smooth sailing. Not so much.

Jim decided he would move to New York in May right after graduation. During his senior year, he contacted a variety of employers in both banking and nonprofit services (his two main interests), participated in several career fairs in New York City, and made a lot of connections. He even found a roommate and put a deposit down on a place to live. And then he got the e-mail from the registrar's office: he was missing three credits needed to graduate. Suddenly his carefully laid plans started falling apart.

He knew that any job offers would be predicated on receiving his degree in May. He also knew that his school required that the last credit be taken on campus, and the class he needed to take wouldn't be available until the fall.

His great future in New York City was quickly vanishing. He couldn't get his deposit back, he might have to pay rent until his roommate could find a new roommate, and he didn't relish the idea of staying in his college town for six more months—not to mention the cost and time of taking a course.

Like everyone who faces this type of crisis, he had a choice. He could get stuck, get angry, blame himself and anyone else within reach . . . or he could take action.

He contacted the dean's office and received special permission to take his last class via an online extension course. He moved to New York when his classes ended in May and started his job search over.

And I'd like to report that all went well. It didn't.

Did I mention his two career interests: banking and non-profit? Banking. New York City. This was 2008. Massive layoffs and bank closings. Nonprofit? Donations at an all-time low. Glut of job seekers who already had their college degrees.

So what did Jim do?

He worked. Part-time jobs, volunteer jobs. He took a quick course in bartending so he could get a job that would allow him to work evenings (keeping his days open for his volunteer work and job hunting) and get good tips. He life-guarded on weekends. And he networked. He attended networking events, job fairs, talked to customers at his bartending job, and made a lot of friends.

Within a few months his volunteer work turned into a paying full-time job—but the story doesn't end there. He's still not earning enough money to support himself, so he's keeping the bartending job. When he goes on vacation for a week he plans to participate in a volunteer project at the resort town so he can add another interesting item to his résumé.

He finished his undergraduate degree and is now taking graduate classes in social work at a local college. By the time he has his graduate degree, he hopes that the economy will be better. Given his action plan, he'll be ready to pounce on opportunities the second the economy opens up.

Jim's story illustrates the importance of *thinking* and *taking action*: the two key factors in surviving career setbacks and two key elements of the Wise Wanderings system. So how can *you* think and act your way out of a career setback? Try these 10 strategies:

THINKING-BASED SETBACK SURVIVAL STRATEGIES

If you call failures experiments, you can put them in your résumé and claim them as achievements.

—MASON COOLEY

1. Revisit chaos theory.

> If you haven't already, it's time to read (or reread) Chapter 1. Review what you learned about chaos theory so you'll remember that the situation is complex and change is a constant. You can adapt to the changes by not getting stuck on the "how's and why's," but rather what action you can take now to move forward.

> Determine what you know and what you don't know, and focus on short-term opportunities to build skills and knowledge that will serve you in the long-term.

2. Determine the nature of your setback and whether it is a deal-breaker or not.

> Analyze the career plan you originally developed and decide if you still want to pursue it (albeit in a newly modified way based on your circumstances) or whether it's time to pursue something different. If you failed a class and still want to go to medical school, you could consider a postgraduate program where you can take (and possible retake) the science classes you need. Do your research to learn whether the setback is a temporary blip on the radar or a final call.

> What was the core idea behind your original dream? And what part of the dream do you most care about now? For instance, was the job most important or the location? Would you be willing to take a lesser job to stay in the desired location? Or would you prefer the dream job even if it were in a less desirable location?

3. Evaluate your mindsets—what are you thinking these days?

> Your mindset is under your control, but when you're going through a rough patch, it's easy to let it wander away from you into feelings of sadness, boredom, or anxiety. The best solution for those moments is change and action: what can you do to start changing things? Put on some music that inspires you. Move around—get off the sofa and turn off the TV. Turn on your strategic thinking: what ideas haven't you considered yet? What new plans could you develop?

> Are you practicing your reflective mindset? Are you taking time to reflect on what you've done so far in the job search? Have you reviewed and revised your Wandering Map? Have you identified more themes or threads you'd like to apply to your next job?

→ Are you staying flexible? Try to suspend judgment about whether your situation is good or bad. Just recognize it for what it is and try to learn more about yourself from it. The "bad" job you have at the local retail store might introduce you to a new customer tomorrow who works in the field you're interested in.

→ In particular, are you practicing the positive mindset? You already know that your thinking greatly influences your mood and your actions, so you need to get your thinking under control. In his book *Learned Optimism*, Dr. Martin Seligman identified the three *P*s that characterize all optimistic and pessimistic thinking: permanence, pervasiveness, and personalization. Optimists see good situations as permanent and bad situations as temporary. Optimists limit negative experiences to specific events, not pervasive trends. And optimists believe they are responsible for the good things in their lives and don't tend to blame themselves when things go wrong. Read Dr. Seligman's book to learn more and develop a mindset that will serve you well in all endeavors.

→ And while you're considering mindsets, always keep the learning mindset in the forefront. As long as you're learning, you will have new skills to show and new stories to tell future employers.

4. Find balance in your life.

→ Wait. You don't have to do everything at once. This may seem contradictory to the calls for action, but it can be helpful to give yourself some space to make a decision, particularly after a long-desired plan has gone awry. Know that part of surviving a downturn economy, for example, is just a matter of waiting for it to get better. Now don't confuse waiting with doing nothing: even in a poor economy you want to do all you can to build your resume and make connections. But it's OK to put some plans aside until the timing is better. Focus on what you can do now.

→ In her book, *Feel the Fear and Do It Anyway*, author Susan Jeffers proposes that to maintain a healthy balance in your life, you identify nine areas of your life that are important to you. For example, you might want to include friends, family, a job, a relationship, hobbies, spiritual life, health, and finances. Then set some goals for each of these areas of your life and work on them every week. In this way, your life will feel more whole and balanced even when you don't have one piece of it—such as a job.

5. **Remember that this situation is temporary.**

I once saw a sign outside a church advertising a sermon entitled, "Hell in the Hallway." It intrigued me and I asked the minister what it meant. She said, "Well you know how everyone always talks about when one door closes another opens? Well, nobody talks about the hell in the hallway, while you're waiting for that other door to open." She has a point. It's a lot easier to endure a waiting period when you know what's coming at the end. But while you're in the "hell in the hallway," it's important that you take care of yourself and find time for friends and fun. In the great scheme of things most setbacks only hold you back for a short time. Determine that you will survive whatever your setback is and come out stronger for having experienced it.

Keep your emotions in check. It's OK to feel angry, disappointed, sad, lost, frustrated, etc. Express those feelings in a healthy way with friends and confidants, or even a counselor—just not on your Facebook page or in a public blog.

Now that you've got your thinking under control, it's time to focus on actions.

ACTION-BASED SETBACK SURVIVAL STRATEGIES

6. **Revisit your plan of action.**

If you developed your action plan based on your original career goal, before you experienced a setback, it's time to revisit your plans. How are you going to take advantage of the situation at hand? That may seem like an odd question when you're staring at the word "NO"—in the form of a graduate school rejection, job loss, or other setback. But it's really the only valuable question to ask: what are you going to do now to move forward? Do you have another clear career goal in mind or are you wandering? If needed, go back to Chapter 6 and decide whether you are now on a probable, possible, or intention-setting path. Start outlining the steps for the next best plan. Here's what Jim had to say about switching from his probable plan to a possible plan:

> *Put your possible lives on your wall: cover it with the Post-it notes of the steps to attain your goal. Look at it regularly to make sure you're keeping up with your plans. If you can only work part-time,*

then take classes if you need more education. Volunteer and turn it into a full-time job.

Go back and read your Post-it notes on your wall again, and then go work out. If you sit at home, you will lose your motivation, get depressed, etc. When I didn't have a job, I worked out for two hours every day and took classes at the gym. I figured, if I am unemployed, I better be sweating from all the work.

I also suggest getting all your personal to-do things done when you don't have a job. Revise your résumé, get your suits altered and ready to go, etc. Get your life organized, so you are prepared to go into a job interview at any time.

Notice Jim's focus on action: he is constantly moving forward even though he doesn't know where he's going to end up. He controls what he can control.

⇨ Did you determine that certain actions could restore your original plan? Write out those actions and start doing the first one in the next 24 hours.

⇨ If you experienced a setback because you lack a certain education or experience, what can you do to start acquiring that education or experience now?

⇨ How could you branch out into areas that are related to your original plan but more easily obtained?

⇨ Revisit or create a new Possible Lives plan (Chapter 5). If one part of your career plans isn't attainable right now, what other parts are?

⇨ Go where the jobs are. If you're living in a more depressed area, do you need to move, or are there opportunities for working remotely?

⇨ Go back to school, but know why you're there. Your goal is to acquire knowledge or skills related to your career plans.

7. Design a "gap" experience.

A "gap year" is a British term for taking a break during a time of transition. It is usually taken between high school and college or just after college graduation. It's a time devoted to trying a new experience—traveling, volunteering, working at a temporary job, or otherwise taking time out from the linear pursuit of a career to do something interesting, adventurous, or novel. Although labeled as a year, gap experiences can be a few months or extend into many years. Based on your financial and personal situation, you can design a gap experience that will take you to another country on a mission, develop a community service project in your hometown, conduct independent research on a subject of interest, write a book, or do a postgraduate internship in your field of interest. A gap experience can give you time to:

- ⮞ Chill out from years of intensive education. You may feel like you've been on an academic treadmill and need to recharge with a completely new experience.

- ⮞ Try out another possible life. Surprisingly, this might be the best time to try out a risky possible life—that music, art, or writing career you dismissed as impractical.

- ⮞ Go on an international volunteer mission. Many provide basic food and housing—you won't earn much (if anything), but you'll gain valuable experience.

- ⮞ Teach English abroad or find other international work that will broaden your horizons and give you a global perspective. You can learn a new language or improve your skills in a language you've already studied.

- ⮞ Focus your goals. Gap experiences offer a chance to get out of your routine and discover what's really important.

- ⮞ Look into pre-professional internship programs (paid or unpaid). Many are part-time, which would give you time to take a job to pay your bills.

- ⮞ Create a unique volunteer community experience in your hometown. Look for an agency serving a population that interests you or a community issue that needs to be addressed.

- ⮞ Build your résumé with a unique experience to share with employers. (See Chapter 8 for ways to creatively describe your adventures on your résumé.)

8. Create your brand.

Your "brand" is your image: it's everything from your résumé and cover letter to your interview outfit to your online presence. Taking time to think about your "brand" will help you focus on your key strengths and give you confidence in the job search. To put it simply, you analyze yourself in terms of the marketplace, identify what will be the most effective presentation of your talents, and promote that.

- → Start by re-analyzing your Wandering Map for threads and themes you want to highlight to employers.

- → Review your résumés and cover letters to make sure they are targeted to the new career plans you've created. Make sure you're selling your accomplishments, not just your skills. What value will you bring to an organization? How will you help them save or earn money?

- → Identify the three key items you want an employer to know about you after they've interviewed you.

Did you know that your online presence is part of your brand? Leave it to adults to take the fun out of everything. Here you were having a great time on the Internet, creating MySpace and Facebook pages with your latest exploits only to learn that employers are now checking out your online presence. With over 50 percent of employers using the Internet to check up on job candidates, you can't afford to have a lot of "digital dirt" out there. How do you deal with it?

- → Try to get any negative material removed. Obviously, if you put it up, take it down. Even though Facebook and other accounts are "private"—they're really not. Employers can find ways to read them. Ask any friends who have "tagged" you in less-than-flattering photos to take them down.

- → Create positive entries. Create a professional account on LinkedIn. Consider developing a Web page or blog that highlights your portfolio (if you're hoping to get into a field like marketing, advertising, writing, etc.). Show off your talents and skills.

- → If you're a good writer, consider creating a blog that deals with your professional area of interest. For instance, if you're ultimately seeking a social work position dealing with adolescents, start a blog about issues related to adolescents. Include information you've gleaned from research you've read, or volunteer experiences you've had, etc. A blog can be a great way to get noticed and build a professional reputation.

- → Just remember—even if you take down the blog or an old Web site, it can still be found in cyberspace. The Internet is not the place to publicly complain about problems, how much you hate the job search, etc. Save that for discussions with friends or private e-mails. Your online presence should be used to build your career, not destroy it. Consider every post an application for a job: would you want a future employer to read it?

9. Keep developing your network.

As a Wise Wanderer, you know all about the butterfly effect and how an opportunity can appear when you least expect it. That's why you should craft as many small experiments (Chapter 7) as you can—and networking is a great small experiment that will increase your chances of encountering the butterfly.

You already have a built-in network of relatives, friends, your friends' relatives, your connections on LinkedIn and Facebook, and so on, but you can broaden your network even further. Networking can seem a little intimidating, particularly if you tend to be shy or not as comfortable at public gatherings, but it's a skill you can learn. Almost everywhere you go can be the potential source for a new connection: an alumni cocktail party or gathering, a meeting of a club you belong to, a book reading group at the local bookstore, even your customers at your current job. When you have a chance to interact with people, you have a chance to develop a new connection and ultimately build up your network. Here are some tips to get you started:

- Don't think of networking as "selling yourself" to someone—asking for a job immediately or trying to impress someone will backfire. Instead, focus on the person you're meeting. Find out what they do and what they're interested in. If you share common interests, talk about that. Networking is ultimately about building relationships and making new friends.

- Be sure you mention whatever you're seeking. While you don't want to ask someone for a job (it's too easy for them to say no, and then the conversation gets awkward), it's fine to say something like, "I really enjoyed my economics major and now I'm hoping to find a job that will let me apply what I've learned." Say it with a smile and not a look of desperation. Depending on how they respond, you can pursue that topic, or move on to another.

- Remember the marketing axiom "Get out of your ego and into your customer's ego." Can you offer something to the person you're talking to? A piece of advice, some information, a connection for him? Remember, you don't know how this might benefit you in days to come. And even if it doesn't, you're practicing your networking skills.

→ What are you passionate about? What hobbies do you enjoy? Join groups related to those areas so you can meet more people. You already share something in common with them—who knows what else you might ultimately have in common?

→ If you go to a reception, focus on meeting as many people as you can.

- If you tend to be shy, or find it hard to make small talk, think up 2–3 topics you can talk about before you go to the reception. What could you talk about with people your own age? (Suggestions: college, sports, movies, music, travel.) How about people who are ten years older than you? (Their college experience, how they got their job, what kind of work they do, sports, TV, travel, etc.) What if the people at the reception are your parents' age? (Try travel, their career, where they went to college, etc.) You get the idea—many topics will work with a variety of people. Try to avoid personal topics or asking about children unless the other person brings the topic up. If they tell you about their child's musical recital, then it's fine to ask more about the child. Otherwise, don't ask. Unless you're at a religious or political event, it's best to avoid those topics as well.

- Turn off your cell phone (or at least put it on vibrate). And don't interrupt a conversation to take a call.

- Take a business card with your name and contact information on it. (You can create them on your computer or get them printed inexpensively at a local print shop.) When you get a business card from someone, jot down on the back of the card any pertinent information from your conversation. For instance, you might write, "has 2 children in elementary school, plays soccer, possible job at First National Bank." Then, when you contact the person the next day (which you always want to do when you have a solid lead like that), you can mention how much you enjoyed talking about his children and playing soccer before you jump right in to the question about the banking job.

- Don't go hungry. It's hard to network when you're munching on chicken wings. Enjoy a few food items but don't make a dinner out of it (unless, of course, it is a dinner). Never have more than one or two drinks. If you know you might be tempted to have more, consider getting a drink you don't like—it will take you longer to finish it and you'll be less inclined to get another.

10. Hire yourself.

When all else fails, become your own employer. This notion is as much psychological as it is literal, because the best philosophy to take throughout your career is the idea that you're always self-employed. At times, you will have different names on your paycheck, but you are always developing your own career. Whether you choose to run your own business for just the next few months or the rest of your life is a decision you will come to, but while you're seeking the next best employer, you might as well work for yourself.

- ➔ What hobbies or skills do you have that you could earn money from? Can you tutor, teach a musical instrument, provide lawn care, become an au pair, conduct research or fact-check for writers, ghost-write publications or blogs for busy professionals, create Web sites, or develop social media networking outlets for small businesses?

- ➔ What inventions or ideas for a service or product do you have? Many of today's millionaire entrepreneurs started their businesses in the garage or their dorm room. What would have to happen for your plan or idea to become a reality? Is it something you'd like to invest time and money in?

- ➔ Research the basics of starting a business. Who would your customers or clients be, and how would you attract them? What fees can you charge? Read everything you can about the type of business or product you're thinking of developing. Look at who succeeds and copy what they do.

- ➔ Develop a business plan. How much time can you devote to this effort and how will you find income while you're developing your business? What knowledge do you need to acquire and how can you acquire it? Tons of resources are available for starting a business, and the cheapest place to start is your local library and the Internet.

- ➔ Read the business section of your local newspaper and check out the local Chamber of Commerce for upcoming programs and networking opportunities. SCORE (http://www.score.org/index.html) is a great organization and resource. Composed of retired business executives working in conjunction with the Small Business Administration, you will find lots of valuable information and help for starting a business.

Starting your own business may not be your ultimate dream, but sometimes just the process of thinking about the kind of business you'd like to run or the skills you have to offer can help you clarify the career path you'd like to follow next. You may not want to run your own tutoring business, but it might be a short-term option while you prepare for the teaching career you ultimately seek. And always think about the stories you'll have to tell an employer that demonstrate your hard work, initiative, and drive.

FINAL THOUGHTS ON DEFERRED, DELAYED, AND DENIED DREAMS

Remember back in Chapter 1 when we talked about the pressure and lure of the linear path? Many people feel the pressure to know what they're going to do and move toward whatever that is. None of us likes to hear the word "no." And if you had a plan and it's fallen apart, it's hard to do that "glass half full" thing. A famous cartoon by George Booth shows a woman working in her garden tending the flowers. Behind her sits her dog with a decidedly unhappy/annoyed look on his face. The caption reads: "I want you to start thinking good thoughts about someone *new* at our house. I want you to start thinking good thoughts about a pussycat." Now no one is asking you to think good thoughts about a bad situation, but there is wisdom in accepting what is and moving forward. In the great scheme of things most setbacks only hold you back for a short time. Determine that you will survive whatever your setback is and come out stronger for having experienced it.

You hold in your hands the system for finding your path. Take the pressure off yourself to fix everything and make it perfect. Non-linear careers—whether intentional or unexpected—are usually the most fascinating.

I dedicated this book to a talented composer and musician, John Stewart, whom I had the pleasure of getting to know in the last few years of his life. One of his best songs contains the line: "Those aren't clouds on the horizon; they're the shadows of the angels' wings." We don't know what we don't know. We can only view things from our limited perspectives. And given that, I think it's worth assuming that what looks like a setback right now might end up being a gift.

Wander wisely.

ACKNOWLEDGMENTS

This book would never have been possible without my amazing agent, Bonnie Solow; my insightful editor, Alessandra Lusardi; my smart and funny attorney/friend, Margaret (Peg) Anderson; and, of course, Viking Books. A special thanks to Judi Hays and Elizabeth Alexander for their help with the illustrations. This has truly been a magical writing experience, thanks to y'all.

Certain educators are forever burned into my brain because of their kindness, brilliance, creativity, and unknowing contribution to this book:

- Mr. William Shoemaker, my fifth-grade teacher, who always warned us about an invisible sign over the door that read "It's later than you think" and who told wonderful stories while taking us on bird walks on the Gettysburg battlefield.

- Mr. Paul Johnston, my ninth-grade writing and typing teacher at Harrisburg Academy, who taught me the two skills that have helped me land and survive every job I've ever had.

- Professor Carol Small at Gettysburg College, whose Art and Visual Perception course taught me to think visually and who opened the world of art history to me.

- Dr. Michael Yura, former professor at West Virginia University, whose Adlerian approach to counseling and brilliant insights into projective testing taught me to read between the lines and helped shape ideas for this book.

- Dr. Stephen MacDonald, former dean at Dickinson College (now president of Lebanon Valley College), who encouraged me to follow one of my Possible Lives and teach film courses at Dickinson.

- Dr. Linda Ferreira-Buckley, at The University of Texas at Austin, who hired me to run the liberal arts career services office because, as she said, "This is the first person I've met who really 'gets' the professional value of the liberal arts."

➔ Dean Richard Flores, at The University of Texas at Austin, who encouraged me to take my ideas and create the first Major in the Workplace career courses for credit at UT, and Dean Marc Musick, who continues that support.

And to my dear friends:

Judi Hays, who got me through the proposal-writing stage; Gayle Bolinger, the most creative accountant I know, with whom I taught a course at Dickinson College in 1996, The Liberal Arts in Business, which provided some of the early thinking behind this book; Marjean Fieldhouse, Julie Lake, and the other members of our Chez Zee Writers Group who encouraged me to keep writing; my wild and brilliant friends from Dickinson College: Dave Crouch, Chuck Zwemer, and Cindy Samet, who are always there to provide the humor; and the amazingly talented musicians of the South Austin Bakery JAM, whose music provided wonderful respite from writing each weekend.

Don't even get me started on all the writers whose books have inspired, educated, and moved me throughout my life.

And finally, to my students, and my talented and creative career center staff members at both Dickinson College and The University of Texas at Austin, and everyone else I've failed to mention because my editor wants me to keep this short, thank you. You know who you are.

Katharine S. Brooks
Austin, Texas
August, 2008

REFERENCES AND RESOURCES

CHAPTER ONE:
A BUTTERFLY FLAPS ITS WINGS AND
YOU FIND A JOB

Bright, Jim E. H., and Robert G. L. Pryor. "The Chaos Theory of Careers: A User's Guide." *The Career Development Quarterly* 53, (2005): 291–305.

Dickens, Charles. *Great Expectations*. Michigan: Ann Arbor Media, 2006.

Krumboltz, John D. "Serendipity Is Not Serendipitous." *Journal of Counseling Psychology* 45 (4) (1998): 390–92.

——, and Al S. Levin. *Luck Is No Accident*. Atascadero, CA: Impact Publishers, 2004.

O Brother, Where Art Thou? DVD, directed by Joel Coen. Walt Disney Video, 2000.

Parsons, Frank. *Choosing a Vocation*. Boston: Houghton Mifflin, 1909.

Sinetar, Marsha. *Do What You Love, The Money Will Follow*. New York: Dell, 1989.

Sloan, Julia. *Learning to Think Strategically*. Burlington, MA: Elsevier, 2006.

Tetenbaum, Tony J. "Shifting Paradigms: From Newton to Chaos." *Organizational Dynamics* (Spring 1998): 21–32.

CHAPTER TWO:
CONNECTING THE DOTS

Buckingham, Marcus, and Donald Clifton. *Now, Discover Your Strengths*. New York: Free Press, 2001.

Buzan, Tony, and Barry Buzan. *The Mind Map Book: How to Use Radiant Thinking to Maximize Your Brain's Untapped Potential*. New York: Plume, 1996.

Dasgupta, Subrata. "Multidisciplinary Creativity: The Case of Herbert A. Simon." *Cognitive Science* 27 (2003): 683–707.

Hagstrom, Robert G. *Investing: The Last Liberal Art*. New York: Texere LLC, 2000.

Novak, Joseph, and Gowin D. Bob. *Learning How to Learn*. Cambridge, UK: Cambridge University Press, 1984.

CHAPTER THREE:
MENTAL WANDERINGS

Cameron, Julia. *The Artist's Way: A Spiritual Path to Higher Creativity*. New York: Jeremy P. Tarcher/Putnam, 1992.

Krug, Steve. *Don't Make Me Think: A Common Sense Approach to Web Usability*, 2nd ed. Berkeley: New Riders Publication, 2006.

Maxwell, John C. *Thinking for a Change*. New York: Warner Books, 2003.

Pichot, Teri. *Solution-Focused Brief Therapy*. New York: Haworth Clinical Practice Press, 2003.

Seligman, Martin E. P. *Authentic Happiness: Using the New Positive Psychology to Realize Your Potential for Lasting Fulfillment*. New York: Free Press, 2004.

——. *Learned Optimism*. New York: Pocket Books, 1998.

——, and Mihaly Csikszentmihalyi. "Positive Psychology: An Introduction." *American Psychologist* 55, no. 1 (2000): 5–14.

CHAPTER FIVE:
WHY SETTLE FOR ONE CAREER WHEN YOU CAN HAVE TEN?

Dyer, Wayne. *The Power of Intention: Learning to Co-create Your World Your Way*. Carlsbad, CA: Hay House, 2004.

Markus, Hazel, and Paula Nurius. "Possible Selves." *American Psychologist* 41, no. 9 (September 1986): 954–69.

CHAPTER SIX:
EVEN WANDERERS MAKE PLANS

Gelatt, H. B., and Carol Gelatt. *Creative Decision Making: Using Positive Uncertainty*. Boston: NETg, 2003.

King, Stephen. *On Writing: A Memoir of the Craft*. New York: Scribner, 2000.

CHAPTER EIGHT:
MY JOB AS A KRACKEL BAR

Moore, Ian. *Does Your Marketing Sell?* London/Boston: Nicholas Brealey Publishers, 2005.

CHAPTER NINE:
CHANNELING JANE AUSTEN

Cameron, Julia. *The Artist's Way: A Spiritual Path to Higher Creativity.* New York: Jeremy P. Tarcher/Putnam, 1992.
———. *The Right to Write.* New York: Jeremy P. Tarcher/Putnam, 1998.
King, Stephen. *On Writing: A Memoir of the Craft.* New York: Scribner, 2000.
Lamott, Anne. *Bird by Bird.* New York: Pantheon Books, 1994.
Maisel, Eric. *Write Mind.* New York: J. P. Tarcher/Penguin, 2002.
Palumbo, Dennis. *Writing from the Inside Out.* New York: Wiley, 2000.
Sher, Gail. *One Continuous Mistake.* New York: Penguin, 1999.
Strunk, William Jr., and E. B White, *The Elements of Style.* New York: Macmillan, 1979.

CHAPTER TEN:
WANDERING INTO THE WORKPLACE

Shain, Merle. *Some Men Are More Perfect than Others.* New York: Bantam Books, 1977.
Sheehy, Gail. *Passages: Predictable Crises of Adult Life.* New York: Dutton, 1976.

CHAPTER ELEVEN:
WANDERING AFTER GRADUATION

Peaceful Warrior, DVD, directed by Victor Salva. Universal Studios, 2007.
The Untouchables, DVD, directed by Brian dePalma. Paramount Studios, 1987.

APPENDIX

Ferrazzi, Keith, and Tahl Raz. *Never Eat Alone: And Other Secrets to Success One Relationship at a Time.* New York: Broadway Business, 2005.

Jeffers, Susan. *Feel the Fear and Do It Anyway.* New York: Ballantine Books: 2006.

Seligman, Martin. *Learned Optimism: How to Change Your Mind and Your Life.* New York: Vintage, 2006.

Stewart, John. Lyrics from "Shadows of the Angels' Wings."

WEB SITES AND BLOGS
FOR JOB SEEKERS

Going online to research job and career information can quickly become overwhelming. This list identifies some of the best sites available for job seekers. Site addresses can change, so if the address doesn't work, just search for the site on your favorite search engine.

One place to start is my blog, **Career Transitions,** published on the *Psychology Today* Web site: http://www.psychologytoday.com/blog/career-transitions. You'll find the latest job-searching tips for college students, recent graduates, and job changers who are not following the linear path in their careers. Please join the discussion and ask questions or request future topics.

GENERAL CAREER INFORMATION AND JOB LEADS

About.com: Job Searching: http://jobsearch.about.com/
Good starting point for articles related to the job search as well as links to various job boards.

CareerBuilder: http://www.careerbuilder.com/
Large online job site resource.

Career Realism: http://www.careerealism.com/
Career blog originally developed by students at the University of New Hampshire, Career Realism focuses on career issues most relevant to college students and recent graduates.

Chimby: http://www.chimby.com/
Web tracking site that monitors more than 400 career-related Web sites.

Collegerecruiter.com: http://www.collegerecruiter.com/
Devoted to the college student or recent graduate, this site offers lots of career information and job leads.

Indeed.com: http://www.indeed.com/
The rather sparse home page is a little intimidating, but you can find thousands of jobs nationwide by entering a career field and geographic location you're interested in.

Monster.com: http://www.monster.com/
Large and well-known search engine for jobs as well as career information.

Occupation Outlook Handbook: http://www.bls.gov/OCO/
Published by the federal government, this Web site will help you research occupational fields

ONET online: http://online.onetcenter.org/
Useful as an idea generator for possible career options, ONET online provides detailed descriptions of jobs and the skills they require

Quintessential Careers: http://www.quintcareers.com/
Some of the services are fee-based, but this site also has lots of free information for job seekers.

The Riley Guide: http://www.rileyguide.com/
Well-respected comprehensive guide to all aspects of the job search.

SPECIALIZED CAREER WEB SITES

Coolworks: http://www.coolworks.com/
Offers links to seasonal or "gap year" jobs.

TransitionsAbroad: http://www.transitionsabroad.com/
Excellent resource for international volunteer, work, internship, or
study abroad opportunities.

The University of Texas International Jobs Site: http://www
.utexas.edu/cola/lacs/resources/international
I wrote this site that contains resources to get you started on your
international career or gap year experience.

SALARY INFORMATION AND COMPARISON

These sites offer salary calculators to help you compare salaries or
determine the cost of living in your desired location:

Collegegrad.com: http://www.collegegrad.com/salaries
Payscale: http://www.payscale.com/

SOCIAL NETWORKING AND CAREER BRANDING SITES

LinkedIn: http://www.linkedin.com/
The most widely used professional social networking site. Provides
helpful guidance for college students setting up their first site.

Personal Branding: http://www.personalbrandingblog.com/
Dan Schawbel is a leading expert in the area of personal
branding. His blog contains lots of valuable information for job
seekers, particularly related to maintaining online presence, or
brand.

SUBSCRIPTION-BASED RESOURCES

You can access a basic level of service on these sites for free, or you
can obtain greater access if you pay for the service. Before you pay
any fees check with your college career center. They may already
purchase the service for you:

CareerShift: http://www.careershift.com/
Search for thousands of jobs, contact information, alumni, and
other resources.

Vault: http://www.vault.com/wps/portal/usa
Vault provides a wealth of research, publications, and background
information on employers.

INDEX

F

Family influences
   and career choice, 46
   parent-influenced goals, 135
Figler, Howard, 89
Films about workplace, 182
Flexible/adaptive mindset, 73–75
   components of, 73–74
   developing, 74–75
   relationship to workplace, 74
Flow, 66
Foreign experience. *See* Study
      abroad
Foreign language study, 68
Formatting
   cover letter, 244
   résumé, 205

G

Gap analysis, 63
Gelatt, Carol, 146
Gelatt, H. P., 146
Geography, considering in job
      search, 187–89
Global mindset, 67–68
   components of, 67
   developing, 68
   relationship to workplace, 67
Goal setting, 134–61
   barriers to, 134–35
   daily choices in, 157–58
   organizing environment,
      159–60
   Possibility Planning, 146–52
   Possible Lives information in,
      138
   Premack's principle, 161
   Probability Planning, 138–46
   Seeking the Butterfly,
      152–56
Grades
   and earning power, 87–88
   as focus, 87–88
   improving, steps in, 99–108
   See also Studying

H

Haiku cover letter, 245
History major, skills derived from,
      91
Hobbies
   fun versus profit, 129

I

Intentions
   defined, 154
   examples of, 154–55
   Seeking the Butterfly, 152–56
   selective perception, 154
   setting daily, 157–58, 184, 285
   visual reminders of, 155–56
Interests section, résumé, 218–20
Internships
   strengths gained, 178
   value to employer, 178
Interviews. *See* Job interview

J

Job interview, 251–74
   examples of questions, 255–56,
      267–68
   framing your story, 251–52,
      264–66
   interviewer agenda, 253–54
   presenting major in, 96–98
   storytelling, 258–73
   styles of, 257
   SWOT analysis as preparation,
      269–71
Job objective section, résumé, 210–11
Job posting, responding to, 247–48
Job search
   "Chicago Way" metaphor,
      281–82
   college career services office,
      286–87
   cover letter, 223–49
   enjoying process, 284–85
   experimental wanderings as
      preparation, 163–94